Making a Difference

Making a Difference

University Students of Color Speak Out

Julia Lesage, Abby L. Ferber,
Debbie Storrs, and Donna Wong

ROWMAN & LITTLEFIELD PUBLISHERS, INC.
Lanham • Boulder • New York • Oxford

ROWMAN & LITTLEFIELD PUBLISHERS, INC.

Published in the United States of America
by Rowman & Littlefield Publishers, Inc.
An imprint of the Rowman & Littlefield Publishing Group
4720 Boston Way, Lanham, Maryland 20706
www.rowmanlittlefield.com

12 Hid's Copse Road, Cumnor Hill, Oxford OX2 9JJ, England

British Library Cataloguing in Publication Information Available

Library of Congress Cataloging-in-Publication Data

Making a difference : university students of color speak out / Julia
Lesage . . . [et al.].
    p. cm.
Includes bibliographical references and index.
ISBN 0-7425-0079-9 (cloth : alk. paper)—ISBN 0-7425-0080-2 (pbk. :
alk. paper)
    1. Minority college students—United States—Attitudes.   2. Minority
college students—United States—Social conditions.   3. Multicultural
education—United States.   4. College environment—United States.   5.
United States—Ethnic relations.   I. Lesage, Julia.
LC3727 .M35   2002
378.1'9829—dc21   2002001782

Printed in the United States of America

⊗ ™ The paper used in this publication meets the minimum requirements of American
National Standard for Information Sciences—Permanence of Paper for Printed Library
Materials, ANSI/NISO Z39.48-1992.

For our students and colleagues

Contents

Preface: Genesis of This Project

Julia Lesage

M*aking a Difference* has had a number of lives. First it was a video, *In Plain English*,[1] made with students of color at the University of Oregon and then a printed crosscutting of the expanded interviews. Later it was expanded with an analysis and a roadmap aimed at creating institutional change.

The University of Oregon has never had a critical mass of people of color that could make it a place where faculty and students of color find their viewpoints accommodated and valued and their experience validated. Because Eugene, Oregon, is a mostly white college town, police and street harassment of students and faculty of color are all too common. In my second year at the university, I participated on a president's task force for affirmative action. I was acutely dissatisfied when the group's report ignored the experiences that faculty of color had on campus and in the community and, more importantly, the underlying assumptions they held about how a university does and should function. Since my job included teaching video production, I went to the head of the affirmative action office, Diane Wong (not coauthor Donna Wong), and proposed making a videotape about this group of faculty. I wanted to represent their concerns more faithfully than the task force report had. Wong easily convinced me that students of color had even less voice than the faculty and would be a better focus for such a tape. Even then, we also hoped to do a print publication based on the interviews for the tape. This was the beginning of the videotape *In Plain English* and the subsequent interviews published in this book.

In planning the videotape, I relied heavily on people of color on campus for guidance. The first people I sought out for assistance and advice were the staff and faculty of color on the task force. They told me to work closely with the student unions that represent the major ethnic groups on campus. I was glad that I followed that advice. The student leaders interviewed for *In Plain English,* who also appear in this book, had developed their own cogent analyses of the educational system. Since the tape was made, each student union has consequently used it and promoted it extensively.

The tape was made with the collaboration of Dianna Kale, a Native American academic staff person in the Office of Multicultural Affairs who worked for years organizing antidiscrimination workshops.[2] Kale had long desired a tape presenting the perspectives of students of color. We had instant agreement about aesthetics, planning to intercut students filmed against a neutral background, with no intervening voice-over and no authorities "interpreting" the students' voices. Kale participated as an associate producer on this project, seeing it through from the preinterview stage to the final script. She and other faculty of color helped recruit students for preinterviews and later for videotaped interviews, during which Kale herself did most of the actual interviewing while I or an associate did the camera work. This was a key element in the project's success, since Kale's ongoing work with students of color meant that her analysis informed the interview process. Her familiarity with the students as individuals let them feel comfortable talking about a range of issues with her that they might not have discussed in the same intimate way with me.

The tape bears the marks of being a collaborative effort among the students, Kale, and me. Because of Dianna Kale's presence and credibility, the students trusted us and felt safe to express themselves and name things happening in their lives that they would not ordinarily air in public. Especially important to them was understanding the context and reason for the video. First, in a preinterview situation, they told their stories in response to questions focused on education, questions intended to elicit kinds of knowledge typically rejected by those in power. Before the videotaping they had a chance to organize their thoughts around these same issues to think about what they wanted to say.

Kale and I agreed that due to the complexities of video production, I as director would take responsibility for the final presentation of the issues. Because I am committed to media for social change and its collective production, I have reflected on some of the pitfalls that can hinder the process of collective media making. To finish a tape in a prompt and responsible way, it is important to delineate structures of authority and responsibility from the very beginning. Because I maintain production control, I can work very economically, set deadlines, pay for most of the costs up to the online edit out of my own pocket, and distribute the work at no profit, making extensive use of cable access television showings. Because it takes years to make an inexpensive, independent video production, done alongside one's paid work, I try to conceive of and edit the subject matter and its presentation in a way that will not become quickly outdated.

In this case, even though I use no external scripted narration, this documentary—like all documentaries—subtly interprets the experiences about which the people in the tape speak. When I made *In Plain English*, I created a space for the students' voices to be heard and a tape that they could use, but through a production process that I established and controlled. Although I gave the students feedback mechanisms, veto power, and points of input, at crucial points I made the political decisions. Sometimes I made decisions to highlight or enhance certain social contradictions and other times to flatten out contradictions. Such a process occurs in any documentary media making. Both in what the students chose to say to the camera and in how the tape was edited, some issues and contradictions, especially the most painful ones, were not addressed. Some of this was due to my directorial control, and thus it was important to me that both I and the students shared the same goal to direct their voices, analyses, and narration of lived experiences to the larger, white world.

Because the tape features student leaders of color who have an acute analysis of educational process, it has become a major "cultural guide" on campus. It is widely used to teach about the experiences of University of Oregon students of color. Following from what I learned on the affirmative action task force about how faculty and students of color have to teach institutions the same things about race over and over, always starting from zero, I conceptualized *In Plain English* as the equivalent of a classroom panel discussion featuring student leaders of color. When the teacher shows this tape before such discussions, the consideration of racial issues can start on a more advanced plane. A teacher might show the tape and lead a discussion herself instead of expecting a student leader of color to come to her class to explain racism. I have found that the effect of the tape is to empower students of color, but white viewers often resist the demand that they too conceptualize their education or workplace in terms of race. This experience of using the tape, then, has shaped the form of the subsequent book.

Following the release of the tape and its use on campus in numerous classes, two graduate students in sociology, Debbie Storrs and Abby Ferber, expressed an interest in working with me on a print version of the interviews, with the goal of publishing the full interview material and taped interviews conducted with other students of color who did not appear in the tape.[3] At that time, Storrs received a dissertation year fellowship, and so Ferber and I worked together editing and organizing the interview material for the book. We put together a preliminary book manuscript with the interview material and essays by Ferber, Storrs, and myself, as well as Donna Wong, then an administrator in academic learning services who wrote a history of students of color at the University of Oregon.

This manuscript did not yet have a cohesive vision integrating the narrative material by students of color with an activist analysis of university structure. Since we knew the tape had been used widely in diversity work at workplaces other than educational institutions, we intuited but did not yet know how to apply this material to other institutions. Ferber resurrected the project with this goal in mind, to create a book useful to a broad committed readership across institutional lines.

As the new version of the book developed, each of us brought her own specific field of expertise to bear on the project. Storrs, now teaching at the University of Idaho, understood how personal narratives provide an effective tool for conveying the complexities and lived realities of race. Ferber, teaching at the University of Colorado in Colorado Springs, had written about the intersections of whiteness and masculinity and developed a methodology to teach whiteness in the classroom. And Wong, now coordinator of academic support services in the Office of Multicultural Programs at Emory University in Atlanta, brought to bear an acute understanding of institutional structure and the various branches of an educational institution that impinge on a student's life. As these younger scholars helped me develop an analysis of how race issues are worked out in institutions today, my understanding of how to teach and write about these issues grew, especially as I delved into contemporary scholarship around race. The process of writing the book collectively was a dynamic one that involved our ongoing reconceptualizing of its emphasis and address. The interaction and mutual growth among the authors, as we exchanged scholarly resources and gained experiential knowledge from one another, mirrored the larger dialectical process of the relation between personal and social growth: people learn from one another while working together for social change.

NOTES

1. *In Plain English: University Students Speak Out* (56 min.) is available from Julia Lesage Video, 3480 Mill Street, Eugene, Oregon 97405. $40, VHS.

2. Kale moved from Eugene, Oregon, to another position. Her participation in the book project would have been greatly welcome, but unfortunately I could not locate her.

3. In *Making a Difference,* two of the names—Del Carter and Frank Piedra—are pseudonyms. In the time that elapsed between doing preinterviews for the videotape *In Plain English* and writing the narrative section of the book *Making a Difference,* these students could no longer be reached. At the preinterviews, all students in the project signed releases for both written and videotaped presentation of the material they stated to the tape recorder and later to the camera.

Acknowledgments

Many people helped with this project. In particular, we would like to thank those who contributed significantly to the content of the book: the students, Mia Tuan, and Charles Gallagher. Lynda Dickson, interim assistant vice chancellor for academic and multicultural affairs, University of Colorado, Colorado Springs, contributed an earlier insightful essay that did not fit into the current organization of the book, and we are grateful for her commitment to the overall project. Some people read the book manuscript in its entirety and offered useful suggestions that were incorporated into the revisions. These include Andrew Hacker, Dianna Kale, Kathleen Karlyn, and David Li.

Each of the authors is individually indebted to those who read our essays with excellent critiques. Karen Ford, Chuck Kleinhans, John Mihelich, and Quintard Taylor aided both our writing style and our address to a broad readership. The authors worked together collectively on this project, and we learned from one another.

Finally, in terms of the production process, we would like to thank Shari Patterson for formatting assistance and Dean Birkenkamp for excellent guidance as the project editor.

Introduction: Conceptualizing Diversity

Julia Lesage

TALKING ABOUT RACE

Although they do not experience the effects of race and do not analyze it the way people of color do, many white people talk about race at work and on campus, usually in a rather guarded way, censoring their speech according to social expectations. Publicly, white people may express reactions to welfare and affirmative action with worries about "special treatment" and favoritism: "They got in because . . ." "It was just an athletic scholarship." "I worked hard and never received any handouts." Sometimes, on a more vulgar level, you hear assertions about unreasonableness, laziness, stupidity, or criminality based on race and ethnicity; phrased more civilly, people might decry the inner city, illegal aliens, welfare mothers, unwed mothers, or the region's most recent, poorest immigrants. Furthermore, when required to attend diversity workshops or take college multicultural classes, white attendees often say things like, "What does this have to do with me?" "This makes me feel like a racist merely for being white." "Things have changed a lot." "There has been a lot of progress in this area. Why can't they quit whining?"

With common access to even more vulgar racialized speech, all white people have heard racial jokes told in their extended family or circle of friends. To avoid breaking the circle of intimacy with friends and loved ones, many respond by laughing or sitting in embarrassed silence. Those who challenge racism often find it difficult to maintain a sustained conversation if they try to explain why they found a joke offensive, usually hearing in response, "It was just a joke."

1

Furthermore, on other occasions, especially at the workplace or on campus, when more liberal whites want to discuss racial issues openly with their friends, family, or coworkers, they often hear in response a dreary, "Oh, that again, why do we always have to talk about that?" Or "I don't see any problem in . . . I just don't see that going on around here."

In contrast, to hear how people of color regularly talk about and understand everyday life as racialized, consider an incident narrated by University of Oregon student Lisa Rodriguez in part 1 of this book. Students of color were returning to the dorm after a football game, a group of white students walking behind them. The second group began talking about the video series used in their Spanish class, deliberately mispronouncing the names of the video's characters. Rodriguez describes what happened:

> They were laughing and saying racist things like, "Tortilla-eating people." "I'll trade you some refried beans for a cigarette." I turned around and started arguing with one of the white women. She said, "I don't understand why you're so offended. If I said something about economics, you wouldn't be so upset. . . . I don't know why you're getting so defensive."

Rodriguez says she and her companions contested this kind of speech, but

> when we tried to explain, they refused to acknowledge what we were telling them or why what they did was wrong. They didn't know Chicanos were walking in front of them and were surprised that we objected. . . . It helped that we were around other friends saying it's not right and to stand up for ourselves and tell them we don't like it. The white students ended up running off.

Following this episode, the students of color filed a formal complaint about racial harassment with the Office of Student Conduct.

I cite this incident because many white readers might not see this incident as exemplifying "hate speech" or deliberate harassment on the basis of race. But as Lisa Rodriguez describes what happened, her words convey the racism experienced by most students of color and one positive, proactive response to it. This book is about different ways of thinking and talking about race, as experienced by white students and students of color on predominantly white campuses across the United States, but it also could describe many other institutions and workplaces. The impetus for this book comes from its central group of narratives told by students of color at the University of Oregon. Their words have a particular address to students of color who are currently in college or preparing for college life. The interviewees originally spoke with the goal of transmitting hard-won knowledge, and their accounts can offer today's students of color strategies for navigating university life. We hope that these narratives will resonate with the experiences of today's students of color, countering their all too frequently felt sense of isolation and reaffirming their sense of community.

The students who speak in these pages offer their experiences to a wider audience in order to resolve problems that concern us all. They articulate an alternative point of view in an effort to shape a social world to sustain this point of view. As faculty and administrators, we hope to contribute to a national dialogue on how to create change. We want to trace out the implications of these narratives and what we can do in light of the insights they offer, especially through constructing histories of diversity in the institutions in which we work, developing new strategies for teaching whiteness, and working with student protests for change. We conceptualize this book as following the students' lead. Their narratives speak to the complexities of their realities, and as they speak, the students themselves deal with race and ethnicity as multifaceted. Through the presentation of their first-person perspectives, we also address ourselves to a desired audience, an implied community of listeners and readers who might act to move workplaces and educational institutions in a new direction, starting by analyzing issues that concern us all.

RACIALIZED REALITIES

In speaking of race, the book often refers to *race* and *ethnicity*, both of which are contested terms. Race itself is an illogical concept. Biologically, it does not indicate traits potentially useful for taxonomic classification; race cannot differentiate groups of homo sapiens closely enough to distinguish biological variety. In general usage, the term *race* applies only to whites (Caucasian, of European origins) and blacks (Negroid, of African origins). Yellows (Oriental, Chinese, etc.) were also once considered a race, but that has been dropped in common usage; *Asian* is the term now used in a racialized way, especially in pseudoscientific debates about the inheritability of intelligence. To complicate the matter, the students who speak to issues of race in this book talk about their experiences as Hispanics, Latinos, and American Indians, as well as various kinds of Asians. These groups, which are usually described as ethnic, cultural, or national, have shared cultures, histories, languages, and heritages. Furthermore, some terms in common usage referring to race and ethnicity have meaning only as a social distinction important in U.S. culture and law, and they are composite terms that do not refer to a single ethnic group: Asian American, Hispanic/Latino, and Native American. Recognizing some of this complexity of nomenclature but not simplifying it, the U.S. government added more categories and subcategories of race to the 2000 census, which provided sixty-three possible racial combinations for citizens to use to state their racial identity.

These issues of racial/ethnic categorization have serious consequences related to historical circumstances of oppression. Both nomenclature and ways of understanding race and ethnicity are in flux and can be shaped. Ordinarily, people have a working understanding of racial classification. And this common-sense understanding has an ideological base.

> The effort must be made to understand race as an unstable and "decentered" complex of social meanings constantly being transformed by social struggle. . . . Race continues to signify difference and structure inequality. . . . . This racial "subjection" is quintessentially ideological. Everybody learns some combination, some version, of the rules of racial classification, and of her own racial identity, often without obvious teaching or conscious inculcation.[1]

As people go through daily life and think about race, they are not confused by the words they use to talk about race nor by the signs characterizing some people as different. In daily social interactions, "race" means that we categorize people according to certain visual or accented-language traits to "mark" them as racially/ethnically distinct. For those who are "marked," some obvious distinguishing trait shapes how they are perceived and treated as well as how they perceive themselves (many are multiply "marked"): a person is a woman, a Latino, someone in a wheelchair, a child.[2] Although race is a confused category, it is one that people feel they intuitively recognize and easily use in thinking and acting. The result is that people who are unmarked, especially white men, easily—and usually do—ignore whiteness and maleness as their identifying characteristics. In contrast, to the degree that they are marked racially/ethnically, people of color have an identity that seems encapsulated by the racial label. As a result, they are on display and judged for their race.

To give an example of how both commonsense (ideological) notions of racial differentiation and also the historical context affect any extended treatment of race and ethnicity, I will describe how these issues were dealt with in planning for the videotape *In Plain English*, which was the basis for this book. In conceptualizing the form of the video, associate producer Dianna Kale and I chose to present two men and two women from each of the racial categories established by the U.S. government: Native American, African American, Asian American, and Chicano/Latino. (Three Native American women and no men came for the videotaped interviews. At that time, mostly women served in the leadership of the Native American Student Union.) Although race is a precarious category, our adherence to mainstream racial categorization reflected the power of the state to shape identities, groups, and racial politics.

Our use of mainstream categories ran the danger of reinforcing the way that these very categories and their widespread use impute a fixed identity to and lump together racial and ethnic subcultures that are diverse and in constant flux. Additionally, the categories downplayed many of the students' mixed racial backgrounds. Even as we recognized the limits of such categorization, we used the categories to organize the video and to select the interviewees because of the pervasiveness of this way of understanding race within our nation's racial logic. As their narratives show, many students identify racially on multiple levels. Furthermore, they recognize the political and personal benefits from identifying within such categories. This means that despite masking differences, such categories also provided them with a sense of belonging and the energy of participating in a resistance culture that could mobilize to bring about change.

WHITENESS AND PRIVILEGE

Being marked racially has wide-reaching social consequences. Racism's exclusionary and marginalizing practices create a limited "structure of opportunities"[3] within a social hierarchy that frames the way things are. For example, those who are "unmarked" more generally can assume a position and tone of authority since their voices more regularly get listened to and they consequently can expect institutional support. Comments such as "Why can't we put all this race stuff behind us and move on?" express an effort to acknowledge that race exists as a problem but does not amount to much. Such an act of minimizing allows whiteness and white privilege to remain largely invisible. As a white person, I can elect when to focus on race and when not to.

People of color do not have that luxury. What sounds like a complaint to white people is a description of the daily reality experienced by people of color; they cannot just "move on." The lives and experiences of people of color fall outside dominant cultural expression, with its assumptions shaping the media, education, and politics on the large scale and experienced on a more personal scale at school or work. Renato Rosaldo contrasts this unasked-for condition of being marked to the privilege of not being marked.[4] The condition of the marked is second-class citizenship. On a personal level, Rosaldo says, it means not being heard, not taken seriously, and constantly having one's group "reinterpreted" to the culture at large.

Because white people seldom feel the effects of racism personally, they often find it difficult and anxiety producing to hear that their neighborhoods, organizations, workplaces, and country are problematically structured around race. But racial inequalities shape everyone's life in America, and these inequalities lead to asymmetrical conditions of life and possibility for people of color and whites. Certain groups in the United States are systematically marginalized and disadvantaged. Existentially, on a daily basis, racialized social structures and modes of perception consistently affect people of color in an adverse way but remain largely invisible to whites. The cultural isolation and economic disadvantage that people of color face is especially acute because of residential segregation, poorer schools, and economic disadvantage.[5] Racial distinctions cause pain.

In contrast, whites usually deny privilege that they cannot see, especially if they do not condone acts of meanness toward people of color and generally wish them well, advocating equal opportunity within a meritocracy. Yet the system of advantages that white people inherit as the unmarked functions in the following way:

> Privilege generally allows people to assume a certain level of acceptance, inclusion, and respect in the world, to operate within a relatively wide comfort zone. . . . It allows people to define reality and to have prevailing definitions of reality fit their experience. Privilege means being able to decide who gets taken seriously, who receives attention, who is accountable to whom and for what.[6]

I emphasize the concept of privilege because it is the one thing that white people often deny they exploit or even have. Speaking as a white academic, I know that my own culturally privileged, intellectual community, mostly white, both limits and supports change within the university. This peer group, which offers me a stimulating work environment, largely consists of people who make me feel comfortable since they reinforce my thinking and values. However, this intellectual community has structural constraints that limit my effectiveness as a faculty member of goodwill. In particular, as a feminist scholar, I have just begun to understand the degree to which I do not intuitively see the structures of race as permeating all aspects of society, although I study this kind of pervasive structure in terms of gender.

Class and race privilege guarantee that I can do works of social critique yet keep my position of relative power as tenured faculty: I can criticize the dominant order, get a publisher, distribute a video. As a white academic in the humanities, I can move on to some other "important" issue after writing this book. That is, I can study any issue and write about it and know that my perspective will not be judged as "racial." I have extensive class privilege and can choose when to share that power, status, and privilege. When making *In Plain English*, I expected people to want to be in my video, knowing their pressing need.

My position is similar to that of many readers. One of the goals of this book is to start white readers on the road to educating themselves about their own racial location, institutional position, and ability to apply knowledge and work with, not just for, those positioned socially as subordinate or "other." Readers can articulate their own personal and cultural narratives, analyze their own location, and thus use this text in a self-referential way. Hopefully as white readers read the student narratives, they will reinterpret the institutions that they inhabit. The students of color in these pages characteristically refer to racism as white people's "ignorance," perhaps in an overgenerous way. If I look at my mostly white colleagues at work, I see their general ignorance of university structures, of institutional policy that could change, of the feelings of students of color, and of the limits to some people's opportunities. At the same time, my colleagues regularly learn and change. They do so from teaching and working with students and from their own introspective process and desire for self-development, especially their desire to improve their teaching.

Learning occurs on different levels and in different ways, especially with changes in historical circumstances. Also, the process of learning about race is awkward and full of stumbling. All of us working for institutional change have to keep in mind that everyone begins somewhere and moves from that place to understanding on a different plane. Mistakes, uneasiness, and anxiety are inevitable as well-meaning people advance their understanding of how race structures society and individual consciousness and imagination. People in the process of working for racial equity cannot stay within their comfort zone, since misunderstanding, dissent, and disagreement are part of how they learn, particularly in regard to diversity issues.

In this context, it is worth noting a few aspects of what happens when relatively ignorant but well-meaning white people in a position of privilege embark on a process of working for cultural change, in particular, working on diversity initiatives to reshape the institutions in which they work. In many disciplines there is an ongoing national dialogue and disciplinary discussions around these issues—heard at conferences, aired in journals, or presented on the Internet. For students, college is already the place where they try out new ideas and expect to change in many ways; in this regard, college is also an ideal place for white students to "tune in" to diversity issues, perhaps for the first time.

ACTIVISM

Up to this point, it has usually been people of color inside the workplace who have felt it necessary to take on the task of educating an institution. But that creates a great deal of personal stress for them and detracts from working toward professional accomplishments. Student Eric Ward describes this situation in the narratives:

> They want us here because they get more federal funding, we make the university diverse, and they learn a hell of a lot from us. They get much more from us than they

give back because we end up having to teach them so much. . . . I'm not saying anything different or better, but I am saying it. I'm taking the risk of not graduating and getting my degree in five years, when I'll be cut off financially from the support I need to complete school. It's not fair to ask that of students of color. When we open ourselves up to white people, it costs us. Whites play a role in this racist system out of complicity. Why do I always have to explain this? Every time I say something that white people don't see, I have to take my time to explain everything. I have to expose my hurt.

Ward's accusation could have been justly leveled against most U.S. colleges and workplaces for years, but now in some areas, diversity and the climate for people of color in institutions have improved, too slowly perhaps, but there are visible changes. With the "browning" of U.S. demographics, workplaces and colleges serve and have working within them an ever more racially diverse group of people. Consequently, many within these institutions are dedicated to fostering a more inclusive and welcoming environment for people of color. Much of this change has been influenced by student activism, especially that of organized campus groups of students of color, often working in collaboration with women's and gay and lesbian student organizations. Not only have these students served as a major voice teaching institutions about race, as Ward explains above, but their actions have led to institutional changes on campuses nationwide. Over the last thirty years, students of color have led an unheralded civil rights movement within colleges and universities. Despite the emotional and academic risks, students of color nationwide have continuously agitated for institutional change. But it is only more recently, perhaps in the last five years, that major changes in many schools' policies on diversity issues and their institutional structures have begun to catch up. Finally, the student voices are being heard.

Part 1 of this volume provides the reader with in-depth perspectives of people of color, an insider view that can become a starting point for broader discussion. People of color should not have to shoulder all the burden of representing the experiences of their group. We hope that the book provides white people with knowledge and perspectives that they can use to inform themselves and other whites about the issues, without having to rely on people of color to educate them and without having to tokenize people of color to serve on all the committees dealing with race in their own institutions. In that light, and because campuses are another, albeit specialized, form of a workplace, this book has value for those trying to understand and change other kinds of institutions, especially workplaces. For this reason, we conceive of our readership as including college faculty members and students—both white and nonwhite, parents of college students, and administrators and executives of colleges and of other institutions and businesses. Written in a practical way, sections of the book may find their way into diversity training seminars or in courses and faculty workshops, where selected readings can be used to spark discussions on how to move institutions toward greater inclusivity. By tying together the broad literature in this field, we give information about the many resources and organizations and models currently available to assist institutional projects for change.

DOCUMENTARY AND NARRATIVE

This book begins with a lengthy compilation of student narratives, presenting experiences of students of color at the University of Oregon. We feel that such a narration, told in the students' own voices, contributes to a fuller picture of college as an institution and as a place to live, emphasizing that there is no one, universal, or neutral "student experience." By concentrating on the voices of students of color, the narrative section displaces the focus on white college students that is generally taken as the norm. Since these students of color describe a college that is dramatically different from accounts or analyses offered from a majority perspective, this narrative material contributes to literature on higher education and also to our general knowledge about the experiences of people of color in the United States today, and is especially valuable for considerations of contemporary race relations. Interestingly, despite increased discussion nationally of multiculturalism and diversity, student voices have largely been absent or ignored in the professional literature, even though it is often student activism and protest, frequently in reaction to a racist incident, that sparks change.

In terms of its structure, *Making a Difference* is a new and different kind of book in a number of ways. First, it contains materials written with different modes and tones of address and in different kinds of voice. It begins with students of color speaking in their own voices, without extended critical interpretation. We envision that many who use the book will find this part most engaging and teachable. In its address to readers, because this section draws on empathy, the personal narratives can speak to the lived experiences of readers of color while leading white readers to understand the unarticulated problems that permeate most institutions. In particular, we hope that the book has a special address to students of color, whose concerns, analyses of race, and activism are so effectively conveyed by their peers.

The narrative section of the book also shows the project's origin as a documentary videotape. In light of my background as a documentary filmmaker and the goal of the documentary video project, which sets multiple narratives in interaction, my purpose was to strengthen the viewer's engagement with the students' historical world.[7] In the video and now in the book, first-person voices convey the texture of lived experience, while the crosscutting of those voices makes further connections between the existential realities that the students describe. In the documentary tradition that I prefer, voice-over narration is eschewed; rather, the editing, selection, and arrangement of filmed evidence encourage viewers to "see for themselves." Such a style has an ethical dimension and often relies on the strategic, relatively unobtrusive recording of a specific historical moment, which the filmmaker explores deductively, looking for its interacting forces and underlying connections. The present is filmed as living history, and certain moments in it are named, foregrounded, and rhetorically presented with the goal of the work's having a social impact.

In this project, student leaders of color articulate, in formal interviews, issues that are acknowledged in their own communities but not in the dominant culture. They speak about their personal, individual realities in a way that reveals their acute awareness of the structures, institutional constraints, and social relations prevalent in the culture at large.[8] All of the students speak out of their situated, partial knowledge; in a parallel way, the editing strategy of juxtaposing their voices emphasizes that there is no prior unity among these students nor any ontological truth about racism and ethnicity to be reached as a goal of the book. No one person's account is capable of conveying the complexity of race. What the project strives for is to open up a space for individuals who are not usually heard to talk about their experiences and provide a venue for publishing and distributing to a broader audience their firsthand accounts of their lived, historical experiences of racism and race. Left to the audience is the work of thinking through the relation between the way these students conceptualize their lives and how the reader/viewer conceptualizes her own. The first-person narratives may resonate with the audience's own experience or may help them develop an empathy for those different from themselves. By articulating an ordinarily unheeded minority discourse, the narratives make available social meanings that exist dispersed, perhaps demeaned, and certainly not broadly attended to in dominant culture, especially in the domains of politics, law, the mass media, education, and workplace environments.

The narratives begin with students talking about their experiences when they came to the university and their subsequent frustrations. To create thematic categories around which to organize the narratives, we worked deductively, drawing intertitles from student testimonies. Internally, each anecdote is often told in a chronological order, but the prose organization also crosscuts the interviews so as to highlight concerns that the students have in common. In effect the thematic categories reveal and emphasize arguments inherent in the students' thoughts, words, and analyses. For this kind of editorial style, I am indebted to Studs Terkel's *Race: How Blacks and Whites Think and Feel about the American Obsession*,[9] especially as a model of good writing and tone. I admire Terkel's social commitment and willingness to explore both his interviewees' analyses and their structures of feeling.

In doing this project, the students wanted to communicate to the public an understanding of the subjective experiences of students of color and of the structures that have shaped their lives. No single experience characterizes being a minority in a predominantly white institution. The students all differ according to their cultural positioning and individual history, and this multiplicity reveals the value of working from personal narratives to gain a perspective on social formations. The segmentation of the stories under thematic subheadings highlights perspectives that the students have in common and also sets forth their disagreements. These differences are important to attend to because they counter mainstream culture's tendency to conceptualize race in homogenizing, essentialist terms.

Today's reader is media savvy and can read many different kinds of contrapuntal or segmented editing, but too rarely is the prose editing of personal narratives used to teach social structure and contradiction. The narratives provide insight into the working of race, racial identity, and race relations in the United States, far beyond issues in higher education and workplaces. The students' stories reveal the complexity of race and starkly demonstrate how racism shapes the daily life and chances of people of color. The book as a whole builds on and extends their analyses to challenge the structural organization and deployment of privilege within U.S. institutions today.

CONTEXTUAL ANALYSES

Part 2 of the book develops some models for how readers might use, understand, and respond in a socially proactive way to the student narratives. Chapter 4, by Debbie Storrs and Julia Lesage, "The Tellers, the Tales, and the Audience: Narratives by Students of Color," details how personal narratives work and communicate a message to a wider audience. Storrs and Lesage explore how these student narratives negotiate complex issues of racial identity and indicate how personal narratives are structured, why they are told (especially when uttered for the sake of public communication), and how to use narratives in teaching.

Moving from an individual perspective to a larger social context, Donna Wong, in chapter 5, "Diversity in Higher Education Nationwide," offers a brief overview of civil rights developments in higher education in order to point out how understanding the national scene on diversity can effectively enhance the work of those acting for change. Wong advocates for more research, showing the positive effect of a multicultural curriculum on all students. Wong follows with chapter 6, "A Historical Look at Students of Color at the University of Oregon," using original research on the history of racial diversity or lack of it in the institution from which these students come. Not only does Wong present a history that is very common among predominantly white institutions of higher learning, but her work reveals that original, independent historical research is needed to understand the backdrop of diversity efforts in most institutions. This chapter can serve as a model for others to create the same kind of institutional history around race, since such information has rarely been gathered or written at the local level.

The chapters that follow look both at the national scene and at local efforts, especially in the classroom or workplace. In chapter 7, "Hate Crimes, White Backlash, and Teaching about Whiteness," Abby L. Ferber not only analyzes white backlash but also includes a more positive perspective. She looks at the approaches of various professionals, including professors and a business diversity consultant, who have developed strategies to reach whites who have difficulty acknowledging their own whiteness and the privileges it provides. The book's concluding chapter, "This Is Only the Beginning," by Abby L. Ferber and Donna Wong, written from an activist stance, gives specific strategies for acting collaboratively across institutional divisions. This chapter includes two case studies—one from a teacher with a women's studies background and one from a multicultural affairs administrator—to indicate the paths that these initiatives take in real-life situations. Wong and Ferber also focus on classroom strategies, and they show how to evaluate proactive steps taken and positive outcomes within an institution, as well as negative attitudes and institutional barriers that still persist. The footnotes and bibliographies for the articles, as well as a detailed appendix, detail the most useful contacts and resources to draw upon for planning diversity work, including concrete tools such as Web sites, associations, books, videos, and journals. The appendix contains a diversity checklist, a useful abbreviated way for people to evaluate their own institutions, especially those who think they are doing everything they can and those who know that their workplace should do more but need a set of directions and map.

Finally, as an afterword, we include the authors' autobiographical statements to give the reader an understanding of our backgrounds, work experience, and intellectual concerns. As two white women and two women of color, our diverse racial backgrounds show different paths toward working for social change. We value partial perspectives, and in one another's and the students' stories we find narrated experiences and ideas that resonate with something similar in our own lives or elicit empathy for that which is different.

It is important for everyone to explore the reality of race relations as more and more students of color inhabit university campuses. We need to consider the impact of racial diversity in predominantly white institutions. We have seen many faculty and administrators who do not understand or plan for changes in campus climate when the student body changes in racial composition. They may deeply desire peaceful coexistence yet not see the degree to which ongoing processes of change, beginning with a destabilized status quo, are already happening and are necessary.

This book puts race and ethnicity at the center of higher education, here treated as an exemplar of institutional life. We examine attitudes and relations that perpetuate and/or change racism, explore social policy, and advocate change. There are ongoing layers of change, both social and individual. Situations that have come up for us in teaching, working with colleagues, supporting student protests, and working within institutions make us aware that large-scale shifts in attitudes or institutional structures usually occur gradually but sometimes happen in spurts. When circumstances do change or when we feel stalled out, the student narratives in this book and the scholarship we cite are resources that we ourselves return to for new perspectives. We hope that as this book brings voices of faculty and student affairs administrators together with those of students of color, it aids diversity work, encouraging readers to explore relations between race, culture, education, institutional culture, and power.

NOTES

1. Michael Omi and Howard Winant, *Racial Formation in the United States: From the 1960s to the 1990s* (New York: Routledge, 1994), 55, 57, 60.

2. For this argument, I am indebted to Erving Goffman, *Stigma: Notes on the Management of Spoiled Identity* (New York: Simon & Schuster, 1986).

3. Andrew Hacker, *Two Nations: Black and White, Separate, Hostile, Unequal* (New York: Ballantine, 1995), 11.

4. Renato Rosaldo, "Cultural Citizenship, Inequality, and Multiculturalism," in Rodolfo D. Torres, Louis F. Mirón, and Jonathan Xavier Inda, eds., *Race, Identity, and Citizenship* (Malden, Mass.: Blackwell, 1999), 253–61. See also Beverly Daniel Tatum's discussion of definitions of racism in *"Why Are All the Black Kids Sitting Together in the Cafeteria?" and Other Conversations about Race* (New York: Basic, 1999). Following David Wellman in his *Portraits of White Racism* (Cambridge: Cambridge University Press, 1977), she defines racism as a "system of advantage based on race" (p. 7).

5. Hacker in *Two Nations* demonstrates statistically how blacks in the United States have faced greater disadvantage, not only historically but continuing into the present.

6. Allan G. Johnson, *Privilege, Power, and Difference* (Mountain View, Calif.: Mayfield, 2001), 33. See also Joe Kinchloe, "The Struggle to Define and Reinvent Whiteness: A Pedagogical Analysis," *College Literature* 26, no. 3 (1999): 162–95.

7. For an extended discussion of how history and historiography intersect with documentary, see Bill Nichols, *Representing Reality: Issues and Concepts in Documentary* (Bloomington: Indiana University Press, 1991).

8. Patricia Ewick and Susan S. Sibley consider these disruptive narratives because in them, a personal story is told with the intent of making clear the social structures behind the event: "If narratives contribute to hegemony to the degree that they efface the connections between the particular and the general, perhaps subversive stories are those that employ those connec-

tions, making manifest the relationship between what C. Wright Mills called biography and history" (p. 218). "Subversive Stories and Hegemonic Tales: Toward a Sociology of Narrative," *Law and Society Review* 29, no. 2 (1995): 197–226.

9. Studs Terkel, *Race: How Blacks and Whites Think and Feel about the American Obsession* (New York: Doubleday, 1992).

I

UNIVERSITY STUDENTS OF COLOR IN THEIR OWN VOICES

1

School, Language, and Identity

THE STUDENTS: BIOGRAPHICAL SKETCHES

K_ronda Adair_ comes from an African American family and was raised in the African American community in Portland, Oregon. She sees herself facing triple jeopardy as a black lesbian and feminist activist. She says that because of her black skin she will always have to deal with racism and black issues.

Geo. Ann Baker is Klamath and Payute; she does not consider herself a citizen of the United States but rather a member of her tribe and her family. In her own family, she has experienced the generational loss of their indigenous language. She now works closely with the Native American Student Union to form a support system to help native students stay in school.

Del Carter grew up in a small Nevada town where her mother taught her how to deal with the epithet of "nigger," which she first encountered in grade school. When she came to the university, Del felt completely isolated, which led her to see the need to build student/community ties to support black students. She finds support in a black sorority that has, she says, "helped me enhance my identity and learn a lot more about black culture."

Carol Cheney, along with her twin sister, was adopted by a family living in small-town eastern Oregon. She is one of numerous Korean children born to U.S. servicemen and Korean women who were brought to Oregon for adoption through Holt International Children's Services. Cheney discusses how taking a course on Asian American women's biographical narratives, taught through women's studies, has had a formative influence on her identity and self-esteem.

Callan Coleman is the son of an African American professor who founded ethnic studies at the university. Callan completed a master's degree in counseling

17

and remains in Eugene, where his family continues to play a major role in supporting the small African American community in this campus town.

Diana Collins-Puente is Guatemalan and came to the United States with her family when she was eight. She discusses how, as a fair-skinned Latina, she reacts to racial slurs and racialized humor when she is forced to listen to it. She is an activist in MEChA, the Mexican/Chicano/Latino students association.

Kevin Diaz is a Peruvian American who describes himself as very "Anglo" looking and is also active in MEChA. He discusses the dynamics of language use in his family while he was growing up. His younger brother felt isolated because he did not speak Spanish until he took a college language course as a young adult in Mexico.

Leyla Farah has a Lebanese father and an African American mother and is very proud of the tradition of strong, self-reliant women in her family. Her travels and her mixed race experiences put her somewhat outside the African American community of students on campus, and she has found her main support group through women's studies and a black sorority.

Gretchen Freed-Rowland is Ojibwa and Winnebago and was raised in a family that embraced the concept of a pan-Indian identity rather than tribal association. When she entered graduate school at age fifty, after years teaching secondary school, much of it abroad, she faced the humiliating experience of having to get tribal enrollment to qualify for a scholarship, a kind of certification not required of any other U.S. minority group.

Meredith Li is fourth-generation Chinese American yet is often asked where she comes from. She grew up in the small community of Corvallis, Oregon. In the public schools "you could count the students of color on one hand." In her senior year in the Honors College, she wrote her thesis on "The Myth of Asians as the Model Minority."

Maria Mendoza comes from a Mexican American family in a small farming community, where her parents have a history as farmworker union organizers. She is an activist in MEChA and feels she owes much of her success in college to the strong foundation and support she has received from her family.

Armando Morales is a Mexican American who discusses the prejudice he faces because he speaks with a strong accent. Morales's home base is Eugene, where he is a strong contributor to the local cultural environment.

Jon Motohiro is from Hawaii and is active in the well-established UO Hawaiian student association. Of Japanese ancestry, he uses language learning in college both to enhance his business training and to create stronger ties with his grandparents.

Frank Piedra comes from a Japanese and Puerto Rican background and has spoken Spanish, Japanese, and English fluently since childhood. He is working his way through college while raising a younger sister, and he discusses racial insults he has to face at work, in town, and on campus.

Lisa Rodriguez went to the university because her friend Maria Mendoza was already here. Like Maria, Lisa comes from a Spanish-speaking Mexican American family, and her experiences have also led her to become an activist in MEChA. Lisa discusses how jokes that contain ethnic slurs hit her hard and how she finds it important, as do many other students of color, "to spend time socially with other people around who care and who are experiencing the same things you are."

Shelli Romero comes from a Mexican American family, but her parents were punished for speaking Spanish in school, so she did not grow up speaking Spanish. She is relearning the language, a process that leads her to articulate eloquently the "cultural genocide" inflicted on many people of color in the United States. Her father is director of ESL (English as a second language) and bilingual education for the Portland schools, and she feels he has taught her the importance and value of contributing to the community.

Sweeter Sachuo came to the University of Oregon from the Truk Islands in the Pacific; he and his family are citizens of the United States although they cannot vote. Working on a doctorate in education, writing a dissertation on the influence of U.S. education on Trukese children, Sachuo strives to educate his own children in his people's ways, although the children are also very attracted to the American way of life. His brothers also reside here, and as a group of dark-skinned men walking arm in arm down the street together, they are often harassed by police.

Michelle Singer is Navaho. Her parents met as teenagers at the Indian boarding school in Salem, Oregon. They married and stayed in Salem to raise a family while working in the same school they attended as teens. Michelle went to public school but had regular contact with the Native American students at her parents' school. Active in NASU, the Native American Student Union, Singer talks about the toll such work takes on her studies and grades, about her commitment to her community and fellow native students, and about the lack of general support from the university for minority students.

Eric Ward is an African American student from Los Angeles who was originally attracted to the "New Age" liberalism of Eugene but came to see the shallowness of this liberal posture. Like the other dark-skinned men who speak here, he has been harassed by the local police. Committed to a life of social activism, he eloquently explains what it means to have to be on display as a "representative of his race" and to have to continuously educate the campus community about issues of race.

STICKS AND STONES:
EARLY SCHOOLING AND RACISM

"Sticks and stones will break my bones but names will never hurt me." This children's rhyme suggests that children can be hurtful to one another and that name-calling is less harmful than physical violence. The students suggest otherwise, understanding how both forms of violence harm self-esteem. Looking back on their previous education, students discuss the racial incidents that they faced, both explicit and subtle. Central to these students' memories is how dominant group members positioned them as different, inferior, or marginal. While students of color unfortunately have this common experience, they differ in their strategies for coping. For example, as Gretchen Freed-Rowland points out, in predominantly white grade and high schools, Native American students were often useful to teachers as a token or a representative person of color as long as they behaved "in an appropriate way and did not make waves or create discomfort for other people."

In training teachers, only in the past decade have colleges incorporated multicultural education and implemented some diversity training into their credentialing programs, and these programs vary greatly in quality and depth. Such training is important because K–12 educators have to become aware of the ways in which racist comments from fellow students and teachers mar the experiences of students of color in early education and lower their academic confidence and self-esteem. When public school administrators and teachers dismiss racial comments or intimidation as "unintentional" and do not discipline the perpetrators, the resulting educational environment can have a devastating effect. Currently, on the level of K–12 education, more public school districts have begun to implement antiracism policies to foster tolerance and mutual respect.

Del Carter

In third grade in a small Nevada town, I walked up to a girl on the playground and asked her to play. She said, "No, my dad says I can't play with niggers." Because she'd called me a name, not because of that particular word, I went to the principal. Earlier my mom had taught me a little about what to expect, since we were one of the few African American families in town. Now she sat me down and explained racism. She said that people are taught racism when they're young and unless they're educated about it as they get older, they take pleasure in making fun of people because of race. That was the case in junior high where the kids wanted to provoke a violent reaction from me. They thought it was funny to make me cry. I could not tolerate it and fought my way through junior high.

Then I grew up. By high school I'd learned not to react. I kept my reactions inside and dealt with incidents in my own way. For the rest of my life I'd have to face racial slurs and couldn't continue fighting at every one. My white friends did not understand the racist comments and at most reacted with, "I can't believe that happened to you." My mom has been my best friend for a long time and she got me through it, saying, "Small towns breed small minds." A realist, she let me know that there's no way to smooth over racism. Slurs will always come up and you have to deal with them.

Callan Coleman

Here in Eugene, Oregon, white parents typically don't teach their children about black people. I was surrounded by children who didn't understand things about me like my hair. They'd ask, "Do you have to brush your hair?" After a while those comments wore on me. But I had no choice but to get used to them. When the news or a film that we saw in school dealt with black people, only I would feel the issue's intensity. Furthermore, my classmates thought of me in terms of stereotypes, expecting me to dance or play basketball. I didn't like it and was too young to understand that I needed to teach them. Sometimes I did things that I wouldn't do now. Back then, for instance, if somebody said, "Hey, dance for us," I might have danced. I didn't realize what that meant, for a black kid to be dancing around a bunch of white people, and the other kids didn't realize it either.

In social studies class in high school we did role playing of colonial landowners and indentured servants from Europe. I played an indentured servant. Even though everyone knew I was playing a white person, as soon as we began playing the role, we clicked into this harsh master and scared, submissive slave act. The other student yelled at me. I started begging for forgiveness and went out of control. I felt odd afterward but didn't know what I'd done. Years later I realized how movies had given us an image of servitude and how through our unconscious history we fell right into those roles. It felt nasty but I didn't have the words to ask, "Do you understand the repercussions of what just happened?" I couldn't even turn to one of my classmates and say, "I feel creepy about what happened." They'd have responded, "I understand."

Eric Ward

In Los Angeles I'm used to overt racism with people driving by and screaming "nigger" or "go back to Africa." I was bussed into Long Beach for junior high. People would drive by all the time calling slurs. Once we were sitting at the bus stop when four college students, white men, drove by screaming, "Niggers go back to Africa!" We yelled back. They stopped and started to get out. We picked up rocks, threw them, broke some windows, and ran. At school we'd hear, "You're being bussed here so you can get a better education." For us it meant getting up an hour and a half earlier and hearing all kinds of abuse while walking to the bus stop. Usually someone would be screaming. I guess things in the South were worse, but to me it was much the same.

Because I'm black, college wasn't there for me in high school. I never considered it a goal. None of my counselors ever mentioned anything about community college, even though I had a 3.4 grade point average. Nor did they say anything about financial aid since I couldn't afford to go to college on my own. No one ever talked about my going on to a university or even to a city college, much less what college preparatory classes to take. The school had the attitude: "Let 'em come in, give them their degree, and let them move out."

Geo. Ann Baker

On the first day of school we would have to stand up and say our name and nationality: "I'm Suzie and I'm an American." "Hi, my name's Mary and I'm Italian and my father owns this." To start off, my name is spelled differently. It's spelled "Geo. Ann" on my birth certificate. My teachers would argue and tell me that's not the way it's spelled. One time I even brought my birth certificate to which they said, "Your mother didn't know what she was doing." I would stand up and say, "My name is George Ann and I'm named after my mother and my father. I'm Klamath and Payute." When I'd sit down, the kids would start, "What's that? Where are you from?" The teacher would say, "She's Indian." Then they'd ask, "Do you live in teepees? Do you ride a horse? Do you wear a red dot on your head? Do you ride elephants?" They'd confuse me with people from India. I was so embarrassed that I hated the first day of school. Later I'd say my name real fast and "I'm Indian," trying to get it over with as fast as possible.

When I was growing up, my classmates often called me "nigger," but I didn't know what that meant since my mother never allowed the word in our house. She told me I looked like my grandmother and my mother. The earth is our mother and when we're born, we're our mother's color. My grandmother is the night, and that's why my hair is black. In turn, I tell my son, "People make fun of you because they are jealous. They are so ashamed that they don't have something to belong to that they try to ridicule and degrade you and take away what you have. If you start feeling bad about yourself, think about lost people and look at them. People who don't have an identity are so lost that they want to take up some culture or race that is not even their own. Look at all the people who wear turquoise and beadwork here in Eugene."

Maria Mendoza

When I was little I knew I wasn't accepted. My mom said she found me in her room putting Johnson's baby powder all over me. I told her I wanted to be white. She also said that when she used to bathe me, I'd try to scrub away my skin color. In public school Chicano kids either assimilated or kept their culture and heritage. When I was in primary school, I tried my best to fit in and would lie about where my family was from: "I'm from California." Not from Mexico! I faced so many racist incidents in public school, I can't possibly tell about them all. In fourth grade one of the most popular kids came up to me and asked my name and if I was a "nigger." Not knowing what the word meant, I replied, "No, I was born in the United States."

I fought a lot when I was in junior high and a little bit in high school. Still I made good grades, which had to do with my father's influence. If I'd bring home Bs, he'd say that's good but not good enough. I faced a lot of pressure from him but now I thank him for it. He always valued education. He only went through sixth grade in Mexico, where he had to memorize everything and recite it to the professor. He's proud that he can still remember every detail. I gained a lot of pride from my father. He'd say, "My father was in the Mexican revolution" and would go on about Mexico's history. He'd sing old songs, ones that he heard when he was growing up. He still goes around the house singing these songs all the time. I grew up around that background and admired it. Other children admired things like clothes. I had something to be proud about and preferred my father's mentality, one closed off from the white community.

I graduated as salutatorian of the class with a 4.0 average. Yet when I went to the counselor, he told me that I should consider going to community college because he thought a university would be too challenging for me. Or I should look into the army. I was never told about the University of Oregon or Oregon State or any universities outside of Oregon. We students of color come into universities on our own merit. However, it is harder for us to get here, since high schools offer so much discrimination and discouragement.

Meredith Li

In eighth grade I had to deliver a message to a teacher I'd never met before. He wanted me to stay and explain things about China, which I couldn't do. He made me point out on a map where I was supposedly from. I kept saying, "I'm from Davis, California." "No," he insisted, "I mean where you're from." I have a rough idea of where my family came from in China and pointed to that spot. Later in high school, a teacher told our class, "You guys better look out because there's an Asian in this class. Asians always kill the curve. I always hated having

Asians in my classroom when I was in school." He meant it as a joke, but he was picking me out and creating a negative feeling based on what I look like.

Carol Cheney

If I didn't have my twin sister, I don't know how I would have made it through life. I first recognized racism when kids made fun of the shape of our eyes. They put their hands up to their eyes and pulled their eyes apart. We couldn't understand the gesture but we knew they were making fun of us. When we asked my adopted mom to explain, she said, "It's because you're Korean and you look different. They don't understand you." My folks tried to celebrate our Koreanness, yet they couldn't understand our situation because they didn't have to deal with being ostracized by classmates. After we moved to eastern Oregon, my sister and I were the only two children different from anybody else in the town. And eighth graders can be mean. We felt like loners and knew our parents could never understand our feelings. We clung together.

Gretchen Freed-Rowland

Growing up in Oregon, we were often the token Indian family in an all-white community. My mother and her sisters and my grandparents and their nineteen grandchildren all excelled at being "good." I was a Rose Festival princess in high school, which led to college scholarships. As long as we were doing well, the response was, "This is our Indian girl. This is our Indian family." As an adult, I found out that the world reacted quite differently to an outspoken Indian woman, especially workplaces or schools that did not accept my opinions and ways of doing things. For us it's a double bind. If we do it right and people need us to be Indians, then we're Indians. But people may need someone who looks like an Indian but will behave in an appropriate way and not make waves or create discomfort for other people.

SPEAKING TONGUES: LANGUAGE

Through language we affirm where we are from and who we are. The cornerstone of identity, language is often a contested site, a locus of psychological and social conflict. For most of the students who speak here, language has been an issue highly charged with emotion and rife with contradiction. Students here discuss their own histories and struggles surrounding language and frequently want to talk about the complex experience of straddling two cultures and two languages.

While some students are bilingual, others grieve the loss of their ancestors' tongue and analyze the process of language assimilation in their families. They may have encountered the expectation that they know their parents' or grandparents' language, yet they understand the many reasons why the older generation has not passed on its language to the next. In particular, many of the students' parents faced discrimination in primary school, where they were punished if they spoke a language other than English. Currently, with a greater emphasis on globalization, college students' bilingualism may be encouraged since it can have a positive effects on future employment possibilities. However, since most primary and secondary schools do not regularly offer bilingual education and it is not funded as much as it was in the past, in most parts of the United States, immigrant parents usually encounter a sink-or-swim mentality about children learning English.

For the students who speak here, the college experience may have provoked them to reassess their relation to their family's language or to question whose language will be acknowledged and celebrated publicly. Some reclaim their ancestors' language through college classes while others explore the languages of other groups. Still other students discuss how nonverbal language styles differ by racial and ethnic groups, revealing again the power of language in shaping and reflecting personal identity and in establishing or discouraging community solidarity.

Frank Piedra

My mother is Japanese and my father is Puerto Rican. My father was in the military, so we had to move around a lot. Both cultures shaped my life. When my folks divorced, my mother married another military man, and we moved all around the world. I've lived all over the United States, East Coast, West Coast, and also in Europe and Asia. I never lived in Puerto Rico but I lived in New York. I still try to speak all three languages—English, Spanish, and Japanese. I'm proud of my ethnicities. At the university I do not get treated like an American nor like an Asian. The Chicano group treats me well but I'm not Chicano.

Puerto Rico is part of the United States. It's an island in the Caribbean taken over by the United States about a hundred years ago after the Spanish-American War. People expect Puerto Rico to be a foreign country and do not treat it like it's America. Puerto Ricans have a bad reputation. That upsets me. When I was in Japan, I was discriminated against as an American. My Japanese relatives treat me like I am an American, which I am. But I'm also Asian. I grew up spending a lot of time in Asia, and I speak and write Japanese. I never thought that I was a this or a that but an American. I never felt this problem till I came to Oregon. Now it seems I can belong everywhere but don't fit in anywhere.

Lisa Rodriguez

My best friend Maria's mother was my baby-sitter every day and she spoke only Spanish. I didn't start learning English until first grade. At home we throw both languages together. My father knows English but feels more comfortable speaking Spanish, which he has always done, as have all my relatives. My summer work always included translating for people, speaking and writing. Here, a lot of students who don't know how to speak English very well ask me for help, and lately I've worked with Chicano students studying for their high school equivalency certificate. I like being able to do something for someone else, and I'm glad I can speak two languages. My brother didn't go to Maria's mother for baby-sitting but to a neighbor across the street. He understands Spanish but has trouble speaking it. When my father speaks in Spanish, my brother answers in English since my brother can only put some Spanish words together and not make complete sentences.

Many Chicano college students who don't speak Spanish are taking Spanish classes and trying hard to learn it. They feel frustrated when someone expects them to speak Spanish because of the way they look or because they're Hispanic or Mexican. Some Chicano students here grew up in small, closed-minded, racist towns. These kids felt compelled to assimilate into mainstream culture and weave into the crowd. Their parents might not have allowed them to speak Spanish at home, just English, so they would fit in. Schools especially hassle migrant students, since everything is taught in English.

Shelli Romero

My family's first language is English. Even though my parents grew up completely bilingual, they faced a lot of hardships. If they spoke Spanish at school, they would get hit and sent to the principal. They didn't want that kind of thing happening to us. Basically they went through language genocide. I could always understand Spanish but spoke English. I had to study Spanish three years in junior high, three years in high school, and one year at the university to learn all the grammar. Right now I'm at the point where I need to go study abroad to improve my fluency. I studied abroad once in Guadalajara, Mexico, when I was fourteen, but I need to go again. It means a lot to me that I've attempted to be literate in two languages. I've not only learned a lot of words that my parents use, but I've found a way to combat what I think is internal oppression because through language study, I could reclaim myself. Since my culture was taken away from me, I've had to be twice as strong to reclaim it. I've had trouble with people's expectations that as a Chicana I should already speak Spanish. Even here, many Spanish teachers tell Hispanic students, "You should know that."

"You should know how to write it if you're from Honduras." "You should know how to speak it if you're a Chicano." That's not necessarily the case for Chicanos who were born here. Spanish teachers should understand that.

Meredith Li

Although I'm of Chinese ancestry, I'm studying Japanese at the University of Oregon. That's confusing for a lot of people. My family has been in the United States for a little over a century and a half. Nobody asks students from a European background, "Why aren't you taking German? Your last name, isn't it German?" Or, "Why aren't you taking French? Aren't you of French ancestry?" Because I'm so identifiable as coming from another ethnic group, they wonder why I would possibly want to take Japanese when I could be taking Chinese. I find Chinese interesting and consider it valuable to learn about my background, but I became interested in studying Japanese.

It's almost embarrassing when I can't speak Chinese and so many people expect me to. The worst situations have been in San Francisco, where my brother and I have gone to eat in Chinese restaurants. Since we look Chinese, Chinese people there immediately assume that we can speak the language and treat us like we're uneducated when we cannot.

Jon Motohiro

I'm proud to be from Hawaii but am aware that I am Japanese. There's a native Hawaiian race, a very proud group. Out of respect to them, I want to make it clear that I'm not a native Hawaiian. I am proud of Japanese American history, what my people accomplished, and what they've had to go through. At an early age I started to appreciate my Japanese ancestry.

I've studied the language since seventh grade partly because of my Japanese ancestry and partly from my parents' encouragement. My grandparents are very proud of me and every time I write them a letter in Japanese, they'll wake up my parents at 6:00 A.M. on Sunday to read the letter aloud over the phone. Learning the language seems important not only for personal fulfillment but also professionally because of Japanese investment in Hawaii. I'd like to help in bringing the United States and Japan to work together. It's not good for these two strong countries to be fighting each other when so many other countries are forming alliances.

Maria Mendoza

My parents only speak Spanish. My father, who's seventy-eight, came to the United States in 1945. He has pride in his heritage and speaks English only when he has to. My mother knows English, but around our family she always speaks Spanish. I have a sister who was born in Mexico and is seven years older than me, whom I grew up with. She came to the United States with my mother when she was eight and had to repeat the first grade because she didn't know English well enough. As she learned English, I learned through her. She'd practice English with me. We shared a private language. I grew up learning both languages, but when I was young I didn't want to speak Spanish because it was discouraged in school. Now it's an advantage to speak both languages fluently.

Diana Collins-Puente

I came to the United States from Guatemala at age eight with my parents and two older brothers. I learned English in school. Many of my classmates were helpful and would let me write down their names on little sheets of paper. I would stick labels on everything, and that way I learned English slowly. Sometimes I would get taken away from class to help translate for parents who couldn't speak English well. In school my ethnicity was considered positive. My parents spoke English a little, but Mom almost always spoke Spanish to us. Dad would switch back and forth depending on the situation. My brothers took longer to learn English and still have a strong Guatemalan accent.

When I went to Europe last summer, everybody I met knew three or four different languages including English. I feel ignorant speaking only two languages, yet so many people in the United States speak only one. It makes me sad. Language is such an easy thing to learn from birth if it's encouraged. Part of U.S. culture doesn't want to embrace other cultures. Once when my brothers and mom and I were grocery shopping, I found someone in the store who spoke Spanish. As we were talking, a shopper came by and screamed at us, telling us to go back to where we came from and that we weren't wanted here.

Kevin Diaz

My parents speak Spanish and English back and forth but have spoken more English as time has gone on. My brother is seven years younger than I am and didn't speak Spanish. He felt excluded if we spoke Spanish at the dinner table. Last year he got shipped to relatives in Mexico for three months, and now we can speak more Spanish because he understands what's going on. I'm competent in Spanish and understand everything, but I do not know enough about my father's culture.

Armando Morales

I teach Spanish here as a graduate instructor. At the beginning of the term I'd tell a joke: "I know some of you will say, 'Whoa, this guy has a funny accent,' but I'm from Texas." After the class laughs, I add, "Let me tell you why I said I'm from Texas. When somebody from the East Coast comes to this university to teach, you never question his or her accent. And if you hear people from Louisiana or from Virginia, they talk funny but nobody says anything. But when it's a student or professor of color with an accent, then everybody questions him. It doesn't matter if he's born in this country or not."

I learned English in the streets, at community college, and in the university. We Latinos need to learn English if we want to work and to develop here. I'm not saying that we'll reject our culture, but to deal with people, we want to learn English. We also want Anglos to learn our language and our culture if they want to work with us. We need this interchange of ideas for a better society.

Geo. Ann Baker

When I was small, my mother and father both worked, she as an accountant and he as a juvenile police officer. My mother would leave me with my grandmother, who spoke the Klamath language to me. Grandmother was on the tribal council and would take me to meetings, where I'd hang around and listen. The old ladies would all talk in this language and I'd understand them. When we moved, grandmother quit talking Klamath to me. I never knew why.

After I got out of high school, I asked her, "Grandma, why don't you talk to me anymore?" She told me that when she was eleven they had shipped her to a boarding school in Riverside, California. There she was beaten for speaking her own language. She thought that if I went to school and spoke my language, they would beat me. In order to save me, she quit speaking Klamath to me. So I can remember only a very few words in my own language. I asked grandmother to teach me but she still won't do it. She'll say things like "get the water" or "I'm going here," little baby words. I still listen to her talk to other old ladies, but she won't talk Klamath to me or my children.

When my mother and father were still together, my father taught me Payute. Then they got a divorce. I never kept up the Payute language because I'm closer to my mother's side of the family than my father's, so I can only remember a few Payute words. I'm gradually picking up a little Klamath. The Klamath tribe has made a tape and a little booklet and given it to the head of each household so we can start learning our own language again. I lost the tape, but I still try to learn. I practice with a friend at school here who knows a little bit more than I do, but the real old language is lost and has a lot of slang mixed into it now. The tribe even made a dictionary, but it's so complicated that there's no way I can comprehend it. I talk to my cousins who have a little more access to Klamath than I do, but most of the time I ask Grandma, and she'll say a phrase to me.

She's one of the few remaining people down there that can still speak the language fluently. But she has nobody to talk Klamath to. Maybe there are two others, but of the three of them, one is deaf, one is hard of hearing, and the other barely sees. Grandmother was born in 1908. If I ask her, "Grandmother, how do you say this?" or "What did you say this was?" she'll tell me, but I forget and she does too, even though I try to keep it in my head. In one of my classes last year we had to do an interview and I interviewed my grandmother with a camcorder. I asked her, "Do you still speak your language and would you like to do so?" She said, "No."

English is not my native language. If I had my choice, I would learn another language. For my major at the university, I have to take a foreign language and I'd like to learn Lakota. I speak a lot of Lakota since my husband's Lakota. The university said they can't let me do this because they'd have to hire somebody to come in and test me. I said I'd be willing to pay for it and would even hire my own teacher. But no, I have to take the standardized Spanish or French or whatever.

Michelle Singer

My parents speak broken English, still broken English. They very much speak Navaho, and they don't let us forget it. Over the years they've been speaking to us half in English and half in Navaho. My first language was English. My older sister can understand Navaho from hearing and translating but doesn't speak it. My brothers don't understand it, only certain words. I can read Navaho phonetically and understand it to the point where I can carry on a conversation. We have a Navaho Bible and little story booklets comparable to a first grade level. The books have English on one page and Navaho on the other. But Navaho's so complex and has so many dialects that it's hard to understand. My parents would teach us words and try to teach us the language. Sometimes they'd get upset at us because we couldn't learn. Sometimes they thought we didn't want to learn or that we didn't take it seriously enough. We went to school and studied in English and then came home to learn our own language. We tended to stray away from our own language and speak English because school always emphasized that.

Callan Coleman

When I think about nonverbal communication, I think about all the times I get looked at as if I don't belong here. That makes me feel self-conscious. I understand that there aren't a lot of black people here, but when you are the person being looked at, it's upsetting. Sometimes people smile, which is nice, but sometimes they look at you like they suspect you and don't like seeing you here. That's a horrible feeling. You want to stop them and say, "I've probably lived here longer than you. Don't make me feel like I'm an outsider. This is my town, too."

With black people, especially in this small white town, if you saw another African American and they saw you, the tendency would be to look and nod, smile or wave. Some black students who come from areas with a lot of African Americans aren't in this habit. When I see them, I'm surprised when they don't want to acknowledge me, and I tend to forget that not everybody comes from a place where it's a novelty to see another African American. I like the feeling of nodding and saying, "Hi, brother, how are you doing?"

I'm starting to learn in counseling classes about eye contact because they teach us that it is necessary to hold eye contact. Within black culture, constant eye contact does not indicate personal connection like, "I'm there for you," but is received as if I were staring at you. When I sit and speak with other African Americans, we typically don't look into each other's eyes. We tend to look around, then glance, then look around. We usually make that contact when making the final point and then it's while we're summing up. When you're listening, when somebody is speaking to you, it's typical to look around. I've noticed that people who come from Africa don't like to look at you a lot. Culturally it's more of an imposition, more of a hard stare.

Sweeter Sachuo

We don't speak our native language in school, only English. At home we speak Trukese. This causes some conflict and disruption because when we are at school we learn things in English that are not taught at home, and at home we know things that have no place in school. We face that conflict. Here in the United States we talk Trukese to the children, ages seven, nine, and ten, and also English. We mix the languages because there are some English concepts that we don't have in Trukese, like snow. Right now the children are more fluent in English and it's difficult for them to speak Trukese. When they entered school, they had a hard time being accepted because they didn't speak English well. But since they've become fluent, they have more friends.

When I first came here, my accent was bad and I spoke slowly, saying one word, pausing, then saying another. I could sense that people were not paying attention to me. In fact, they'd turn away from me because they expected me to speak fast, like in this culture. In writing, first I think about the concept in Trukese; then I have to look for an English word to translate it into. It's a very difficult process.

Gretchen Freed-Rowland

I didn't know that being a girl or a woman was all that different until I became an adult and observed the hierarchy of power. It's related to who gets to name things and decide how you're supposed to perform. It's related to the use of "mankind" instead of "human kind," "he" as the universal for us all. In the English language, we have a subject and a predicate. He/she, the actor, acts upon something rather than *with* something. Linguistically in many American Indian languages and other indigenous languages, the subject does or acts with whomever or whatever the object is. We accomplish whatever is done within a relationship. We do it together. For example, as Leslie Silko describes it in *Ceremony*, the hunter hunts with the deer and when the deer dies, basically, the hunter shoots with the deer, with the deer's permission. There's a sense of relation that the structure of our language leads us to remember and respect.

My cultural style and thinking style did not blend in with the department where I was doing graduate work in the School of Education. The faculty indicated that I was incompetent and needed remedial English courses even though I had taught junior high and high school English for years. I didn't know academic style. Give me any other kind of exam and I'll do very well. The problem is in how I put it together. What I've learned since then is that I have a storytelling, anecdotal style. I grew up in a storytelling environment where my grandmother could take a story we'd heard many times, a myth of epic proportions, and spread it out several days. She'd build on our anticipation and teach us patience. Similarly, my grandfather liked to stop on the road if he saw an interesting-looking person and go talk to them. My grandmother and I would sit in the car for twenty minutes and then he'd come back and say, "You won't believe this," and he'd tell us a wonderful story about that person. In terms of my graduate studies, I used to think, "They can't just want that. It's too simple." If I give you that simple outline, you don't know what those words mean to me. There's no context. "Precision" is the cultural language trap of academia. Academic language has to be narrow and clear. It has to be rigorous and valid. You end up with a tiny little piece of something and have thrown out all the context. And this kind of writing still uses the adversarial language of "us and them," as if there were an enemy, rather than foster Euro America's own heritage in terms of providing an organic understanding of the speaker's and writer's being in the world.

DEFINING OURSELVES: IDENTITY

The notion that race is a biological reality is a socially enforced fiction, enacted and perpetuated by law, social custom, and institutional and residential segregation and discrimination. Psychologically and socially, everyone in the United States reads race by exterior bodily signs. White people do not usually have the experience of identifying who they are and evaluating their cultural status according to race, nor of having constantly to do so. Here readers will get a "feel" of what life is like when shaped by race and ethnicity.

Students of color cannot ignore the meaning of skin color and other visible racial markers or lack of them. The students who speak here are also self-conscious in how they define their race and ethnicity, understanding the political implications of and complications behind racial constructions. Thus they explore issues such as their relation to the United States as a nation and to "American-ness," the complex intersections of race and gender, and the performative nature of racial and ethnic identity. Kronda Adair, for example, discusses how dark skin or blackness marks an identity one cannot mask, although the meaning of blackness and of participating in an African American community varies for African American students. Many of these students discuss the need to be with people like themselves, but they note that sometimes they do not fit in with the ethnic group formations on campus.

Maria Mendoza

It's always been a big issue whether you call yourself Hispanic, Chicano, or Latino. Many people, including myself, do not accept the word "Hispanic," which is the name given by the government to clump us all together. It is completely Spanish oriented and denies our Indian heritage. Some say, "We are Chicano, Mexican," and do not accept "Latino." I prefer Chicano or Latino, and our organization is "Chicano/Latino" since we have a lot of Latinos in it. Within the group, some people speak Spanish and some don't. I've heard other people whom I know from California say that if you can't speak Spanish, you're denying who you are, and they do not consider you as Chicano or Mexican as the next person.

Here at the university, white students have a lot of hostility toward students of color. Many Anglo students think it's not fair that we are here and they also think that we are admitted to the university and get scholarships just because we're black or Chicano or Native American. In fact, it is a lot more difficult for us to get to the university because there is so much discrimination at the high school level, where we're never encouraged to come to a four-year college or a university. My friends and I were told to join military service or go to a community college.

Diana Collins-Puente

Many people assume I'm Mexican and I hate that. I'm very proud of my Guatemalan culture and my ethnicity. Even though I appreciate Mexican culture, it's not mine. To call me Mexican is not an insult, but it's not respectful of me.

When fellow students ask, "Oh, you're Mexican?" if I sound Hispanic, they do not do it to find out anything about me. Even when I say I'm from Guatemala, they think Guatemala is Mexico, a city in Mexico. Lately I heard someone say, "Yeah, Diana, that Mexican girl." I have to keep criticizing them until they get it and one day stop saying it.

Kevin Diaz

Most people do not know what a Chicano or Latino is and are still using "Hispanic" or "Mexican." The reason we get labeled "Hispanic" in the first place is for bureaucrats who want categories to show "hard facts." The fact that those bureaucrats are generally white shows their ignorance when they try to lump us together like that. I don't have a problem being called Latino, although Latin America is incredibly diverse. I'm not Chicano and would correct someone if they called me that.

Because of my light complexion, people don't think twice about saying things or think that maybe I have something going on in my head that is not going to agree with what they're saying. They say it, of course. If I'm quiet at first, then they start to feel comfortable. It's been agreed that the basis of what we're talking about is a single, monocultural activity. The next thing I know, something will come out and I'll either have to confront them or leave. Many times if I don't clarify who I am when I'm in a group of people, unpleasant things come out. I'm disheartened when I invest a lot of time in someone from a very different background and eventually we have to part in a hostile way. When dating, generally I go out with women who understand what's going on outside the United States. But with my male friends, I've had serious differences over the Gulf War that cannot be resolved. Several friends fought in that war or were very prowar. I came from Peru and know that the Gulf strategy had originally been formulated for Peru. Because I knew it all could have happened in Peru, that made me very antiwar. In fact, I have two separate groups of friends who don't intermesh. When I'm with my Latino or Chicano friends, many are a lot darker than me. Merely for that, I often don't fit in. Also, many of them grew up in a different cultural setting and bring up unfamiliar things or tell me, "You don't know what you're talking about." When I'm with Anglos, almost the same thing happens. They deny my background. If I challenge, "How can you say that?" their response is, "What are you talking about. You're white and are doing fine. You're in college." With Chicanos, there's an acceptance regardless. When they get to know me, they know my commitment to Latinos.

Meredith Li

There's a real tendency not to understand that Asian Americans are Americans. Many people think that if you look Asian, you're a foreigner. Students or staff on this campus who are Asian Americans have been called "foreigner" by people driving by in a car yelling out the window. There's a lot of tension right now due to economic problems with timber that local people associate with the Japanese. When your family has been here for four generations, you feel American. Even though you're proud of your heritage as an Asian American, you are, nevertheless, American. It's disturbing when people constantly refer to you as a foreigner and you've never set foot in the country that your ancestors have come from and you can't speak that language. If students want to ask me, "What's your family history?" I appreciate it because I like to share my background with them. But too often the only thing they focus on is, "Where are you from?" and they don't ask me, "What's your name?" or they don't ask me, "Where do you live? What are you studying?" Instead, they concentrate on, "Where are you from?" That makes me feel like they're treating me like a foreigner.

Leyla Farah

My father is Lebanese and my mother is black American. We moved to Kuwait when I was nine and we moved back here when I was around thirteen. My father hoped being there would help me identify as an Arab, which it didn't. However, everyone there is "of color" in U.S. terms because Arab people range from blond to black. Because I am the color that I am, I looked very natural there. Everyone assumed that I was Kuwaiti or Palestinian and treated me without regard to my color. My problems were purely in regard to my sex, which was another issue. I lived those developing years with no reference to my color ever and did not have to deal with that growing up. Coming back to the United States was quite a shock.

My mother never thought it was her job to give me a "black" experience. She comes from a long line of strong women and looked on black men in a neutral if not negative way. It is a black thing, this strong woman thing. Usually the black woman is the one holding up the family, at least in my mother's experience, and because of that black women harden quickly. White women don't usually have to deal with this. My mother told me to be strong, and that was one of the best things she could've done for me. When I started dating white guys, they didn't know what to do about my sense of self. Not that white women are weak lumps of Jell-o, but black women have a distinct sense of self.

Because I came from such a strong womanly background in the United States, going to Kuwait upset me. The boys had more privileges in terms of their free time, the way they dressed, and whom they associated with. I wanted to play soccer but girls did not do that. When the boys were out playing cricket, the girls had to jump on the trampoline. We had to line up separately from the boys, and the boys always went into the classroom first. We had to wear different kinds of clothes from the boys. The girls were watched more and expected to be lady-like. And because I was only nine, I made an unfortunate mistake. I was so upset by the way I was being treated as a girl that I decided to reject the whole culture. I never identified as an Arab, refused to learn Arabic, and had a horrible bias against the Muslim religion for the way it treated women. I couldn't have articulated it then, but refusing to learn the language was my retaliation. Now I think it was stupid. I should be able to speak Arabic. In those four years I could have mastered the language.

In the United States, we moved to West Linn, Oregon, a lily white suburb of Portland. Because I'm light enough, a lot of students thought I was Hispanic and said things like, "Are you like a foreign exchange student from Spain?" Or, "She's not black. She doesn't act like the black people I know." Or more frequently, "She doesn't act like the black people on TV." I don't have black English speech patterns, and culturally I don't have a lot of black culture thought patterns because I wasn't raised in the United States. The worst thing happened in a class at which I was not present. A student was presenting figures on the number of black-on-black crimes and black males in prison, implying that blacks are bad people. Another student asked, "What about Leyla?" The student doing the presentation replied, "She has white blood in her." I heard about it immediately. It was the first time I felt that sickness: "My god, it's right here." I never confronted the student who did the presentation because he was powerful in the school, was male, and I was not in a position to challenge him. I didn't know how to fight back. I was afraid that if I reacted, it would confirm his opinion of me. One student told me, "But we all told him he was wrong." And I said, "Oh, thank you."

My feelings about West Linn are mixed. Everything was fine as long as I was like everyone else, which I was most of the time. I always felt I had to act good because they didn't know any other black people, and if I weren't good, they'd think that all black people were like me. Now I can function anywhere. Whether or not it's healthy is beside the point. I can be a representative and I can be relatively comfortable with that.

When I came to the U of O, it was a lot more diverse, which scared me. I was used to being different. Here, I wasn't, and that was both comforting and scary. Beyond that, even though I was a representative for black people in high school and had an "of color" experience in Kuwait, I did not have a "black" experience. Suddenly I met all these black people who had totally different life experiences and lived in a world completely different from mine. I found myself retreating into safety, which meant maintaining an aloof and even antagonistic West Linn "aura." That's what scared me. I would ask myself, "Is what I'm thinking what a black or a white person would think? What am I thinking? I don't know." My expectations going to a university were completely unrealistic.

Once here, I didn't have the background to function well socially, and trying to wing it didn't work.

Here I was all of a sudden with all these black people who automatically expected me to relate to them and understand where they were coming from. I couldn't understand them when they spoke. I couldn't understand them when they were talking about their shared experiences. I couldn't relate to their point of view on a lot of issues. I would find myself arguing with them. At times I felt like a southern white racist saying words falling out of my mouth in response to things I simply did not understand. It was scary because I thought I could fall into U.S. black culture here by virtue of being my mother's daughter. I did not know I would face such a huge, disorienting problem.

The kind of experiences I've had at college have been intertwined with my sex and my race. It's hard for me to separate racism, sexism, and homophobia, and it's hard for me to talk about racism and not want to bring in all my other aspects. White men think I'm like an exotic island girl, not too intelligent. Both black and white men think I'm easy to get into bed, but for different reasons, for different stereotypes. White men desire exoticism and black men see me in terms of ownership and community. I can't say it's bad for a white man to come up to me and say, "Wow, you're beautiful," or, "Your features are so different," or, "Your hair is neat looking. I've never seen anything like that before." I can't tell when someone comes up to me and says, "Hey, what are you doing Friday night?" if they like who I am or they heard what I said in class and thought it was intelligent and want to get to know me, or if they looked over and thought, "I've never seen that before. I wonder how she is in bed." There's a line and you don't know when it's being crossed. When it gets bad is when a man will take me out because he wants other people to see him with me or he wants everyone to think that he has something special, a new and improved item. I think that mixed women often face this problem, not just African American mixes, but all kinds of mixes as long as they're mixed with white. Somehow we look a little less different. We're not white but we're not quite not white. It's easier for many Euro Americans to look at an Asian face that is not completely Asian. It's easier than looking at a black face, since it doesn't have the features so associated with clashing and conflict.

Michelle Singer

In Salem public schools my brother and sister and I were the only Native Americans. In the kindergarten Thanksgiving play I was an Indian girl and I dressed up in my outfit. That's when I knew I was different. Not very many kids that age wear jewelry, but I had silver bracelets that my mom or dad or aunt or uncle would make and I'd wear those often. When I was in fourth grade, my grandparents on my dad's side were in a *National Geographic* special on Navahos. My school posted all the magazine pictures. The teachers got a kick out of it. For them it was good public relations. I didn't like the attention. That was a turning point where I knew I was different from everybody else. In show-and-tell time I'd get questions about my relatives, especially my grandparents. When I said that my grandpa didn't know English, the kids laughed. They thought I was lying. When my grandparents came to visit me in school, they looked completely different in long skirts, buns, jewelry, and they're obviously darker. My classmates would make fun of them, which upset me a lot. I was very feisty at that age, especially if somebody insulted my family. I wanted to go beat somebody up. I wanted to become violent but I didn't. It was then when I first started thinking about discrimination.

I went to Oklahoma the summer before my senior year. I stayed at Riverside Indian School in Anadarko and was one of three Navahos, the only one selected from Oregon to go. There were a hundred students there, mostly from Oklahoma. This was a turning point in my life. In high school I faced an identity crisis because I was the only Native American in eighteen hundred students. At that age girls feel self-conscious about personal appearance, and obviously I looked very different from a typical blond-haired, blue-eyed girl. That changed when I went to this program and learned things at my academic level and about Indian cultural background. I met all these different tribes for the first time and leaders who had made an impact on Native American life. I felt deep awe and respect for these people. They were professionals, people who'd made a mark in life and it was a big honor to be with them. That month changed my life and is my most memorable experience. I still keep in touch with those friends and return to Oklahoma every summer.

I also spend time every summer in Arizona and New Mexico with my grandparents and uncles and aunts. The scenery is completely different, and people down there are traditional. There's a lot of respect and a fine line of what you can cross. Although my parents are very lenient with me, there I have to stay mute and listen. I have to watch what I say. Sometimes the relatives think I'm crazy because I'm so outspoken. My parents speak Navaho there all the time and they want us to do the same. I can speak Navaho about fifty-fifty and can understand and translate it into English in my head and then answer somebody who talks Navaho to me. But I can only answer in English, or half in Navaho and half in English. My cousins and relatives call me a light Navaho because I grew up in an urban surrounding and act differently. All I'll do is listen because I know I'm either going to make a fool of myself or be better off not saying anything.

When I go down there, I hang out with my cousins and herd sheep and visit the relatives and drive around. The area has a completely different atmosphere with barren, beautiful scenery. Everybody has a tie to their home. Even though I did not grow up there, I know I have to go back. That's where I belong. It's my dream. When I finish here and establish a career, I'm going to go back to the reservation.

Geo. Ann Baker

My family consists of me, my sister, my mother, and my father, who divorced my mother when I was seven. My father is full-blooded Payute and my mother Klamath and Modoc. My grandmother lived near Klamath Falls on a ranch. When the reservation was terminated, we moved to Portland. I went to school in Portland, but every weekend until I was in the second grade we went back to Klamath Falls. During the summers and holidays we always went back to Grandma's house.

My father's people originally came from the Nevada area and my mother's people came from east of Klamath Falls. When my grandma talks about the past, she wishes she could go back to reservation life because it was more communal and everybody supported each other. When the government paid us, then everyone separated, which was government's whole purpose: to isolate us and kill us off one by one. Each living individual on the tribal roll received $154,000 to pay for the timber and land we held in trust. When people without money suddenly get that much, they are going to spend it because they don't know what else to do with it. All the merchants in the surrounding area came to us saying, "We'll sell you cars, houses, and this and that." Mother was an accountant, which saved us. We lived on the ranch for three years and then moved to Portland, where my parents purchased a home and sent me to school.

My mother resents what happened to the reservation and does not talk about it much. My father talked about the things he used to do and how he missed that life of hunting and fishing and going to see his brothers whenever he wanted to. When he finished work on Friday, we'd drive six hours to Klamath Falls when it wasn't snowing. We'd get there early Saturday morning about 1:00 A.M., stay all day Saturday, and then have to start back about 4:00 P.M. Sunday night. We couldn't see who we wanted to see and my father couldn't do what he wanted to do. Still, we had a closer-knit family than a lot of my friends did. My family came first. My friends came more from within my family than outside my race or culture. I didn't realize at the time I was growing up what an impact this closeness would have on me.

I don't vote because I don't consider myself a citizen of the United States. People are shocked when I say this. Yet Indians will get screwed no matter who's in government. Show me the benefits. I'm denied my own education, my language, and my religion. The notion of my belonging to something has no meaning for me. I believe there are no boundaries between Canada and Mexico. We belong to the land; the land does not belong to us. The only thing I can belong to is earth, the whole earth. I was put here for a reason, and I wasn't put here to be told where to stay and what to do and who to vote for and how to speak and how to walk and how to dress.

I teach in a multicultural camp where the children always ask, "What do you want to be called? Do you want to be called Indian? Or do you want to be called Native American or indigenous?" I know I'm native to this land. As long as you know that I belong to this continent, I could be Native American, American Indian, or indigenous to this land, whatever you want to call me. Don't call me the negative names. I consider myself a member of my tribe and my family. When Anglos come and start to push their values on us, they group all native peoples into one big tribe, "Indian," and think we speak the same language and have the same values and religion. But we do not. Each Native American tribe is a separate nation. I'd rather be called Klamath or Payute. But you don't know that from meeting me. Other native people can tell which tribe I'm from.

Sweeter Sachuo

I'm from the Truk Islands, which are 120 islands scattered in a vast area of ocean. Only a few islands are inhabited, but the indigenous people have been there for a long time. The Truk Islands are a part of the United States, and we are U.S. citizens, except we don't have the power to vote.

Our family has been here four years. The children want to stay in the United States. I tell them we have to go back to the islands. They now like the American way of life and may have a difficult time when they go back. My wife and I are training them to understand Trukese ways: different ways of approaching people, different kinds of relationships, different ways of doing things, and different ways of behaving around older people and around their peers. Back there, people expect my wife and me to get an education and come back, but not to bring back a different way of life.

Lots of students who come to the United States have problems when they go back home. They come home with American lifestyles, thinking processes, and ways of doing things that are unacceptable to the community. It's often very hard for those students to be transformed back into their culture. My brothers will face this because they are undergraduates staying here to go to school. Some returning students have been ousted from their own families or clans because they no longer behave like people in their culture. Some have even had to go to other islands to live. Students here who become so immersed in the system that they take on the American way of life may find that when they go back to the islands, there is no way of reprocessing them so that they can resume their old culture.

Carol Cheney

When we were thirteen months old, my mom and dad came to Korea to adopt us. They used to tell me, "You're a GI baby." They came over to Korea, looked at all the babies in the orphanage, and thought we looked different from all the others. For a long time I was proud of that. Now I think some man from the United States military went over and got a Korean woman pregnant and left her there with us. At the time I thought, "Oh goody, that makes me a better person because I'm half American." How sad and awful that I had to qualify myself like that. My folks always told us about how we were so sick that they had to put us in the hospital right away in the United States. During my lifetime I always felt grateful to them for "saving" me and my sister. But I've lost a lot of my heritage and know that I'll never be able to find my real mother. Who knows who my real father is or whether he's Korean or American? At this point I don't care. I would like to find out more about the culture my mother was from and who she is and maybe what kind of trials she had to go through.

Kronda Adair

I grew up primarily in an African American community within Portland. I miss diversity. It's not that I run into so many racist people at the U of O, although there are those, but I miss seeing people of color and having diversity. That's hard to adjust to. When I came to the U of O, I expected culture shock because the school is so bland racially, but I moved into the cross-cultural dorms, so I didn't face much of a transition.

I haven't experienced racism here as much as pressure to fit in more with blacks. I get this pressure from black people in a blatant way. Most of my friends are white, which bothers my mother. For example, when I had to drive my mother to California this summer, she didn't want me to return to Oregon by myself, so I called the first friend who came to mind who I thought would do it, a white man. We then phoned my grandmother to say we were bringing a white guy. Grandma asked, "Is he prejudiced?" My mother answered, "Well, he's friends with her." Half joking and half not, Grandma replied, "That's not saying much. She's more white than black." I was pissed but didn't respond angrily. I told Grandma he was more open-minded than she. My mother thought it was very funny and agreed with Grandma. They'd be very happy if all of a sudden I started hanging around with a bunch of black people and fitting in. My mom and I are very different in a lot of ways. I think I may be more radical. We argue over and over again about how I need more black friends, as if I hadn't met my quota. I see her concern about my not identifying with my culture but I resent it when the family makes jokes about me not being black enough. How can you not be black enough? If your skin is dark or if your parents are black, even if someone paints you, you're still going to be black.

I don't fit most of the stereotypes. Language is a very personal thing for me. I don't talk black, whatever that means. I don't speak jive. My parents have always impressed upon me the need to speak well, especially in mixed company. Since the fourth grade, I can remember being with my friends and correcting them when they said "ain't." I don't correct people anymore, but it seems important to me to set a good example because there's a stereotype that we don't know how to write or talk well. Other people have the right to talk jive and I don't want to stifle or censor somebody and say, "You can't talk this way because other people will think badly." But when people are using slang and the whole group assumes that's how people talk, I cringe. It's a charged issue and I'm not sure how to deal with it.

I face what I call triple jeopardy. I often talk to students on panels organized by GALA [gay, lesbian, bisexual student organization]. The audience asks common questions: "Why are you so blatant? Can't you live your life and not tell anybody about it?" At the only panel I did specifically in a multicultural class, there was a lot more hostility, with students having the attitude, "Prove to me that I should accept you." One woman there said that she thought black men were more homophobic than white men. When people like those in this group ask unsympathetic questions, panelists from our organization talk about the need for gays and lesbians to be out.

People most easily picked out as gay are often those who fit the stereotypes, fringe people who conform to what a common definition of a gay/lesbian person is. Many students don't see as gay all the "normal-looking" people who walk by them all the time, whom they interact with and work with and have classes with. That's one of the points I always try to make. I look "normal," whatever that means. That's why I consider it important to be out. It's a statement: "You can't stereotype me because I don't fit." Some people do fit the stereotype, and that's fine with them. But I feel that by being out, I can break stereotypes and say, "You can't assume this about people." I also emphasize that for those who are struggling as an oppressed group, a multidimensional approach is the only good strategy. When we're struggling with an issue and trying to get people together to work on it, we can't isolate that issue. In particular, there's racism in the gay community and homophobia in the black community. We have to work with other people and acknowledge that many of these people happen to be different from each other. We need to respect each other's rights no matter what those differences are.

2

Hopes and Coalitions and the Realities of Campus Life

HIGH HOPES ABOUT COLLEGE— STUDENTS' EXPECTATIONS

In a unified voice, students discuss the great hopes and sense of excitement they brought to the University of Oregon. They juxtapose their initial anticipatory expectation against the disappointing, difficult reality they faced once they got here. They reveal that finding a support group is necessary for minority students' survival in a predominantly white institution, since too often the university does not acknowledge or meet their needs.

Some of the students' experiences point to a chilly campus climate on predominantly white campuses, which often affects their decision to stay or leave. Student affairs programs now attempt to address and improve the climate by setting up clubs, offices, and activities that support students of color as a whole and as separate ethnic organizations.

Michelle Singer

My sister, who's nine years older than me, went to the University of Oregon. I came down often to visit her. I saw all the big buildings, all the people, and knew college was for me. I went with her to register so I learned how that whole process went. I went with her to the bookstore to buy books. Professors would even mistake me for being a student. When I went to her French class, they gave me an exam and I had to say, "I'm sorry, I'm just visiting." We went to basketball and football games. She was part of the Native American Student Union, which at that point was strong. There were a lot of Indian students at that time,

43

and I went to their powwow at Mac Court. I liked Eugene better than Salem because it was much more liberal. It seemed diverse, always having something to appeal to me.

I knew I wanted to come here. I planned to go to school and not worry about anything else. I thought I'd be like everybody else. In the public school system I blended in with the other white kids, so I didn't figure myself to be different. The issue of self-identity came out for me and a lot of other students of color once we hit this campus. When we were in high school or grade school we weren't classified as minorities, like we are coming into this school. Once we came here, people wanted to put this label on us and, if we were students of color, immediately push us aside. As students of color, we were either a token or a quota. It made me wonder why I was here.

Through the admissions office I learned what enrollment numbers have been. There are surprisingly few Native American students here and few minority students in general. There are hardly any faculty of color. The retention rate for students of color also surprised me. This university is structured in a way that systematically overlooks minority students. Like most colleges, the university glorifies something in order to attract students. Once I got here, I saw the reality of it all and felt let down. I regarded the institution so highly that when I got here I thought my previous expectations were a lie.

The first year I was disappointed but shrugged it off. My sophomore year I became more active but during fall term almost considered dropping out because I felt so uncomfortable. A good friend of mine was so upset she dropped out, and I almost followed her lead. She was upset with school, especially the curriculum, which presented a one-sided Euro American viewpoint. She hated being around white people in general. It made her homesick. The school offers no strong support for Indian students. It was so hard. I felt alone. No matter how hard I've tried to work for my people and other minority students like me, I always face such an uphill battle. I never know if I am going to have any success at all. That battle still goes on.

Lisa Rodriguez

My hometown was so small; we had two African American families there. Out of my senior graduating classes of sixty-five, only four of us went to a four-year college. I was seriously discouraged by my counselors from coming to a four-year university. They said, "Maybe you should go to a community college for one or two years before you come to the university." One of my counselors had been to the U of O and said it'd been tough for her, so she didn't think I could handle it. I didn't want to go to a community college but I wanted something better.

To broaden my horizons, I wanted to go to a school with more minorities, more Chicanos. My best friend, Maria Mendoza, went here and loved it, so that made me want to come to the University of Oregon. My current friends say there are too few minorities here and that the campus is closed-minded, but when I came, I thought, "Wow!" Seeing other students of color encouraged me, made me feel I'd made the right decision, and made me comfortable here. Maria knew her way around the university and opened a lot of doors for me. She told me which programs were good and which weren't. I think I would have been lost without her. She had a room reserved at Adams, the multicultural dorm, and asked me to move in with her.

In fact, Maria didn't think we were going to get along when I moved here because we hadn't talked for a year. We'd felt a big gap between us when she left for college and did not keep in touch. In high school she was more academic and I was more social. But at the university we automatically clicked and got along great. I met her friends and their friends. I was lucky in the way I came into the university, knowing people and what to expect. Many students don't have that opportunity and come in alone and scared. They have to figure things out for themselves. I was also fortunate to live in the multicultural dorm my freshman year, which let me see other people's backgrounds and cultures. People here are very friendly and helped me grow as a person, to learn about other people and myself. My grades were average fall term. I didn't know how to take a midterm or what to expect. Winter term I did well but spring term when it started to get nice outside, I began partying and slacking off.

Eric Ward

When I graduated from high school, I didn't have a goal. I worked for a while but L.A. was so stressful, I wanted to get out. When I was twenty-one, two of my friends were coming to Oregon to go to school so five of us who are close all transplanted together to Oregon. I doubt that I would have done it by myself. Wherever they were going I'd probably have gone too. And if some of them had not gone to college, I would not have taken that path either. Eugene, Oregon, was luck. I grew up in concrete. Eugene didn't seem real because there was grass and trees everywhere. It felt like Disneyland with everyone walking around with peace symbols, beads, and tie-dyes. In September '86, it seemed interesting and progressive.

I'm a first generation college student and the second person in my family to get a high school diploma. My relatives are proud of me but don't understand why I'm up here in Eugene. I'm starting to wonder too. We call Eugene the twilight zone. It is so strange. I wish you could have grown up with me and looked at Eugene through my eyes. People here are liberals, beautiful but racist, mostly in an unconscious way. My parents never want to come to visit since they think of Oregon in terms of horror stories.

The reason I went to community college was because I wanted to come to the U of O and I needed a good way to build my study skills. Then I went to school in France for a year. There I applied to the U of O through the French mail system, which is always going on strike. This was the easiest place to apply because I knew people in Eugene who would run the errands back and forth that I couldn't do. Now I think maybe I should have gone to another school but I'm too close to graduating. I would definitely go to a different graduate school because it's hard here for students of color, especially once they become conscious of what's going on around them. The percentage of students of color here is 8.6 percent combined.

Jon Motohiro

I wanted to go away to school, but not too far. I wanted an affordable school in a clean area like the U.S. Northwest. One thing I looked for was the ratio of Asian American students because I didn't want to feel out of place. Joking around, I said, "I'll go to Michigan and get killed," remembering Vincent Chin. U of O alumni in Hawaii managed to get our names from the admissions office. They contacted us at home to invite us to a summer picnic in Hawaii. They talked about what it's like here and steered me into a solid academic program here. Also many of my high school classmates came here, and seeing familiar faces helped.

When Asians come here, they don't want to go far from campus alone. In the dorm I am a casual, easygoing person but also able to stand up and be assertive for myself. However, I try to avoid going to places by myself, especially when I'm far away from campus.

Del Carter

Almost every day, other African American students ask me, "Why did you come here?" I used to run track when I was in high school, and the University of Oregon was considered the track capital. Then I had a series of knee injuries and we couldn't afford for me to have surgery, which ended my athletic career. But I came up here anyway to take a look around. The first thing I noticed was how pretty and green everything was compared to Nevada, where everything's dry. As I talked to a few of the faculty members on campus, they told me how culturally diverse Eugene is: "Oh, you're from the Bay Area. It's a lot like Berkeley. It's diverse." Later I realized how far they stretched the truth.

The first day of registration was my first day at work. It was also the first day

that I walked through the campus full of people. I was behind the dance ...r-
ing trying to find my way to work without getting lost when a couple of girls
walked by making racial comments. It hurt so bad because I had all these expectations about college on my very first day on campus. I didn't say anything but
turned around and stared at the girls with my mouth hanging open. I thought,
"I can't believe it." All day long, I had this problem and no one to talk to about
it. It was hard holding in a thing like that for nine hours, yet I was new at work
and didn't know or trust anyone yet. Finally, when I got home, I cried because
I still couldn't believe it. I said to myself, "This is college. You're supposed to
be an adult, and things like this shouldn't matter any more."

When I first got here, I missed dorm registration and had to live off campus.
The staff was sympathetic: "Oh, you're a freshman, and this is a whole different
state for you, let alone a different town." But I didn't get support from African
American students. I expected the African Americans on campus to be more
unified because we're so few here. But each person and group is separate—the
predominantly black fraternity doesn't mix with the athletes, etc. I did not feel
like I fit in and was alone my first year. I survived freshman year with a lot of
calls to mom, a lot of tears, and a lot of letter writing back home to friends and
relatives. I worked in the administration building, Oregon Hall, and the few
people I met there, Euro Americans, I clung to because I didn't have anyone else
here.

I was thrown into this environment and expected to sink or swim. I'd looked
forward to the culturally diverse campus everyone told me about and arrived
with a lot of expectations, only to be let down. It took a big effort to meet people
of my own culture. I told myself, "I'm a freshman and need to focus on school
right now, so I'll put social life aside." Yes, I'd expected to meet people and form
a support group, but I had to set my mind on education. I managed to get
through although I badly wanted to go home. My mom, who's like a backbone
for me, encouraged me: "It'll get better. Stick it out one more year, and then if
you don't like it, we'll see about transferring." My sophomore year was better
but I still wanted to leave. I was tired. I didn't think I could do the full four
years. Support from people of my own race started improving, which made it a
little bit easier.

Gretchen Freed-Rowland

When I went to apply for the Indian Fellowship out of the Department of Education in Washington, D.C., there were specific regulations. At the time, one of
them was that I had to be certified. If I didn't have an enrollment number, then
I had to go to the secretary of the interior and his office had to certify me. The
issues were very painful for me, getting out my birth certificate, obtaining a roll

number, and dealing with what that meant. I didn't realize how painful it would be.

My birth certificate says I'm half *R* and half *W* and has my grandfather's signature on it. Having the *R* and *W* on the birth certificate means red and white. If I were on the reservation, I would be a half-breed, but if we were living on the reservation, the whole family would be Indian as far as the federal government or the tribal people were concerned. I'm two tribes, which makes it even more complex. My sister and I had attempted earlier to be enrolled on my grandfather's reservation with the Winnebagos. I found out since then that my mother and her sisters were enrolled on the White Earth Reservation, the Ojibwa reservation. It would have been easier to go through the Ojibwas, but we didn't know that at the time. I took my birth certificate and called and wrote people and was told that the birth certificate wasn't enough. The secretary of the interior had to sign a letter verifying that I was Indian. Then I found out that the enrollment clerk with the Winnebagos could say, "Yes, she is Winnebago, but she's not enrolled yet." That was enough to begin with. I received a piece of paper from the secretary of the interior that allowed me to apply for scholarships. I got my first-year scholarship on that. But the government keeps changing its mind, depending on who's been elected into power. We have to deal with all these changing trends in Indian affairs.

The next year, Congress passed a new law, another new law, that declared unless you had a tribe willing to enroll you as one-quarter of that particular tribe, you were not eligible for any money as a Native American. This legislation said if the tribe had not yet enrolled you, even though they verified your blood quantum, it didn't count. In effect the legislature said, "Indians can no longer be Indians unless they have an enrollment number." I got so depressed that I didn't do anything for two weeks. I wondered, "What do we do now? Do we tattoo a number on our arms so people can't take our identity away from us? We're invisible." In the last five years, the issue resolved itself when the government started computerizing enrollment. That's how my sister and I were enrolled. My sister got her enrollment through the Winnebagos using the computer. My brothers have also been petitioning for enrollment, as have my Butterfield cousins. Hopefully, computerization means it's just a matter of time for them too. These issues of enrollment, in terms of getting a scholarship or establishing one's identity, plague Indian people, plague all of us growing up. We tell about it in Indian stories, but these issues aren't presented in textbooks or picked up by the media. There's never enough of a context given to explain how this issue of enrollment affects us.

BUILDING COMMUNITIES AND COALITIONS

Like most students, students of color seek out friendship, support, and a sense of community when they enter college. Unlike white students, students of color at predomi-

nantly white universities share an experience of isolation and exclusion. In response, many students of color actively search out others like themselves in hopes of finding a comfortable and accepting network of friends. In the racially charged environment of the university, such friendships and networks become challenging to maneuver. Because students of color are few in number, many students rely on ethnic student unions as a way to find friends and to learn more about their own communities. While many have found havens of support here, others critique the groups' use of authenticity tests—tests that determine who is and is not a true member of the group. While the students discuss the need for community and challenge the borders of such communities, others reveal how gender and sexuality intersect with race as dimensions in friendships. These intersections are revealed in students' discussions of dating, black sororities, and fraternities, beauty standards, and stereotypes.

Diana Collins-Puente

When I came here, I became more involved with Latinos. That's been enriching for me. Yet because I've gotten to know many different students of color and because I'm so much more involved with their communities than I was before, it makes me realize how much I miss having more people of color on campus. It's hard. When I go down to visit my brothers in California, every time I turn around I see a person of color. It's such a different feeling, it makes me wish I went to school in California or somewhere else with more representation.

Eric Ward

In my part of Los Angeles, I get back much more than I give. The city is so alive. People have negative impressions about L.A. from television, as if the urban city were a war zone. Sometimes it is, but it's also a place with a lot of life, strength, and hope. People haven't given up. They are still struggling. To me there's beauty in that. I may be idealistic about my community, but I get strength and support back from it. Whatever support I get here makes me miss my home because I know how much more I'd get there. I don't want to fantasize about L.A. It'll be harder to go home now, since I understand the dynamics of why things are happening. I know I can't change poverty and racism and health problems overnight nor can I do it individually. It's a process that I'm just one part of.

Geo. Ann Baker

When I came here, I was eighteen years old. In high school I was chosen Ms. Oregon Indian, 1971. I had a sense of who I was and pride in that. I'm thirty-six now and am beginning to find my identity again. When I got here, I was so lost. You talk about culture shock. I couldn't relate to anybody. I had to live in the dorm and hated it. I cried the whole time and wouldn't come out of my room to go to classes. This went on for almost a week. One Indian person going to school here found me and said she had an apartment and wanted me to move in. I was packed and out of there in an hour. After I moved, I began going to classes and getting "into" it. I learned about the Native American Student Union, which became my support system.

My main concern now, working in the student union, is to offer support for all the other Native American students. There are so few of us at any one time, and each of us has wanted to drop out. We're helping each other stay here. If one or two of us leave, the numbers get pretty low and it's time to think about dropping out. I think of dropping out all the time because I get so tired of the system and of trying to fit in and explaining myself. As each one has wanted to give up and quit, the rest of us have said, "No, you can't do this. You made it this far." We help each other study. We're there for each other in case we run into a problem. We tell each other, "Don't take that class." Or "I've taken that class. I'll help you. You need to know these things." That's the main reason our student union is here.

When things get low, I always call my friend in Albuquerque. We don't even listen to each other. We get on the line and start yelling and screaming and hollering. By the end of the hour even though I spend a fortune on my phone bill, I feel a lot better. That's one of my survival skills. Another is I go home a lot. With classes and work, I rarely have anything scheduled on Friday after-noons or Mondays because I leave on Thursday night and travel maybe ten hours to interact with other Indian people. In the springtime, I'm not here any weekend, and it's like that until September and Labor Day. I need that support system from other Indian people. If I didn't, if all of a sudden my car broke down or I had to hitchhike, I think I'd drop out of school.

Michelle Singer

Native Americans are constantly asked to prove who we are. Where is our enroll-ment, what's our number, what's our blood quantum? Are we real or not? These tests face us because of the system. I'm a scholarship recipient. For the admis-sions office and the scholarship application, we are asked for tribal verification. We have to photocopy papers saying we are Native American and enrolled in a tribe, or we must get an original and submit it to the university. Somebody who misses the quota in their tribe but identifies with their Indian heritage has no chance whatsoever of getting the scholarship because they're not enrolled. His-panics and Chicanos don't have to go through that.

People have a stereotype that Native Americans are getting a free education. Native Americans are supposedly rich and have many benefits. I didn't automatically get these things. I had to work for admission like everybody else. I had to work in school for my grades, writing essays like everybody else. I followed the standard application process for applying for a scholarship. But I did not have to go to my tribe and say, "My family's poor. I'm a first-generation student. Here are my tribal papers. Please give me money." We don't look for sympathy, and we don't ask for sympathy. The money comes from treaty rights that are one of the historic trusts that the government has to respect. On the reservation, the government gives us food, education, and housing, but they got everything from our land, gained from what they took away from us. They are far better off then we are now and if they can make cuts in our benefits, they will.

We also have a test among Indian people, discrimination within our communities pitting urban Indians against reservation Indians. Who ever defined anything? Nobody did. Yet some Native Americans think, "I'm full-blooded and this person is a quarter." It seems that the full-blood wins and is more of an Indian than the other. Who has the real advantage? An Indian growing up in a reservation, living close to the environment, being around people who speak her own language, and learning her own heritage and traditions? Or an urban Indian learning white values and white systems but getting educated at a so-called normal rate rather than in the disadvantaged schools on the reservation? I get into arguments about these issues that sometimes stir up hurt feelings. It's another way society has of pitting you against your own people in order to upset you and make you fight among each other.

People think we're quiet. We don't argue with each other and are a passive people. There are not very many Indian men here on campus. And if there are, they're young and lost. They're in a predicament, like I am now. Some come from urban areas. Either their parents grew up in bad times when it wasn't right to be Indian, or the parents threw aside their culture and values and gave into white society and brought their children up only in it. These students are twisted when they get here. Here the struggle is the same for both Native American men and women because we're Native Americans on this campus with an expectation set upon us. But other issues for Native American men and Native American women are different because the issues are different within our communities. We place a lot more emphasis on the woman than the man because the woman is the primary center of life for Native American communities. The whole community always looks to women for leadership and direction.

Lisa Rodriguez

Many Latino students feel secluded and alone when they get here because they do not know many students of color. I know some students who were unhappy and wanted to drop out of school because they felt there was no one else like them. Through MEChA [the Chicano–Latino Student Union] Latino students have gotten help and support. The student unions are a good way to touch base and are where many people go to keep in touch with their background, ethnicity, and culture. That's how many students have had their eyes opened, expanded their outlook, and gotten in touch with other like-minded students.

Del Carter

Black sororities, which are popular in black communities throughout the United States, are more community based than other sororities are. I didn't go through "rush" but when we started forming an interest group for a national black sorority, I felt it was something I could be part of. It's helped me enhance my identity and learn a lot more about black culture. And through it, I try to do a lot for the community. Right now some of the African American students, especially freshmen, feel we *are* the community here on campus. But all black students, especially the incoming ones, need to meet some of the African American families all over Eugene and Springfield who are supportive of us. I've gotten close to one family since I've been here and wonder what it would be like for me without that contact. There are many African Americans in the community who would be willing to support our student union. As I work in the Black Student Union, establishing student-community ties is my main goal.

Leyla Farah

My college peer group was mostly white. I compensated for that by getting closer to older people of color, whom I found more willing to accept me without expectations and who talked about larger political or environmental issues. Now I'm joining a black sorority. For so long blacks were working toward desegregation and integration and molding into society. Now I see the need for separation. People of color are getting tired of dealing with the same issues over and over again. We are moving away from the struggle for integration and saying, "We have to find ourselves. We have to combine as a unit out here before we can go in with you with any amount of strength or power." As black women, we're getting together. We want to preserve our heritage, culture, and history in some tangible form and we're trying to do it together. It's disconcerting. Intellectually it makes me cringe, but inside it feels great.

Eric Ward

I don't know if I should be putting us black men on the spot, but I'll be honest. One of the complaints black women have is that black men say, "I'm dating white women right now, but I'm not going to marry 'em. When I go home, I'm going to marry a black woman." That's sexist stuff.

Callan Coleman

The black male falls under this mystique that he's an athlete and a seriously sexy man. I wish I knew better what black women have to deal with. I know people do not pay them the respect they deserve and need. Sometimes I have been hesitant to approach a black woman because of the vibes I get from her. It is because of the way people have treated her.

Growing up, I wanted to date a blond woman. I didn't realize why I wasn't attracted to black women. When you're watching television and going to movies, it's the blond woman who's the gorgeous one, so when you walk down the street and see blond hair, you're automatically looking over to see how pretty that woman is. It took me years to get over that. For a while, I dove right into the game. All of a sudden, wow, it was like being in a candy store. I partied and went out dancing until I realized it didn't bring me any emotional satisfaction. Now I'm finally pulling away from that as a waste of my time. I want a social life and to spend casual time with friends. It's a matter of how you do it.

In the dorms I learned a lot about myself and others. After we'd been living together for seven months, my roommate disclosed to me that he was gay. I was the third person he'd ever told and he was twenty-five years old. When I was confronted with this other dimension of him, it didn't change our friendship. His telling me was a wonderful experience for me because of all of the stereotypes and negative things that we put on gay people. Here was somebody whom I'd grown very close to who was gay. It opened my mind. I realized that all those negative preconceptions mean nothing when I'm face to face with a friend who is generous and supports me. That taught me a lot about the things other people go through. I can't hide the fact that I'm an African American, but here's somebody who had something within him that he had to hide.

Del Carter

This year some men drove by in a pickup truck. They had a speaker fixed so you could hear what they were saying, things like, "Hey, nigger." I was walking at night alone, something I try not to do. I blew it off at first, but it really bothered me. When I got home and talked to my boyfriend about it, he didn't have a lot to say. He tries to tune those things out and in an irritated way said, "You have to deal with it. Don't worry about it." He was supportive but maintained the attitude, "It will happen. Ignore them. Go on and do whatever you have to do." I haven't heard from him in about two years. We're no longer friends. That incident had something to do with our breaking up.

After many negative experiences dating white guys, I chose not to date them any more. It's not that I'm prejudiced, but I already have to deal with racism and discrimination against women. I do not need the added pressure of trying to teach a man I'm dating. Not only that (this is a touchy subject) but on this campus, it's not okay for black women to date white men, but it is okay for black men to date white women. I have several friends who are dating white guys and everybody's minding their business: "Why are you dating him?" "What's wrong with you?" "Why can't you date someone black?" I understand it. Dating white women has always been forbidden to our men. In some places, it was illegal even to whistle at white women. Because it was forbidden for so long, now young African American men are jumping at the chance and like to show off with the attitude: "For so long we couldn't date white women, but now we can. Hah, hah, I have one." Other black men here say, "I would talk to this African American woman, but she has an attitude. She's stuck up and I don't want to deal with that." I have never been comfortable with the opinion that it's wrong for African American women to date white guys. Why is that taboo? I know that some white fraternities won't let African American men into their parties, will simply not let them through the door, but will welcome an African American woman just because she is a woman.

Kronda Adair

My best friend, the only close black friend I have, is an incredible role model. She's so together and is goal-oriented and outspoken. If she has something to say, you will know about it. She doesn't let anything slide. Sometimes when I hear something offensive, I don't know what to do. I might go up to that person later and say, "Look, you said this and it wasn't cool." For me, it usually depends on the situation, on what was said or on who else is around, especially if it's a large group and I'm the only person who'd say something. But my friend will speak out right then and there.

Meredith Li

I am concerned with the stereotypes white society puts on us. For example, it commonly happens that people think my name is Kim. There are no words sounding like Kim in my entire name. People do this who have heard my name a few times and I've been introduced to them as Meri. They start calling me Kim. Teachers call me Kim. People I used to work with call me Kim. Other students call me Kim. I almost respond when I hear Kim because it's happened to me so often. When people look at me, I guess they think, "Kim," probably because Kim is a pretty common name for Asian women.

I had a friend in my dorm my freshman year who was Korean American from Hawaii, my first Asian American friend. When we walked around together, I wondered if people thought, "Those Asian Americans always hang around together." Because I'd never had an Asian American friend, it took me a while to become less self-conscious.

Especially on TV or in the movies, an Asian woman is portrayed as an exotic seductress or an obedient, servile person always in the background. There's an expectation also for Asian students of both sexes to get top grades and be obedient, successful, quiet, and even-tempered. I am aware that as a large group, Asians have had a lot of success, yet there are also a lot of Asians who are struggling, especially the Asians from Southeast Asia who've recently emigrated. They may still be trying to learn the language and are put at a disadvantage because of the myth of the model minority.

Diana Collins-Puente

Some people have the stereotype that I should be this airhead and are surprised that I know as much as I do or that I can be eloquent. Many people don't want me to be so outspoken. They are uncomfortable if I approach them with something they don't want to hear.

Lisa Rodriguez

Many Mexicans and Latinos don't think I'm Chicana because my skin and hair are fair, not dark, and they are also surprised when I start speaking Spanish. Even within our culture, some people have an image or a stereotype of what we're supposed to look like. Dating on this campus seems more interracial than anywhere else I've seen. I think it's a good experience and don't have anything against it. Most of the Chicano guys I know date white girls. That's a big gripe Chicana women have. More of the Chicanas and Latinas and other women of color on campus date minorities. A lot of us would date anything in minorities rather than a white male. For men of color, it's the reverse. A lot of them date Euro American women, and that upsets many women of color. Many students of color feel that there are so few people of color on campus that we have to get together. Many social functions I go to have all students of color. I usually don't go to kegger parties or white fraternity and sorority parties, but if I go to a party at Kappa, the black fraternity, I like it because we dance. For a lot of students of color, it's important to spend time socially with other people around who care and who are experiencing the same things you are. Even though you're a

Latina from Honduras or Spain, you feel very isolated when you get here, so social contact is very important for us all.

Shelli Romero

A lot of people don't see me as a Chicana. They have a stereotyped view of what a Chicana or African American or anybody should look like. I don't fit the stereotype. I'm fair skinned and am often mistaken for Italian. I feel a special bond with and a tie to other people of color because I can relate to their difficulties and oppressions. I have the same ones. All of the things that I hear, all of the jokes, hurt and they hit hard. Women of color especially have to face the stereotype of being exotic. We're often thought of as difficult to get in bed but once in bed capable of exceptional sexual performance. It's a lie. Humans are humans.

Sweeter Sachuo

There is closer physical distance among the Trukese, what you call personal space. Personal space is less among Trukese. That caused me problems when I first came to the United States. I got close to people to talk and they'd back away. There is a distance in relationships between people here, and to grasp that, I had to come to understand some concepts that do not exist in Trukese culture. For instance, in Trukese we call everybody mothers and fathers and brothers and sisters. Your concepts about relationships create distances between people.

Gretchen Freed-Rowland

At first I found a lack of acceptance in the Indian community here in Oregon. On campus, when I came, I wasn't "dark enough" and didn't have my enrollment number. It's still a very controversial term, but I was raised as pan-Indian, with a commitment to society versus tribal affiliation. I didn't have close ties to my tribe and did not get to know them until I got my master's degree. I've never fit anywhere. I can remember feeling the pressure of my famous Indian family to publicly establish my Indian identity. Being fair skinned means it's important, as it was in my family, that we name ourselves as Indian. Yet in the Indian community, particularly with reservation Indians who don't know you and who are dark skinned, you are immediately suspect. Their first question is always, "What's your enrollment number? Where are you enrolled?" There's a constant testing of who you are. Even my husband, who is from England, says I'm not a real Indian and don't do real Indian art. It is because I don't fit the stereotype. He knew me over there and not here in the context of my own place. The

English are very pro-Indian and know the social issues; they caught me up on all kinds of material that the U.S. press and literature hadn't presented.

When I first came to the University of Oregon, I found the Native American Student Union right away. I wanted some sort of Indian affiliation. It meant a lot to me when I found out that there was a Native American community here. We had a longhouse and several of the Indians who were in the university at the time were from the local Indian community. They used the longhouse each week for drumming and getting the families together and teaching the children some of the traditions like having the elders always go first, then mothers with the youngest children go, then the rest of us mixed in there together. We had traditions that we've grown up with, pitching in with cooking and cleaning. They allowed me to come and eat their food and not bring anything for a year and a half.

Some Indian women, at times, have felt about me, "Gretchen, you're talking too much, which you're not supposed to do in the Indian community when you're around Indians. That's only for when you're out there by yourself in a non-Indian situation." They said they feel the same way, that they have to speak up in the Anglo world but that none of us are old enough yet to be able to do it back on the reservation or with our own people. To be an elder is a gift that's given to you. It's not something you claim with, "Okay, I'm ready." An Indian man from a reservation, educated here in Oregon, told me that he doesn't know how it comes about or what it is, but between sixth grade and age thirty-two, we tend to lose our people, particularly our men. He said, "If we are physically still alive by the age of thirty-two, we seem to come back and say, 'I need the community and I'm ready to accept some responsibility for that.'"

RACISM IN ACADEMIC ROBES:
CLASSROOM INCIDENTS

What marks the students' comments here is pain. Daily in their classes they face racist comments and, more frequently, racist assumptions. Too often their professors fail to speak up to counter the negative stereotypes expressed by other students in class discussion, or professors themselves unthinkingly say these kinds of things in the context of a lecture. In light of the hopes they brought to college, this confrontation with racism in the classroom is a shock. Students of color come to college expecting the curriculum and faculty to be open, respectful, and inclusive. When they encounter overt racism, they face this reality with disappointment, anger, and self-doubt. "Why did I come here?" they may ask. When they hear racist speech and ethnic slurs, students of color usually feel forced to speak up, since otherwise such remarks might go unchallenged. At the same time, they also feel compelled to monitor closely what they say in class because their words are often taken to be true for all people of their ethnic group.

White students are privileged in that they are not pejoratively "marked" by their accents or physical traits in the same way, nor are they assumed to represent their race. In general, especially in a workplace setting, white people can stay in denial about how racism functions there and may consider the distressing incidents they do observe, especially those involving denigrating language, as regrettable individual acts. In fact, people often stand by and do nothing when such an incident occurs because their social environment makes it easy to remain silent. This kind of passive nonaction undergirds racism and is one of its main supports.

Michelle Singer

A Native American friend of mine had a professor who made a point in a large general lecture that she was a scholarship winner. He assumed that she was driving a BMW or some nice car because she had an advantage most kids don't have. That was blatant racism, but you also hear subtle discriminatory remarks. On a broad scale people make ethnic jokes. You hear them in history classes and psychology classes from teachers and students. A history professor of mine made a joke in class about prohibition, referring to drunken Indians. I was mad but didn't do anything. I sat there because I had to. That was my freshman year.

Also my freshman year, I was sitting in the back of the lecture hall with my best friend in a history lecture of about three hundred students. The professor was talking about the early Indian wars and an incident that gave an early sign of the downfall of Native American rights. The colonials wanted to seize Indian lands, so after Pontiac's war in the late 1700s or early 1800s, the U.S. Army gave Indians smallpox-infested blankets. The Native Americans were killed right off from these blankets because they didn't have an immune system to fight the disease. The professor pointed out how this strategy affected Native Americans' future. A student behind me said, "Good, I'm glad that they gave them these blankets. We should get rid of all of them." He was about my age, eighteen. I was sitting directly in front of him with this long black hair, but it didn't dawn on him whom he was sitting near. He was so stupid that he had to say that in front of everybody. I didn't have the nerve to turn around but I was mad. I'd been getting a little more daring but I didn't do anything. I'm just like anyone else and didn't know what to do. When you hear things like that, what are you supposed to do? I wanted to bop him one. I came this close.

Surprisingly, none of his friends said anything even though they must have heard him because he said it loud enough. I hated all of them. Their not saying anything implied that his behavior was all right or that they had the same attitude but didn't say it out loud. They didn't have enough guts to say something to a friend who was wrong. They just had the attitude, "Oh, he says stupid things."

This year in my sociology class we were watching an *Eyes on the Prize* episode about the Martin Luther King era. It opens with a cartoon that has little black figures dancing and singing an upbeat jazzy song. Two big guys behind me, Euro Americans, were laughing and saying "Sambo" and "Mammy," and ham-boning all these jokes as if they were speaking "like a nigger." I couldn't believe it. My friend turned around and stared as did other people, but nobody said anything. Those two made snide remarks like this all through the movie. Finally I got so mad, I couldn't take it anymore. I told the one talking to shut up. He did. He had made everybody around listen to what he had to say. Why didn't other people say anything? If people don't say anything, then it becomes all right to say slurs because the person talking got away with it. You've got to insist that you don't like what they're saying or if they have such an opinion, they better keep it to themselves.

Callan Coleman

In a psychology class, the professor was illustrating problem-solving with a hypothetical example called "cannibals and missionaries." Those words made me straighten up. He said we should figure out how to get some missionaries across the river; one missionary can't be in the boat with the cannibals because he'll get eaten. I thought, "Here I am, black, imagining these cannibals as dark skinned because that's the way I've been taught. Hell, I used to have bad dreams about savages chasing me, because of Africans in movies. It's ridiculous." I went and spoke to him after class. At first he was adamant in not seeing the problem. He said, "I hadn't thought about it that way. I didn't realize it was like that." I elaborated, "Every day I have to prove to people that I actually go to this school. When I speak to them, I have to let them know, yes, I am a student on this campus. To perpetuate ideas that dark-skinned people are backward savages hurts people like me. It helps to keep that ideology going. You can use the same concept with goblins." He said he would change it.

Eric Ward

In one of my classes a professor talking about violence in the classroom said, "I had a friend who worked in a school district in north Portland and one day this black girl pulled a knife on her." That statement may not seem so exaggerated, except that earlier that day I walked past four skinheads sitting on the corner.

white people were also walking by but acted like the skinheads didn't exist. For me skinheads are symbolic in terms of what they stand for. It upsets me. I'd much rather go home and get my baseball bat and confront them then go on to class. Recently a black woman got attacked by a white woman on that street and there were skinheads all around, chanting and yelling. No one, not even the white graduate instructors standing nearby, intervened. We don't even know who this white woman was. We've never seen a report of the incident. That is such a contradiction because if I go out and start an incident, I'll probably go to jail. I know they have a crime gang task force in Eugene, that works with store owners, so anytime a clerk sees a black person whom they think is in a gang, he or she will call the police. Skinheads can sit out there all day and nothing happens. The police drive on by.

That is why I went to class in a bad mood. In class, as I listened to the teacher talk about classroom violence, I thought, "If the student who had pulled the knife on a teacher had been white, the professor wouldn't have said that a white girl pulled a knife on her friend." It seems like a little thing, but it bugged me. I blew up. People always tell me it's better to confront my teachers after class when no one is around so I don't put them on the spot. But I was rude and I upset her. She didn't understand my anger because she hadn't spent the whole morning with me. If I had gone to class in a great mood, I probably would have waited until after class and said, "Did you realize you did this?"

In another class we were considering the abortion debate and someone from Family Planning showed a videotape, *Abortion Stories, North and South,* which builds its argument on "overcrowding in the world." It shows images from Africa and India and says this is the reason why we need abortion and it should be legal. In fact, people in Asia and Africa are dying because of racism and economic oppression. Statistically if any group is overpopulating the world, it's people of European descent, based on a percentage of what they consume, which is more than anybody else in this world. If the developed countries had not gone in and messed up these other continents, there might not be overpopulation. Students can get into a dialogue about whether or not legal abortion might be a significant factor, but they should discuss all the related factors.

What is scary is that students already believe myths about overpopulation, so when a film uses this as evidence, students agree that, of course, it's that way. The media uses whatever it wants to make a point, and many groups use *us* to get their point across. If the country wants more law enforcement, then the news will show blacks on TV shooting one another. I can deal with overt racism but subtle things like this videotape chew at me because other people don't see the issues. I can sit in a class with sixty white students and be the only one who realizes what's going on. It feels like someone's come in and whacked you on the head and no one else saw it. I want everybody to realize it and feel the same hurt I do.

Maria Mendoza

Some people expect me to be quieter in the classroom. They find out that's not true. In a political science class with four students of color out of about 130, a student said that Native Americans are genetically defective and tend toward alcoholism because it's in their genes. We four sat there looking at each other, "Did he just say what he said?" I was so mad, and the professor let it go and did not address it. I said, "I don't mean to disrupt your lecture, but this must be an ignorant class. You just let a student make a racist comment. It's wrong to let something go by that isn't true. Most people aren't educated when it comes to ethnic groups, so if students don't know any better and hear something like that, they're going to assume it's true." After that, as I'd walk into class, students would roll their eyes as if thinking, "There she comes, trying to cause more trouble."

Geo. Ann Baker

Eventually I quit going to school because I couldn't handle it any more. Four or five of us, all Indian students taking a science class, studied together. We were all accused of cheating on the final. I wouldn't even go talk to the professor. I said, "This is it," and I dropped out. I didn't come back until last year.

This year I had to see a counselor about my grades, which were terrible. There'd been a death in my family and my sister was very ill, so my niece came to live with me. When I tried to explain this, the counselor said, "You have to buckle down." I said, "My family comes first. If something happens to my family, I have to go to them." He said, "Ignore them. You can't get caught up in this." I said, "You don't seem to understand. This is my culture. I have to do it." Then, reading my grades, he said, "You got a low grade in this and this and this and that's typical of minority students." I sat there. He added, "You got an A in your writing class? How did you do that?" I picked up my stuff and left. I went to another academic adviser and told him what had happened. It's discouraging to a minority student when a counselor thinks the color of your skin has some bearing on your command of the English language. That attitude is widespread. Until you show you belong in a class, the other students and the teacher look down on you. As I walk in, everybody looks at me as if I were in the wrong class. When the grades come back, they ask, "What did you get?" If you get a good grade, they esteem you since you seem like something rare. Even the teacher tends to ignore you until you submit good work. Then it's as if, "Oh, I didn't know I had this intelligent person in here." Minority students aren't supposed to do so well.

Many Anglos think we minorities got in here because of our race. They think that we had low grades in high school and were admitted because of the color of our skin. I got in on my grades. When I first came to school, I didn't check the admissions form to say if I was Indian or Hispanic. I left it blank. It makes me so angry when people in class say, "You took somebody else's place because you're Indian and provide the university with a certain percentage of that group." The money I get from my tribe is deducted from my financial aid. One woman told me, "When I registered for school, I checked the box 'Indian' because I wanted more money." It's ridiculous. She must think the tribes are both rich and stupid. The Native American Student Union gets the names of three hundred new Native American students each year from admission forms, yet in our office we see at the most twenty.

The other thing I don't like is when they start talking about a minority issue and the whole class looks at you. If they start talking about something like Eskimos, the professor will ask me about it, but I'm not Eskimo, I'm Klamath. I know Eskimo people, but I can't speak for them. The class expects me to speak for the whole Native American race or all minorities, and I can't. I'm there to learn too. I'm not the authority.

Del Carter

I'm taking a class called the African American Experience, with surprisingly only two African Americans in the class. Neither of us feels very comfortable speaking out in class although our instructor is African American. My own experience may not necessarily apply to other cases, but students often take what I say as if it were gospel and true for all African Americans. Or the other students speak and I don't agree with what they've said, either because something different happened to me personally or because I can look at it from an African American perspective. I'm afraid if I say something in response, everyone's going to switch their focus from that person to me, and that's not what I want. I don't want to cause conflict in the class. I want us all to become educated.

Shelli Romero

My roommate, Lisa Rodriguez, and I were taking a psychology class together and were required to participate in three one-hour experiments per term. When we went to sign up, the woman there said, "But one of the requirements is that your native language has to be English." That was a really sick example of racism.

Armando Morales

I was taking a mechanics class at Lane Community College and every time I raised my hand to answer, the professor never called on me. One day he was going student by student, so he had to ask me a question. He asked, "Morales, what is the color of the blackboard?" I didn't get it because at that time I didn't understand much English. The students laughed. But I didn't understand why he'd asked me this question. I went to talk to the multicultural affairs counselor and explained my problem. That professor received some kind of punishment for racism.

Later I had already finished my college of education requirements and needed to take an exam to prove my credentials. If you don't write good English, then you can't get credentials to teach Spanish. But I don't want to teach English; I want to teach Spanish. In U.S. society, they measure your knowledge by quizzes and exams. Yet one exam can never reflect your knowledge of your own history. I know people whose lives have been damaged by these exams.

3

Reframing the Educational Process
and the Community as a Whole

WHOSE KNOWLEDGE? WHOSE HISTORY?
THE CURRICULUM

Students of color come to the university expecting a liberal education inclusive of cultures and respectful of differences in learning styles. Here the students offer a sophisticated intellectual analysis of the limits of a Eurocentric curriculum and note what alternatives might consist of. They also highlight their positive learning experiences, especially in women's studies and ethnic studies.

Meredith Li

I'm an honors college student. In the honors college we're required to take a year of Western civilization. While it's important to take Western civilization courses, they don't offer Eastern civilization or Southern civilization. I know that there are some professors in the honors college who would like to see Southern civilization or Eastern civilization taught, but they don't have the expertise. They don't want the curriculum to become tokenism and want to get students to question what has happened with Western civilization. What's commonly told to me by the administration is that there is no money to offer Eastern civilization or Southern civilization because the university would have to bring in other faculty and doesn't have money to do that. That decision sends a clear message that there's no priority in the administration to teach about these other civilizations.

A good example of their policy is the fact that in the course catalog for the past nine years, there's been a listing under ethnic studies for a course on Asian

American history. It has never ever been taught but the listing sits there because the administration wants to give the image of celebrating cultural diversity. When it comes down to it, they've never offered the class. Recently the Asian-Pacific-American Student Union petitioned to get this class started. When it takes so much effort for us to get a class started that was advertised in the bulletin for so many years, that tells me there's talk but no real commitment to offering a multicultural curriculum.

Maria Mendoza

All the other classes I've taken present only a Euro American point of view. Classes like Chicano literature or Chicanos in U.S. society offer our point of view. We get to speak about our experiences and our history. This subject matter should be included in other classes, but it's not. In a lot of my sociology classes, we have our one lecture on racism. Blacks, Chicanos, Asian Americans, and Native Americans all get dealt with in one or two lectures. It's neither realistic nor fair. It's sad that we have to get our own classes to learn anything about our own people because it's not going to be taught in regular classes.

Jon Motohiro

I had an African American woman instructor for a sociology class—Race, Class, and Ethnicity. She was talking about the history of different groups and spent a solid day each on African American history, Native American history, and Hispanic history, during which she brought up many interesting issues. When we came to Asian Americans, we had a "catch-all" day. There're so many groups, but the teacher only covered Japanese and Chinese Americans and finished her lecture early. When I talked to her afterward, she looked at me and said, "I'm sorry that I couldn't get into it any further but that's not my field. If you are interested, I want you to do it on your own. It's probably the hardest thing to do, but go on and do it yourself." Her encouragement impressed me favorably.

Callan Coleman

This year, I began graduate work in counseling psychology and spent my first two terms learning basic skills. Sadly the required curriculum did not deal with counseling diverse populations, which we study spring term. That was a valuable class which presented the issues that come up when counseling Native American, African American, Hispanic, Asian American, disabled, and older clients. I was disappointed that the basic procedures had been taught from a Euro American perspective, teaching us, for example, to maintain eye contact and forward trunk lean. Now, after I've adopted this habit, I realize it might not be as effective in working with, say, a Native American client, with whom I wouldn't want to make prolonged eye contact. These multicultural perspectives should be taught at the very basic levels but in the basic courses we got this map, and it only dealt with one perspective. The book that we used in Theoretical Foundations had a few paragraphs at the end of every chapter about dealing with multicultural clients. You'd read the whole theory and then at the end read a little snippet of how this would apply to people of color. That approach didn't do me any good and I don't know what it did for anybody else. When we all started seeing clients winter term, many of the counseling graduate students had minority clients but they had not been taught the cultural factors that go into working with such clients.

Sweeter Sachuo

The curriculum merely reflects a specific cultural perspective, so multiple perspectives should be integrated into the curriculum even at the university level. Sometimes I feel frustrated in class because when I talk it seems that people don't accept what I say as intellectual. In these circumstances I feel disappointed, but I know my own way of thinking is the best.

Geo. Ann Baker

The oral tradition is valid for me because that's how our history is passed down, by word of mouth. It's not written; we're educated through oral traditions. In a paper I wrote for speech class, we had to list our resources. I wrote, "My grandmother." My teacher and I argued about this. He said, "You can't use that. It's not a written source." Finally I wrote the speech out, gave it in class, turned it in my list of resources as my grandmother and my own personal experiences, and wrote that if the teacher didn't accept them, he was denying my educational right to learn through oral traditions. I ended up getting an A out of the class, but these things make me angry. I'm learning from educators who are biased to begin with, and I'm being taught in a language that is not mine. I am learning from the perspective of a different value system, one that is not mine, and I'm learning things that are of no concern to me at all. But I have to do these things in order to survive in this society.

Lisa Rodriguez

My multicultural affairs writing class made a great deal of difference to me. The class was small, about twenty people, which allowed for a lot of open discussion. I got to hear other people's viewpoints. I'd never thought about things that way, so I learned a lot. Everyone in there was friendly and we all got along, all of us from many diverse backgrounds and cultures. We had a chance to get to know each other, express our concerns, and learn.

Book work doesn't come easy. I'm a person who has to try very hard. But sometimes I feel discouraged about the way a class is being taught. My first day in Spanish class with a Euro American teacher turned me off. Even if the teacher knows the language and the book work, it's discouraging to me that there are so few faculty of color on this campus that the person trying to teach you your own language is not of the same culture. The teacher would sometimes pronounce things wrong, but she made me feel like she thought she knew everything. If I'd correct her, as I did a couple of times, she'd say defensively, "No, I said it right" or "The book said this and the book said that." I replied, "I'm sorry but personally I don't go by the book. I know how it's supposed to sound and I know how to say it. The way you learn the language is by hearing it and speaking it. You don't learn the language out of a book. Even if you've had four years of Spanish in high school and go to Mexico, very few people can speak one sentence to someone except for asking very basic things." After that, I didn't feel like trying very much. I didn't feel I had to prove something to a person like her.

Carol Cheney

One of the things that upsets me about the curriculum is that in my major, English, we have to take pre-1500 literature classes. There isn't anything more important about that particular period or that particular country than is found in the literature of many different countries, for example, that of China, which had such a long history and so many amazing early advances in science and art. We don't learn anything about this pre-1500 culture. Even though we're learning English literature, that period in England seems irrelevant in this day and age.

I've enjoyed taking women's literature classes and also an ethnic studies literature class. I'm taking a class right now on Asian American women from Alice Yun Chai. It's brought together many Asian Americans who are going through the same thing that I'm going through. We are talking about where we're from, who our mothers were, and how important our mothers and heritage and culture are to our own sense of being and own self-worth. It's been exciting to share that with other women who are like me and celebrating it.

Kronda Adair

Winter term I took Introduction to Women's Studies. It was the first class I took that actually had to do with me. I would rush home to do the reading because everything that I read for that class I could relate to. This was a great experience. I would read and think, "This is me." Previously, I'd read mostly about white men. Another women's studies class integrated the issues I'm concerned about. I read things about lesbians, about women, and about people of color and about people who are all of those things, which is also me. We read Audre Lorde and other writers who are multidimensional. That was my first class ever which did not pretend that people have just one aspect but assumed that a person can be a whole bunch of things and integrate them in her life.

Leyla Farah

The classes I've taken from female professors have all been gender-oriented classes. Those classes make me feel I have a reason to be there. I always have something to say. I have someone to back me up if I'm getting interrupted or if I am trying to make a point that a male in the class is not getting. A woman teacher makes me feel like I can do what she's doing. I've always been exposed to strong women through my mother and her family, and I never thought that there was anything strange about that at all. But I never had concepts to label women's experiences with. I understood what sexism was but could never have labeled something with the concept, for example, of taking up space. Large women are bad because they take up too much space or we women and girls are supposed to sit with our legs crossed and our hands together. Women's studies has also given me a lot of statistics to explain why things happen. But I get torn, because when I'm in the black movement, I'm the gender wing and sit in the back saying, "Remember, we're here too, as women." Then when I'm in the feminist movement, I'm the color wing.

Eric Ward

To me the curriculum is awful. I'm not talking about women's studies or ethnic studies. The core curriculum is awful. It's Eurocentric, which isn't a bad thing when in balance with other perspectives, such as African American and Asian perspectives. The curriculum doesn't give an honest picture. It's like looking at an accident from one viewpoint. Instead of asking the four or five witnesses what they saw, it asks one person, "What happened here?" This curriculum teaches me how to deal with white society, its games, how it thinks, and how it reacts to situations. But I've mostly had to teach myself through independent study. I'm taking my first class focusing on African Americans and race. Here I'm attentive and find it easier to speak even if people don't agree with what I say. In this class, everybody doesn't look at me like I'm way out in left field, and the subject matter concerns things I can use, things that I can think about in relation to my life.

The university says its end goal is diversity or multiculturalism, but it is hedging and cutting steps to getting there. The way it views multiculturalism is like what Malcolm X said about integration: White society invites us to dinner. We sit around the table, but we don't have any money in our pocket, so we have no power or destiny over our own ethnic community. That kind of power for self-determination is essential. It's the only way the university community can sit down together and decide that this is what we want. Multiculturalism can't be forced. Right now, the curriculum damages students of color on this campus, even more than the lack of professors of color. What is portrayed and the information that is dispersed are atrocious. We students of color should make a stand and do whatever needs doing to change this, even if it means not going here and completely withdrawing or refusing to register for school.

THOSE BEFORE US: FACULTY OF COLOR

The students draw on a wide variety of perspectives to argue for more faculty of color. Some discuss the difference it makes when there are sufficient minority faculty to be a regular presence on campus and serve as role models for students of color, increasing the students' self-esteem and giving them greater academic motivation. Others say that faculty of color teaching about minority communities have a greater grasp of the cultural context of what they are teaching, that they understand and can teach the structures of feeling that inform specific cultures; otherwise, the teacher may only teach what comes out of a book and not the context behind it. Some students also point out the role community members can play in teaching about a culture underrepresented among the faculty.

There is a controversy among faculty and students of color about who is most qualified to teach ethnic topics courses. On the one hand, students and faculty all benefit from courses that are regularly taught rather than postponed, further perpetuating ignorance and a monocultural curriculum. Also, faculty of color may wish to teach other courses, such as Shakespeare or French history. Research and teaching among all the faculty should not be limited by race. On the other hand, sometimes when white faculty teach race-related courses, they do not have the lived experience within the subculture being studied to treat a given theme as deeply or with as much understanding as someone from that subculture could. Regardless of their race, instructors can always supplement the curriculum with speakers of color who have expertise related to a particular topic in the course.

Shelli Romero

All the faculty need to take a workshop on un-learning racism to learn to be more culturally sensitive, to watch the biases in their language, and not to teach from one perspective but from different ones. I had an ethnic studies teacher who had to bring in a Native American woman to talk about Native Americans and a Chicano to talk about Chicanos. As a professor, he should know that information. He's getting paid for lectures that he's not even delivering. On the flip side, I had a wonderful English professor who taught a women writers class in which all the books were by women of color. And I've had great experiences with a professor of color. If I'm going to take Spanish or ethnic studies, courses that interest me, I try to take them with professors of color because I feel they have a more realistic understanding, culturally, and historically, and reach out to students of color more.

Gretchen Freed-Rowland

We've been taught that the expert "knows." As teachers we've been taught to stand in front of the class as the "expert." I had a professor, a Seneca Indian man who remains in contact with his language, ritual, and culture, who modeled a form of reciprocal learning in an education class, a way of teaching and learning that draws out students' personal experiences. He had already made an outreach into the local community from a multicultural perspective, which he did as much for himself as for others, since he was also a foreigner coming into this environment. His class made me feel like I was coming home. It validated me. I found another person from my culture, a professor, who said it was okay to teach the way I did and bring material into class the way I did. With him, cultural authorities didn't have to be an expert or talk big words.

If we teach from our perspective of involvement, as he has done, what happens is that students of color feel they can come back to the university. I've heard it over and over again: "I'll only come back if you're going to be there," or "I'll only come back to this class." I spoke with the director of Chicano affairs at another university who said, "We have no trouble with bringing the numbers in now, but it's like a revolving door because there's nothing here that makes them feel comfortable." And that's what is happening at this school. We have lots of well-meaning teachers who have only their own cultural perspective to teach from. Many of them haven't actually lived in other countries. They don't come from ghetto areas. They haven't worked with the homeless. How many university professors have done such things?

Kronda Adair

In school there are four black professors on campus. My friends said of one of them, "If you get a chance, take a class from him." So I jumped at the opportunity to take his course, Women in the Mass Media. In that class important things get addressed. He doesn't shirk issues at all, such as the problem with athletes on campus getting passed through the system. Although it wasn't actually said, in a class with a black professor there is an atmosphere where we both know that black people have to do twice as well to be considered as good as these other people. It's an unwritten rule. I don't consciously think about it but know that I have to be the best and do the best I can.

Geo. Ann Baker

When I was a senior in high school, the principal had different speakers present community issues at assemblies. I came in late for one assembly and was sitting in the back not paying attention. I'd brought out my books and started to read when I started listening to this voice talking about Native American rights and issues. I looked up and said, "Native American rights? I didn't know we had any rights." Then I realized there were six Native American men standing on the stage discussing our rights and our differences. I didn't even hear what they were saying, I was so grateful to see somebody of my own skin color, my own culture, my own background, standing up there telling what it was like, telling me we had options. At the end of the assembly during question time, I jumped up and said, "I'm Klamath and Payute. Can you please help me?"

They met me after the assembly and talked to me. They told me all the things I needed to hear, things my grandmother had been telling me all this time which I hadn't listened to. She'd say, "Be proud of who you are. Be proud of the color of your skin. Be proud of your hair." And I'd answer, "Grandma, it doesn't do any good when everybody else has blond hair and blue eyes, and they think you're ignorant." These men put me to work in the American Indian Action Center. They were protective of me and took me among Native American cultures as if I were their sister. They raised me and brought values I'd learned before to the surface where I could see them again. They were all educated. One had a master's, the other a doctorate, and I realized they had already attained the goals I was striving for, so I had something to look forward to. I'm an older student, and the main reason I'm back in school is because I remember what they told me.

I'm taking a class from the only Native American professor on this campus. It's a lot easier because I don't have to explain myself. When I submit work in other classes, I have to explain things. Teachers always ask, "Can you elaborate on this?" or "What does this mean?" It gets tiring after a while. When I talk to someone from my own background, I can get on with other things instead of having to step back and explain everything step by step from the beginning. In an ethnic studies class I'm taking from a Chicana professor, I can see the difference in her teaching. Her learning is through books and through experience, so she has a better feel for ethnic issues and can explain them well. We need faculty of color teaching in areas like ethnic studies and anthropology. I signed up to take a class about Native American religions taught by a white woman. In our culture women have a lot to do with religion, but it is basically the man's job to teach it. I was highly offended and dropped out of the class. Everything the teacher learned and taught came right from a book. I'd read some of the books that were on her syllabus and said, "This is total garbage," and left. But even if we get faculty of color, we'll still need to have voices from the community, voices from different peoples of color who may not have a degree. These people understand their own heritage and culture.

Lisa Rodriguez

We need more faculty of color. I feel very frustrated that we don't have these teachers to teach the subjects most closely related to students of color. It's good for the university to offer as many kinds of multicultural classes as it can, but it would be nice to have someone from that culture teaching that class. A Chicano/Latino class should be taught by a Chicano. You can relate to the course material more and it encourages you to do a lot better in the class since you're more interested and focused and willing to do more on your own. In some schools you can major in black studies or in Chicano/Latino studies. Here if we can get one or two classes we're ecstatic.

Callan Coleman

It's an incredible feeling to have an African American teacher telling the class about things you know about and teaching you things you didn't know before but understand because you both live in the same spectrum. Some students are resistant but others are into the subject matter and do not feel threatened by reality. I had Introduction to Ethnic Communities with a Native American teacher, where I learned more about Native American peoples, their history, and their present conditions than I ever could have otherwise. I know where this person is coming from. Even though he's from a different culture, he still has the same minority status. Our perspective is the same. I can feel the pain and the pleas that this person is putting out. I know from the personal experiences this person tells the class that this person has felt some of the same things that I have.

Michelle Singer

There are so many different perspectives within our culture that can't be expressed by somebody who's Euro American. White teachers trying to teach

Native American literature don't hack it. There's so much that they do not understand because they weren't brought up to understand it. They do not have a grasp of what they're teaching as opposed to a Native American teacher. There are qualified Native American professors out there, but they're not here, only one. Taking classes from Native American professors makes all the difference in the world because you identify with this person. This person knows you and you know them because of how you're brought up and what you believe. They know about your background. He or she is somebody to look up to because you know this person made it. It isn't the teacher–student situation but much more personal. These people reach out to you with open arms. It's vital that we have faculty of color here. When a Native American student coming to a university sees faculty of color, it's a big asset because the student knows there are minority professors here too. It's an added support for both the faculty member and the student because they need each other.

CULTURE ON PARADE: REPRESENTING THE RACE

Students talk about what it means to be a token yet also be placed in the position of constantly having to educate the whole university community about race, as if racism were a "problem" faced only by people of color. White students do not have to assume these extra roles.

As Eric Ward puts it, "Tokenism is being here at this university." In a classroom setting, when there are few students of color and an issue comes up about race, the white students or the teacher often expect the student of color to respond or explain; they then take that student's words as speaking for the race. Often students of color are asked to speak on a panel about race in their classes or in the dorms. They may do so out of a strong sense of responsibility but with mixed feelings since they face difficult choices about what to say. They also would like to be considered an authority on subjects other than race.

Furthermore, when asked to educate whites on the topic of race, students of color may not want to open up their life to strangers, may feel vulnerable if they speak the truth, and may face a variety of consequences. In this light, silence can also serve as a form of resistance since students of color may not speak out due to their cultural upbringing or reluctance to put themselves forward to challenge teachers with their disagreements. The students' stories here explore multiple forms of resistance under these circumstances.

Shelli Romero

The university loses students and faculty because it tends to use them as tokens. Since I've been at the University of Oregon I must have sat on at least fifty panels. I don't like people to consider me as "Shelly who represents the Hispanics on campus," or the token student of color who represents all students of color because that's not how it is. I can't talk for everybody. I can only talk for me. If my group, MEChA [the Chicano/Latino student union], says "Okay, Shelly, we want you to represent us for this panel," I can represent MEChA. But I'm not representing all of the student unions or all of the other students of color on this campus. In classrooms, instructors should specifically tell the students not to have these kinds of expectations. For example, if students of color are in a class reading about Malcolm X, everybody turns to the only black student. Why should that kid know any more about Malcolm X than anybody else, especially coming out of our educational system? It's not fair. Students of color should not be responsible for teaching the others or sharing their feelings if they do not feel comfortable doing so.

Racism is everybody's problem and people don't acknowledge that. They see people of color lagging behind and say that we must get out by ourselves. They think that racism is a problem that we have: "If you're upset, it's your problem. You are being discriminated against so you should do something about it." It's not my responsibility to tell white people what's going on because racism has stemmed from them and they need to start helping too.

Geo. Ann Baker

We educate everyone else. We go to classes and talk about being Native American. We sit on a lot of panels. Even the public school system will call us and ask us to send one of our students to a grade or high school. Often we are the token Indian, but by doing these things we find out how the system works and we can use that to our advantage. We go to a lot of boring meetings which do not deal with anything that concerns us, but we may meet somebody there who will help us in the future.

Leyla Farah

I now refuse to say, "This is how black people think," because I know that I don't know how black people think. I will say, "This is how I think and this is how history thinks." Oregon is not a hospitable place for blacks to be human. Wherever blacks live in Oregon, there are more whites. So any black person draws the response, "There's a black person." I'm not Leyla, I'm "Leyla the black person." People assume, "We need a black person. Call Leyla." In my women's studies class this year when we set up panels, I refused to be on the one dealing with women of color. I said, "I'll do anything else but I'm not doing that one. Someone else can." It's valid for us to get tired but it doesn't mean racial problems have gone away.

Maria Mendoza

Because there are so few students of color here, we tend to get spread out everywhere. I don't usually mind, but sometimes I think, "Why should I be trying to educate white people?" I do it to get my point of view across. I don't want to say I speak for "our people." That's a big issue for us, whether or not we represent our entire race when we serve on panels and committees. I don't like doing this kind of work because I feel that people take what I say as the general perspective.

Michelle Singer

I'm one of three codirectors of the Native American Student Union. That plus the fact that I'm a student of color sometimes makes me feel like a token. I'm one of the university's quota. I get calls saying, "You're a student of color and Native American. Can you come and serve on my panel and answer questions in my class?" These panels deal with everything from racism and discrimination to what is it like to be a minority in a classroom setting, or to be a woman of color. I'm also asked to serve on many committees. We get asked half a dozen times each term, but usually we each only do one thing. Because it hurts. I have mixed feelings about this work. I feel good that people want to listen and learn, yet I have a problem being put on a pedestal where I'm expected to open my life up to a bunch of strangers.

Jon Motohiro

They count you toward the diversity that makes the campus unique, and they count you as a minority for public relations and federal money. Yet when it comes to helping Asian American students out financially, which a lot of us need, they assume that there're enough of our people here. If they are going to count us as a minority in some areas, our status cannot be a sometimes thing. Now their attitude is, "You're a minority, but you're not a minority for scholarships." Some people think we don't need scholarships because we can afford tuition or because many Asian Americans already come here. It blows my mind. Who gets to establish what's underrepresented? At what point has the university drawn the line between adequate representation and underrepresentation? They're establishing a quota. They'll still accept us in but only if we can afford it. That's definitely going to decrease the numbers coming in. There're so many

Asian American groups: Japanese, Chinese, Korean, Vietnamese. I can't name them all. How many Filipino students do you see out here? How many _____? Go down the line. There aren't many of *those* people. It's almost like we're being black-balled. It's hard to accept that.

Carol Cheney

I'm frightened by this whole theory of Asian Americans being a "model minority." It's a ploy or strategy that says, "Look at this group and how well they're doing. Therefore, they don't deserve any special treatment. They don't deserve what other groups are getting." That's harmful. Institutions are taking statistics that are skewed and using them against a group of people based on race. The myth causes competition between ethnic groups who should be trying to build a coalition. It's a good way for the government to undermine the progress that we've made. I'm an average person who tries hard to do well in everything I do. My dad always told me, "If you're going to do something, you might as well do the best you can." I'm no different from anybody else when it comes to brains, and neither are a lot of people I know. The concept of a model minority is a complete myth and a scary strategy that harms people.

Kronda Adair

My priorities are sexism first, homophobia second, and racism third. But I can't separate them because I'm all one person. The issue of combating racism has been around for a long time and has a certain acceptance. However, when I tell people I have to keep fighting racism on campus, they often respond, "Why are you doing that? Everything's fine." Still, most people acknowledge there's racism in the world and a lot of work needs to be done around it. They know the same about sexism. Combating homophobia doesn't have this kind of credibility or get this kind of social attention. People don't think it's worth the same effort.

To combat isms—sexism, racism, heterosexism—you cannot separate those problems and combat them effectively because you have racism in the gay and lesbian community and homophobia in the black community and in other cultures. In order to combat social problems, you need to network and not just work around single issues. As a lesbian activist, I thought about my own safety before I came in here. This is taped and the video will be around for a long time. Who's going to see it? I worry about my safety in a general way. Anything could happen to anybody at any time so I'm not going to go around paranoid, saying "Oh, no, I'm not going to go out because what if . . . ?" Safety is something that I remain aware of: that if I do this, something could happen. Am I going to let such concerns stop me? Am I going to let them box me in? The answer has to be, "No."

Eric Ward

Tokenism is being at this university. They want us here because they get more federal funding, we make the university diverse, and they learn a hell of a lot from us. They get much more from us than they give back because we end up having to teach them so much. Even though they want us here, they don't want us to say anything that's going to force them to have to stretch to do something or put themselves on the line. To me tokenism is being on this campus because the faculty and administration do not want to sit down and make the changes. Rather, they make excuses why it can't be done. It goes back to that whole paradigm of power. Recruiters tell students of color to come to the University of Oregon with the pitch, "On this campus we want to build on diversity. Racism and discrimination aren't allowed here."

In fact, the university *doesn't* support us if we want to deal with these things. Furthermore, anything I do around discrimination helps white people understand their own sickness and, more often than not, takes time away from my studies, classes away from my degree. The administration doesn't want to deal with problems around race but wants us here. We people of color are the ones who have answers for racism, yet the administration doesn't want us to do anything. If they did, they would support us more and make our struggle easier.

Many people say, "Let's get Eric to speak." There are about two hundred African Americans on this campus who can tell the same things. I'm not saying anything different or better, but I am saying it. I'm taking the risk of not graduating and getting my degree in five years, when I'll be cut off financially from the support I need to complete school. It's not fair to ask that of students of color. When we open ourselves up to white people, it costs us. Whites play a role in this racist system out of complicity. Why do I always have to explain this? Every time I say something that white people don't see, I have to take my time to explain everything. I have to expose my hurt. When they feel guilty, I'm supposed to redeem them from their guilt.

I've had times when someone will be talking about African Americans or racism and everyone will turn and stare at me. The stare means they think I'm the spokesperson for the black race. I never look at a white person and expect them to speak for their whole race nor do I judge their whole race by them. It is a matter of privilege to be able to do that. If I do something good, I'm an example for my race, to live by and to strive for. If I do something bad, I'm a detriment to my race. We don't do that to white people and I don't know why it comes back that way to us.

Gretchen Freed-Rowland

In a large art class, the professor talked about her experience in the Southwest, where she met some Indian potters peddling their wares. When she asked about the origin and design of the pots, they said, "We don't know what it is." She said to us, "You see, there are no real Indians anymore." We Native Americans do not exist when we don't meet stereotypical images of what we are supposed to be about. I said, "I question that the potters didn't know what the designs were about. We tend to have our own prejudices, our own humor about these situations that we may not want to share. Or we may give answers we think the person wants to hear." She replied, "Well, I was there and I know."

Afterward, I went up to the other two Indians in the class and said, "Did I goof? How do you feel about what I said in terms of representing . . . ?" Each one said, "No, what you said was right, but I never would have spoken up." "You don't speak up," is what I hear over and over again from Indian people in this community and at this school. Whenever they protested, they weren't acknowledged or were slapped down or told that they didn't know. Only the expert knows. They've also seen that it affects their grades and getting out of school, so they learned to be silent, like Indians on reservations learned to be silent. For example, right now you are using students to speak about their experiences, but we're very vulnerable. We can be seen as troublemakers whom other universities won't want to hire or medical school won't take because we're seen as whistleblowers. Euro Americans don't have to take the risk. They can step back from it. We have no other choice, except to assimilate and be white. If we're going to be Indian, we have no choice. And blacks or Chicanos or Latinos have no choice. If we walk away, it makes us ill.

LIFE BEYOND CAMPUS BORDERS

The students express hurt and anger when relating the racial harassment they and those they know have encountered in town and in the state, especially in working-class or rural environments where economic hardship has been interpreted in racialized ways. The students describe specific discriminatory incidents that support their construction of reality; accumulated memories and common subcultural wisdom among students of color affect how they engage the dominant culture. Some students are reluctant to go to certain areas of the city or state or to leave "campus–town" borders because they and their friends have had prior negative, racially based encounters. Some of the students discuss discrimination they have faced at work. Dark-skinned men, especially in groups, regularly face challenges from campus security and the police.

All who have spoken out publicly in reaction to these incidents of discrimination describe gaining a sense of empowerment in spite of the threat of further violence. In a proactive way, ethnic student unions at the University of Oregon videotaped testimonies from local people of color to take to the state legislature for hearings on racial profiling as practiced by state and local police.

Sweeter Sachuo

My brothers and I were stopped by the police because we were walking in a group along the road. Two policemen stopped us and asked what we were doing. I told them we were walking. About ten minutes later, a little further from where they had stopped us, another policeman stopped us. I got mad and said, "What are you doing? Do you have to do this to us because we are a different color and from a different cultural background? We're not doing anything. This is our culture. We walk together in groups. Me and my brothers don't drink, we don't smoke, we don't take marijuana." The officer said, "I'm sorry. I was just suspicious."

Frank Piedra

When I first moved here in the beginning of summer, I spent time in Springfield [a working class community adjacent to Eugene, the university community]. That created a big culture shock. I had a man point a gun at me as he drove by in a truck, then laugh and drive away. There wasn't much I could do, you know. It made me feel scared. I moved out of Springfield after another racially motivated incident. I'd been working in a lumber mill, where a fellow employee called me a "stupid fucking wetback." I wanted to say that I wasn't stupid, I was attending a university, and wasn't a wetback but was born in Illinois. But I hit him. He had a lot of friends, which scared me, so I left town. I don't have a problem getting jobs because they always need somebody with a strong back. Finding *good* jobs is difficult. I was never asked for a green card until I came back to the United States, but when I apply for jobs, I always get asked for a green card, which as a U.S. citizen I do not have. Often, after talking to a person for forty-five minutes, it will come out of nowhere: "You speak good English." I have a sense of humor and respond, "Oh, sank you." They ask for it.

I don't know if it's racially motivated but I have a hard time walking on campus, especially at night, without getting stopped by security. Most other people I know have never been stopped. Once I was lying on the grass resting by a tree and two security cars pulled up. One pulled onto the sidewalk near the grass where I was lying and the other pulled to the side. The security police both jumped out as I was about to leave. They stopped me and said, "We thought you were in trouble." That was bullshit. It was so obvious. I had gotten off work and was on my way to my girlfriend's dorm. Obviously I wasn't hurt if I was getting up and walking away. I was upset. I said, "No, I'm fine. I'm a student here." They gave me the run-through, checked my ID and put me through the computer. Not thirty minutes later, I got stopped again by different officers. "What's the reason I'm being stopped for this time?" They said someone had called in and said I looked scary: "If anybody calls in, we have the right to stop you." Every time they have a reason! So I can't officially complain!

Eric Ward

If you don't go to school on this campus you can go for days without seeing another African American in Eugene. I've read about the history of Oregon and how blacks were chased out of the state and not allowed back until the 1900s. When I first got up here, it seemed like there were no more than fifty black people in Eugene, because I did not see any except for one of my roommates whom I moved up here with. But I found out that Eugene has its own kind of racism, not expressed as overtly as in L.A., where you hear racist slurs all the time. When we came up from Los Angeles, we had the kind of rent money we would've needed down there. Because we were a group of five and rents were a lot cheaper here, we could rent a big place in a nice neighborhood. We came rolling in there, five of us, two black, one Hispanic and two white, all punk rockers.

After a week, a policeman walked into our house while I and one of my friends, Chris, who works at Chicano Affairs, were watching the L.A. Raiders on TV. All of a sudden, I look up and see a police officer standing in our hall. He didn't even knock. He walked in front of the TV set and started asking us questions, took down our names, and called in to the station while right inside our house. Then he told us, "Now that you're here from Los Angeles, you don't need to root for the L.A. Raiders." How stupid! About a week later, my other roommate, Ted, got pulled over and photographed with a Polaroid camera down by the bakery. After they took his picture, they asked him if he'd ever thought about joining the Eugene Police Department.

People look at me and think, "Look, he has dreadlocks. He must get stoned and listen to reggae." I do listen to reggae, but that's about it. Until people hear me speak, they think something else about me, a collective stereotype they have because I'm a black male. Last year, after the Human Rights Fair on the day before Dr. Martin Luther King's birthday, I stopped for some coffee with a friend. When I left for home, it was right at dusk. As I was going up the alley toward 14th, a police car pulled around right into the alley. I couldn't see into the car because the headlights were flashing, but I heard clicking noises that didn't sound like they were coming from the motor. When I got out of the headlights' glare, I turned around and looked at the policeman. He had a 35 millimeter camera and was taking pictures of me. I couldn't believe it but I'd been hearing all year that this was happening, that police were photographing African American and Chicano students. We hear also that they keep track of where we live.

Last Tuesday the student newspaper ran a big picture of a black man on the front page, accusing him of date rape. Date rape is wrong. Any rape is wrong, but I've never seen a picture in the student paper of a white man accused of rape. That kind of image plays off old racial stereotypes about black men as rapists and is dangerous for black men. It's also dangerous for women because most likely that's not the person a white woman is going to be raped by if she's raped. I don't want to defend what happened. That's not the point I'm making. It was racist and shows a lot of shallow irresponsibility on the part of the editor, who can be held responsible. After we explained the issue to the editor, who didn't have a clue as to what we meant, we asked him, "Would you do it again?" He said that knowing everything we just told him, he would do the exact same thing again. People like that do not see their own racism because they don't have to.

Callan Coleman

There are places I won't go because I don't like the thought of people staring at me. As I walk down the street I imagine, "Do I look suspicious right now?" It's a waste of my energy to have to think about what other people are thinking about me. But I do know what people think about us, and their constant stares indicate that this prejudice is ongoing. I often hear coworkers say paranoid things about black people while I am standing right in front of them. I have to say, "Look at me. I'm as black as the people you're talking about. Why are you doing this right in front of me?" It's so offensive. Also, at one point I was being stopped by the police for no reason. I had to prove to them that I owned my car and lived in town. Those moments are always scary because I don't know what's going on in a policeman's mind.

In an interview for an internship in clinical psychology, the director of a program told me she wasn't sure I'd be suitable because her clients don't always want to see men. I could accept that. A few weeks later, I spoke to a male colleague who'd gotten a position at that place. I asked, "Did the woman who interviewed you tell you that you wouldn't get any clients because you're a man?" He said, "No." Another man in our program also interviewed with the same person, and she never told him that either. I want to confront her, but I don't usually do that. I don't know how I'm going to deal with it but know I'll have to bring it up to her.

Armando Morales

Another way racism appears is in how people measure your intelligence. Many times when I enter a professor's room, he pats my back and says, "Aye, Morales, come on." Then if I enter with some Anglos, the teachers never pat them. The teachers don't treat them that way.

Geo. Ann Baker

I knew this a long time ago. If you go to Springfield and are by yourself, stay in your car. I'll drive through Springfield, go straight to where I'm going, get my business done, and leave. When I walk into a store, everybody is blatantly so leery of me that I can feel it. I'm made to feel uncomfortable. At the coast the Ku Klux Klan is strong, so I don't go over there at night, only in daytime. We do certain things to prepare for a car trip that we take for granted. I get gas before I leave Eugene and I only stop at certain larger cities where I've been before and other people of color have been before. I'll stop at a public beach if it's crowded, but if I'm by myself or there are few people of color, I'm leery. That's second nature to us. We'll stop and look to see who's there. If it looks like people could be a threat, we won't stay. I don't like it, but it's a way of life.

I cannot stand going to powwows in Eugene but I go to see other Indian people. A lot of white hippies show up with their beads and braids and no shoes on. They look ridiculous as they get out on the floor and hop around. Our dances have been passed down for a long time. The hippies have no respect, no idea what they are doing, but want to be Indian so badly they think that if they dress like us they are going to see God and get the peace and serenity they think we have. It's as if I bleached my hair and pretended I've got a tan because I'm from California. It's just not going to work for them.

I parked next to a car yesterday that had a bunch of sage in the window, so I moved my car. We use sage like Catholics use incense in church. We use it to pray with and it's sacred. It's wrong to play with religion. The sacrilege is the same as if I went into a Catholic church and got that little cup, the chalice, and took it to my house to have a glass of beer. It's the same thing for us with sage, which people don't seem to realize. A lot of Native American religions believe that if you mess with something you don't understand, it will come back to you. I believe that if you disrespect religion, the first person affected is your child. Since I have such a high regard for my children and my grandmother, there is no way I am going to abuse sacred things. I tell people, "You've raped our religion. You've not only raped the religion, you've raped the land and you've raped our women."

Diana Collins-Puente

I went to a Corvallis house dance at the coast with a friend from a neighboring university who lives in Corvallis. A student there started talking about "spicks" and "niggers." I couldn't believe the things he was saying. The words he was using were so derogatory. I almost cried because I was so frustrated and angry. What affected me even more was that so few people said anything. It was me fighting and arguing against him. I wanted him to realize what he was saying but he was so sure of his ideas, so definite, I knew that anything I'd say he'd brush off. The silence of the others made me feel like they agreed with him, especially since they all knew him. They were mostly people he went to school with and their silence told me that they weren't about to help me out. My feeling of safety was diminished. There were only two people there that I knew. After that I stuck with my friends. I've learned to do this, especially if people are drinking and it feels like it's a question of safety. I'm not saying that someone will do something to me, but I am not going to take that risk. Being a woman, it's hard to be around men who don't see me as an equal or even as important as another woman, a white woman.

Meredith Li

As a woman was walking with another Asian woman, a car drove by them. The men in the car pulled up their eyelids and made ching-chong noises and then turned around and drove back, calling racial slurs and spitting on the women. These women made an easy target. Women in general are susceptible to such harassment because they're thought of as easy victims, and Asian women especially are portrayed as quiet servile types or exotic seductresses. Either type tends to make them appear helpless. When one woman called public safety, the police said they'd check on it. She called them back a few days later to see if they'd come up with the men's names because she'd turned in the license plate number. The public safety office had no record of her call. When she went to talk to the administration, they were sympathetic but had no formal grievance procedures for someone who experienced harassment in town on the basis of race. I would like to see a formal grievance procedure made, so that students, if they do experience that, can do something about it. Right now we feel powerless. You hear all this talk on campus about how the administration is committed to diversity and how harassment will not be tolerated, but it becomes only rhetoric if the university doesn't have a procedure where we can empower ourselves to do something about it.

Jon Motohiro

The further out I am from campus, the more uncomfortable I am. Only on campus do I usually see a Japanese American or an Asian American walking down the street. If I go a little further out, I stand out. In Hawaii I'm part of a majority. When I came here, I became a lot more aware of how racism feels. If I hear talk about the Japanese "taking over," it bothers me because we're not diabolical. It reminds me of the "yellow peril" attitude except it's not as harsh. People in the United States are afraid of other groups because this economy is not accustomed to having other economies compete on this level and be more successful. I don't see the Japanese taking over. In the U.S. workplace, you can't name a prominent Japanese American CEO. Look at the Japanese corporations that are here. Taking over is not their goal. For the most part, the Japanese work ethic is so strong that corporation executives and workers are willing to make a lot of sacrifices, which makes them successful. People here see this as a threat and they think it's a conspiracy. But we don't meet in a cave somewhere and say, "Okay, let's try to take this state, then on to California, and then we'll take New York after we get Virginia."

Del Carter

Overhearing things, walking down the street and having people stare at you, hearing whispers and comments, all that was shocking when I first got here. I tried to pretend it didn't exist. I thought, "I don't have to deal with that anymore. People here are grown up and have been educated. They've learned." But that's not true at all. As I was walking through a shopping center with a white male friend, the looks that we got were incredible. We heard, "Oh, my god," and "Oooh, gosh, what is he doing?" Things like that bothered me because I thought, "Eugene is supposed to be so diverse. What's wrong with these people?" On another occasion, I stood there for the longest time in a shop in the mall waiting for help. The clerk sat behind the counter doing everything she possibly could not to help me. When a white woman approached the counter, the clerk was quick to help that customer. Rather than make a purchase, I left everything at the counter and walked away. I made sure not to go there again.

Last year ten or fifteen black students were hanging out by the bookstore, talking about what to do that day. A police officer came around the corner and slowed way down, entirely too slow. About three minutes later, another police car drove by. A few minutes after that, a policeman on a motorcycle drove by.

As I looked in the bookstore window, I saw a security person standing there, as if we were going to rush the bookstore and steal everything. At that time it was funny because I was with so many other black friends who understood. We all noticed the suspicion and tried to laugh it off.

Carol Cheney

A man in a store walked up to me and inquired, "You probably know where the nearest Japanese restaurant is?" I'm Korean American but that had nothing to do with it. Anybody would probably know where the nearest Japanese restaurant was, yet he chose me out of the crowd because of my looks, my race. I said, "I feel that's a racist comment because you singled me out of a group of people because of my looks and are making a lot of assumptions about me. One, that I am Japanese, and two, that I eat Japanese or Chinese food. You know nothing about me." He realized I was very angry and tried to apologize, but I didn't want to listen to him. I shut down when I hear such things and I either walk away or tell people I consider what they said racist and don't appreciate it. I also do that about women's issues because I'm a feminist, I would even say radical feminist. It's all part of the same thing. When you're a member of one group that's been oppressed and are also a member of another group that's been oppressed, it all works together. You can see those cross-oppressions happening in your life. And if I don't say anything, I go home with a knot in my stomach. I feel pent-up anger and have bad dreams of frustration. By saying something, I feel better.

Lisa Rodriguez

I thought this town had the reputation of being liberal but if I'm walking with other students, especially African American students, we get stared at. If we're walking down a sidewalk and meet other people, those people expect us to move. If I am waiting in a checkout line, I notice the person in front of me writing a check out and paying; but when Maria and I go to pay, the cashier asks for identification and gives us a hard time.

Until last weekend I never in my life had been in a fight with someone over insults to my background, culture, or language. After the football game everyone was walking back on the trail to the multicultural dorm. We were my roommate Maria and I and about ten other people. Three white students behind us, a man and two women, started talking about Spanish class and the video series used all year to teach dialogues. They were trying to pronounce the names of the video's characters in Spanish but not doing it well. Maria and I kept looking at each other. They were laughing and saying racist things like, "tortilla-eating people."

Suddenly the man said, "I'll trade you some refried beans for a cigarette." Maria turned around, pointed her finger in his face, and said, "You better shut up now before I make you shut up." He was thrown off. He looked at her as if she should know he didn't mean it.

I've never been so angry in my life, ready to hit somebody for what they said about my culture. I turned around and started arguing with one of the white women. She said, "I don't understand why you're so offended. If I said something about economics, you wouldn't be so upset. I didn't mean anything personal toward you. It wasn't directed toward you." I responded, "But it was directed toward me because that's what I am, that's my culture. You're not going to say anything about it. You're too ignorant to know what you're talking about anyway." She continued, "I don't understand you people. I don't know why you're getting so defensive." The other guy was sounding off to Maria. We were so angry and were this close to getting in a fight. We couldn't believe that people would say something like that, so ignorant that they didn't even know why they were saying it. Then when we tried to explain, they refused to acknowledge what we were telling them or why what they did was wrong. They didn't know Chicanos were walking in front of them and were surprised that we objected.

The big group of minority friends walking with us kept saying, "What? I can't believe that. Go ahead, go ahead, say something. Tell them." It helped that we were around other friends saying it's not right and to stand up for ourselves and tell them we don't like it. The white students ended up running off. We were ready to defend ourselves if we had to, but we were not going to throw the first punch and start a fight, which would put us in trouble for their ignorance. We acted like, "You better leave now before you get hit."

A lot of people don't think racist things are racist. They only notice racism when something extreme like a riot occurs. They don't understand the racism in name-calling or in the way we get treated with a stare or a hassle. This was the first time anything like that had happened to me or Maria, and we were both in shock after we got home. That was a new experience for me, hearing something racist and reacting to the person who said it. It was the first time I'd set prejudiced people straight and was willing to defend it. I feel really good about that. I remember looking at the woman and thinking, "I can take her. She's my size." I knew Maria could handle her own battle.

Now we both have more courage and are willing to stand up for what we think is right. If someone says something racist to me or about me, I'm not going to let them get away with it. It makes me angry that people say these things without realizing it. At least I'm going to let them know their behavior offends me, that they're saying something inappropriate and should've thought about it. I notice racism a lot more now. I notice when people say something offensive or do things to hassle me. I didn't notice these things as much in the past. Now I see why. Now it's easy to see that it's happening to me because of what I look like or because of my skin color.

I don't know any students who go into Springfield. I can tell it's a redneck town because of the feeling I get from people's stares and behavior toward me. I would not feel safe going there by myself. A lot of my friends are minority students and are scared to go places alone at night. We're a very small group at the university. Many of us don't like white people. I don't know how to explain this. Students of color see how white people get so much and how our own cultures have been taken away from us. We have to fight harder to get anything and everything is twice as difficult for us. Often we feel anger, even hatred. Many of us won't talk to or are rude to whites. I too am growing to dislike white culture. I don't feel hatred, but more and more white culture makes me angry and sad and very aware.

REFRAMING POLITICS AND POWER: COMMUNITY RESPONSIBILITY

The students want to participate in an institution that often excludes what they say. Their voices reveal their urge, an impatient urge, to shape the events and educational processes that shape their lives and their future. They hold the university accountable for its obligation to provide a learning environment and experiences that will prepare all its students for a diverse, complex world. Especially when an institution has a relatively homogeneous population and a dominant white institutional culture, its authorities have to plan deliberately for diversity initiatives. In higher education, such initiatives have been developed only through the provocation and protests of students, who seek and gain support of faculty and finally reach the ears of administration.

Many of the students who speak here have been active as leaders in the ethnic student unions, from which groups they have received crucial support to stay in school. Now they want to give similar assistance to the next generation of students, since they see that the university often fails to provide a support mechanism for retaining students of color. They first learned from their parents that they had to be self-sufficient and show that they were "better" than more privileged whites; now they often speak of their future goals in terms of responsibility to their community rather than the more typical individualistic goal of success.

Jon Motohiro

I was nervous about coming to the University of Oregon. I barely knew where Oregon was, much less Eugene. The Hawaii Club helped me settle in. They regularly arrange for a pickup service where they meet new students at the Eugene airport. I've done this, too, for several years, in a "giving back" process. As president of the Hawaii Club, I've seen problems of adjustment and transition when Hawaiian students leave home. Last year I tried to get to know the freshmen by name and keep in touch with them. It helps to have somebody out there who knows you and checks on how you're doing. I've seen friends go through problems here, and I offer to be there if needed.

Frank Piedra

I'm doing a lot better this semester. I have more money. Last year, I was working all night as a janitor and going to school all day. It was rough. I was helping raise my little sister and managed to put her through high school. Now she's graduated. I talked to her and she's on her feet and working. I offered to pay for her college. That's why I'm working. It's important to have role models, and I like knowing that my little sister uses me as her role model.

Armando Morales

People often say, "Armando Morales has wonderful ideas and works well but his problem is his accent." I know that. Sometimes I feel like a disabled person. With practice I can polish my accent and do better in the future, but an accent should not prevent me from entering into and participating in society. If you have a funny accent, they won't let you enter into this society. That's wrong because the United States could learn from us, and it is missing what we Latin people have to offer.

Callan Coleman

My parents told me that in this culture white people won't take care of me. If I'm in the street, they won't pull me into their house and feed me. I need to learn how to take care of myself. I know the expectations white people have of blacks and how they assume we can't do this and can't do that. That makes me want to demonstrate the complete opposite. My parents also taught me that if I do well, it doesn't mean I'm suddenly king of the world and everybody else is dirt. Maybe if I had lived in an African American community, I might understand more how much of a responsibility I need to take. I feel like I've fallen through the cracks of oppression where a lot of African Americans have been buried. I sometimes wonder what would've happened to me if I'd grown up in the ghettos of Los Angeles. My mind might have snapped, you know, yet many people come out of there with strong minds ready to face the world. If they could survive like that and if God has given me this good start in life, then I should give something to society.

Meredith Li

Many Asian Americans find it difficult to speak up against racial comments or jokes. It is hard for me too, but I'm learning that I have to. Many Asian Americans don't say anything because they were brought up not to stand out or draw attention to themselves. I can understand where they're coming from. In some instances I feel too intimidated to speak up, especially when racist men say things and I fear for my safety. But my parents tried to bring me up to be feisty. If I hear something that's offensive, I'm learning to say, "That offends me." Until people realize that their comments make others uncomfortable, they're going to continue doing it. They may not even realize that they're offending anybody or in what way their joke is inappropriate. Once people know, they often will stop doing objectionable things.

Kronda Adair

If you're in a group that is in a position to oppress someone else and someone says that you've done something to oppress them, believe that person. Oppressed people are in a position to know things that you do not know. Instead of getting defensive, figure out why they're upset. I've been in a position where someone's called me on something. My first reaction was, "I didn't do that" or "I didn't mean it." It's hard work to say, "I'm sorry. I'm going to work on that." This is what needs to happen. People need to take responsibility for their own education. It's not my job to go out and educate everybody about racism even though I may take some responsibility for that. It shouldn't be anybody's job to go out and educate the oppressor. We know all about the oppressor. It's time for other people to take responsibility for what they're doing.

Gretchen Freed-Rowland

We knew that our family was an Indian family and that we had to stick together. Beyond the door lay "out there," a place where we had to keep up our guard. We had to prove that we were as good as Anglos by being better. By age seven, I knew I had to stick up for other people who got treated like Indians get treated and to show that we weren't all dirty, stupid, savage, or drunk. Many Indian men and women tell me their parents have actually told them, "You have to go out there. That's your job for us." I have an understanding of individuality that differs from the Euro American concept. My individuality rests in my acceptance of responsibility for my community. I have no choice. It's who I am. When I avoid that responsibility, I don't feel good about myself.

Shelli Romero

My dad is the director of the ESL [English as a second language] bilingual education program for the Portland public schools. His social commitment has been a big influence on me throughout my university career. My main goal is to give back to my community what it has given me, which is strength and support to keep going on. There are very few people of color in higher education. As a personal goal, I want to show people, "Yes, it can be done. We are smart people." My community also needs reinforcement for having developed its own alternative ways of thinking. If you encourage open-mindedness and many different perspectives in education, students have more potential to grow.

A lot of culture is lost through cultural genocide. I feel a responsibility to learn and teach our culture to young people so that they never have to go through what I did. At a young age I lost my language but came back to reclaim it. Younger students should be able to grow up in an environment where they can use both languages comfortably and not have to deal with discrimination in the educational system. It would have meant a lot for me to have some teachers of color in grade school as mentors and role models, people who would have supported me in whatever it was that I was doing. Grade school is a child's tenderest years. What children learn about themselves in those years, their self-concept and self-esteem shape what happens in the rest of their life.

Sweeter Sachuo

In my dissertation, I'm examining the impact of U.S. education on Trukese children. I plan to go back to the islands and work through the educational system to reform it to be more culturally responsive, by which I mean that the medium of instruction should be Trukese. English should become just another subject offered in schools.

Eric Ward

I don't want to live in a mainly white community and wouldn't want to raise my kids in one. I plan on going to law school and then back to my community, maybe not Los Angeles but to an inner city. I know I can survive. I've survived on the streets and I am not afraid of going back even though poverty is painful and hard to look at. Some students are here just to earn more money and get a better job, but getting a job is not my main concern. While I'm here I try to build community. Right now the most important thing to me is the black community on campus and building relations between African and African American students. I'm not satisfied with the system we live in and I say it. I've always been the one who's different, alternative, more vocal, more challenging.

Michelle Singer

Once Indian students get here, they go through culture shock or just get lost. There's no support system for them, and the Indian community and tribes get upset about that. As director of the Native American Student Union, I feel an obligation to help these students stay because they need to go through college and get an education like I am and need to know the opportunities that are there for them. But doing this support work hurts my grades and I'm on academic warning right now, which stresses me out a lot and upsets and frustrates me. I know that I need to succeed both for myself and for other Indian students who want to continue their education. To do this, I have to be good at time management, but I still don't know how I handle it all. When I think about all this responsibility, it amazes me and I don't know how I've gotten this far.

It's hard being here at this university, being one of the very few, wondering if I can make it, wondering if I can deal with how things are now. I wonder if the university will ever come around and really see the needs, the silent cry of the minority students here, instead of just having them be quietly oppressed in a subtle way that people don't see. And will the student population, the student body itself, come to see how we really are being treated, and how many other people out there are struggling just like me? If they don't, it's because they're blind.

We are a modest people, we don't brag, and we don't go out and tell our problems. We share problems among ourselves or we choose not to, but we can sense it—that there's a lot of frustration, anger, and disappointment among the minority students here. It's just a matter of whether or not we can act on it. But acting on it is always hard. It is easier to believe the bad things and get to feeling down, put into a spot where it seems better just to give up. These problems are always ongoing. They happened when my sister was here nine years ago and they still happen today. There are people here who have suicidal tendencies, and I have had them myself. I don't know that the university can do anything for me other than address the needs of minority students. I deal with it by myself or by talking to a few close friends whom I can trust. I don't want to be a quitter even though the university more or less thinks I want to quit. I know if I quit, I'm just another number. That's what institutions, what the whole history of our people has been, just to give up.

Sometimes I think, "I'm only twenty and I'm so tired," but I've accomplished so much in two decades—which most people don't even realize. My parents raised me never to give up, to fight and survive, so that's what I have to do. When I almost thought about dropping out, I couldn't because so many people relied on me and expected me to do something, be somebody. I didn't want to give up with all those other people who look at me as a role model.

My parents are proud of me and understand the efforts I make, how many places I go. They know I do a lot here for Indian students and how I recruit Indian kids for college, telling them how important it is to go through school. When I attend conferences and throw events for the Native American Student Union, I do it for me and my family and Native American people. That's what I have to do. It's what I've been brought up to do and it's part of me.

II

RACE AND ETHNIC RELATIONS
IN HIGHER EDUCATION

4

The Tellers, the Tales, and the Audience: Narratives by Students of Color

Debbie Storrs and Julia Lesage

When I, Debbie, teach race and ethnic relations, one of my goals is to rouse students from their indifference to and passivity around racial issues. Narratives—experiential stories from people of color, whites, and students themselves—can offer insight into the ways in which race operates in daily life. Importantly, moving students, both minority and white, to examine their own racial stories creates the conditions under which they can challenge dominant racial paradigms.

Because I teach in a predominantly white university, a principal goal in linking the theoretical to the experiential is to move the majority of students in my classes, who are white, to see how they too are racially positioned and therefore implicated in the unfair distribution of societal rewards and status. Griffin describes a similar movement, stating that once we are

> stripped of the shroud of our innocence, we can breathe and move; our silence broken, we can make whiteness articulate. In doing so, we compromise whiteness, we problematize and subvert white absolutism. White becomes a color, a heavily weighted color, rather than a blank ground against which all things are projected. And we become a people with skin, participating in history, writing our story, rather than baleful, evasive ghosts, dragging the chains of history behind us, vanishing through the walls. (Griffin 1995, 231)

Like Griffin, I believe that once students' "shroud of innocence" is removed, the whole class can openly discuss what McIntosh refers to as the "knapsack of white privilege" (McIntosh 1988). The class discussion challenges class members, both white and minority students, to address racial inequities and biases in the context of private interpersonal relationships, classroom interactions, and institutions.

Using narratives as a vehicle for teaching about oppression and social change challenges the positivistic approach widely found in universities. This pattern of investigation is particularly dominant in the social sciences, where it posits both a methodology and an outcome, seen as "objective truth." However, such an approach limits what counts as legitimate empirical knowledge, and it has been countered over the last three decades by numerous challenges from feminist, postmodern, and critical theorists. In particular, feminist scholarship has emphasized the value of learning from personal narratives. Influenced by these counter-currents in my field, I expand students' understanding of the "truth" about race by routinely assigning heterogeneous reading materials including short stories, personal narratives, poetry, and empirical research articles.

My critique of objectivity also shapes the assignments I give. Assignments designed to facilitate students' abilities to construct discourse encourage multiple ways of expressing knowledge. Using such multiplicities also teaches students to challenge the presumed neutrality of empirical research as it encourages them to read empirical research critically, noting potential biases, and to value more explicitly subjective forms of knowledge. Furthermore, it has been my experience that students of color most eagerly embrace such a use of counter-discourses; pedagogically this tactic legitimizes the knowledge of those who come from communities with a tradition of oral stories, narratives, and other ways of preserving and passing on knowledge.

I'm often struck with the ways in which students' own subjectivities determine their ability to move beyond hegemonic ideas about knowledge and practice. For example, in a recent race and ethnic relations class, I asked students to think of themselves as committee members selected to inform the masses of Americans about the nature of race and racial inequality. This governmental committee's goal was to help the masses move beyond two basic hegemonic beliefs: that racial inequalities are no longer significant and that friendship between racially different individuals provides the primary solution to any racial tensions that may exist. Because I also question the validity of objective standards and rules for evaluating students' critical capacities, I encouraged students to use counter-discourses in the creation of knowledge rather than formal papers. I received a number of critical and oppositional discursive responses ranging from children's short stories and collections of poetry to Web sites. But, interestingly, the majority of Euro American students chose to respond in traditional academic prose and term paper formats.

One Native American student's project in particular reinforced my earlier

Explains how narratives shed light on racism to other races.

The Tellers, the Tales, and the Audience   97

assessment that subjectivity and expression of knowledge are tightly linked. Brigette Hernandez responded to the assignment by verbally narrating her family's personal experiences in an attempt to reveal the varied dimensions and personal consequences of internal colonialism. Through sharing the stories of family members, she lured the audience into understanding the barriers American Indian women face. The format Brigette selected was linked to her subjectivity as a Native American woman. The oral tradition, deeply imbedded within Indian culture, was selected over what the academy typically values, the written word. Brigette's decision to use narrative was linked to her cultural tradition of sociocentricity and was captured in how she explained the format she used: "Since the times of my ancestors, this is how we kept track of time. Let us not simply look at policies or years, but rather, focus on the lives of individuals and the quality of those lives."

Brigette understood her own life and her future in ways similar to Pawnee/Otoe-Missouria writer Anna Lee Walters, who notes, "My future is in my past, the values and vision of a collective past" (see Carroll 1992). Not surprisingly, Brigette did not include her own narrative in her family lineage. Rather, she began her family lineage with the family's matriarch, her grandmother, and then moved to her mother, her sister, and finally her young niece, "the firstborn daughter of my sister and our future." Not based on Eurocentric ideals of individualism, Brigette's sense of self resided in relation to her family members. Brown characterizes Native American storytelling as ultimately about maintaining community; its purpose is "to explain a world, not an ego" (Brown 1995). Brigette understood herself and her future in relation to the collectivity of the family and to her larger community of Indian peoples, and this explains why she was not the center of her lineage and narrative. Brigette used family lineage and the experiences of her female relatives to tell a shared story of colonization and, importantly, to explain how her family continued to thrive across generations despite these difficulties.

Brigette is not unusual among students of color in higher education. Institutional arenas that ignore alternative styles of learning and expressions of knowledge that students like Brigette bring to the classroom do a disservice not simply to the students of color but to white students and teachers who are currently blocked from learning from Brigette's and other students' subversive views of the world.

THE TELLERS: THE CONSTRUCTION
OF SELVES AND REALITIES

Like Brigette, the students of color in this collection are storytellers. Telling such stories as theirs serves a number of functions, particularly in terms of their address to an audience. On a general level, it is through stories that people come to know themselves and make themselves known to others. As Stivers argues, the self

> is an essentially narrative phenomenon; people conceive of themselves in terms of sto-
> ries about their actions in the world, using them to make sense of the temporal flow of
> their lives. We find identity and meaning as a result of the stories we tell about ourselves
> or that others tell about us. Therefore, a narrative approach to self-understanding is not
> a distortion of reality but a confirmation of it. (Stivers 1993, 412)

However, self-naming and self-understanding through storytelling occurs in the context of larger, dominant stories told about us by those more powerful. These student narratives can thus be viewed as contesting who the students are and what their realities are. A large gap exists between the students' stories and those told by those more powerful; in particular, students of color find that the domi-nant stories about communities of color, expressed both in the curriculum and in the surrounding environment, fail to capture the multiplicities of experience and realities that they know. Stereotypical generalizations surround them at all levels of their university experience. To a large degree, the stories from students of color shared here are attempts to construct a counterhegemonic reality con-cerning themselves and the communities they have come to represent.

As students attempt to construct a counterhegemonic reality, they craft a common construction of selfhood. They define themselves through stories of their personal experiences in three distinct ways. First, students define them-selves as complex and multiple subjects; this construction of multiplicity con-tests the hegemonic construction of students of color as unidimensional objects. That is, the hegemonic narratives of race in the university neglect other facets of students' selves and posit students of color as unidimensional beings with race as their most salient marker. De Danaan explains:

> The assumption of the speech of the typical classroom (and on the part of faculty and
> students) is that "people" are white people and usually middle class. Otherwise modifi-
> ers are used. She is Black. Otherwise she is simply a woman. That is to say, white is the
> general in the speech most whites use. White is not a race in the way most whites think
> of it. There is white, the general, and there is Black or brown, the particular, the races.
> (De Danaan 1990)

Given the many ways in which white experience is associated with the general and the norm, students of color often find themselves positioned as the "other," objectified, and stereotyped. Students who previously lived in other countries or more diverse communities within the United States are surprised upon entering college at a predominantly white institution to find themselves cast as different—the other. The narratives of students of color in part 1 thus illustrate the shock of being marginalized experienced by many students of color when they enter a predominantly white university setting. As the students maneuver through the racially charged environment of the university, their racial status is constantly reflected back to them in cross-racial and same-racial interactions. The constant imposition of race and its variable meanings leads to the salience of their racial identity. Michelle Singer, a light-skinned Navajo student, reveals this process in her revelation that "the issue of self-identity came out for me and a lot of other students of color once we hit this campus." Despite her regular contact with Native students during her secondary school experience, her own identity as such was never as salient until she entered the racially charged environment of the university.

This saliency was reinforced for students of color by the faculty's and white students' assumption that their actions, statements, and attitudes represent their racial group. The narratives of students in this collection provide myriad instances of their being called on in class to represent the "black viewpoint" or the "minority point of view." Geo. Ann Baker's experience is typical of other students of color who share their narratives: "The class expects me to speak for the whole Native American race or all minorities, and I can't. I'm there to learn too. I'm not the authority." Given the immense cultural diversity among American Indians, Geo. Ann's knowledge and identity as Klamath and Payute makes it impossible for her to provide what the class expects. Her reluctance to speak is also due to her frustration at being placed in the role of teacher. Part of this frustration comes from a student of color's inconsistent positioning as teacher by those in power. Students of color often speak of faculty who naively expect their assistance in informing the class of the minority experience while simultaneously rejecting their subjective knowledge in papers or other assessment methods. Beyond being called on as the expert in the classroom, many students report receiving dozens of calls throughout the year, asking them to visit classes or serve on panels, where they are expected to provide the "Native American perspective" or to field questions about the "Asian-American experience."

Chicana scholar Mary Romero critiques such requests, explaining that

> Euroamerican academics and administrators are searching for noble savages—once again our "exotic" difference is to be celebrated. After five hundred years of rape and genocide, if we can still be identified physically as the "other," our phenotype is in demand for photo opportunities, posters, panels, guest speakers." (Romero 1992)

In addition to celebrating exoticness, requests for representation assume homogeneity within communities of color, erasing diversity and multiplicity in identity. Recognizing this risk, students of color respond in two ways. First, they are quick to make links between their multiple forms of oppression. The women of color in this collection are particularly adept at pointing out relations between gender and racial oppression. Kronda Adair, a self-identified African American lesbian feminist, reveals the multiplicity of self in her discussion of how to fight oppression:

> To combat isms—sexism, racism, heterosexism—you cannot separate those problems and combat them effectively because you have racism in the gay and lesbian community and homophobia in the black community and in other cultures.

Similarly, Leyla Farah's narrative rejects a simplified racialized sense of self:

> The kind of experiences I've had at college have been intertwined with my sex and my race. It's hard for me to separate racism, sexism, and homophobia, and it's hard for me to talk about racism and not want to bring in all my other aspects.

Using experiential examples to illustrate their complex subjectivities, these women reject the metanarrative of race that excludes gender, sexuality, social class, and other viable and important social locations.

Furthermore, students of color monitor what they said for fear that listeners will assume all members of their racial group feel or experience the world in the same way. Self-censorship becomes a necessary practice given the possibility of misrepresenting a larger constituency. The freedom to speak, to narrate identity, without such caution is an unearned entitlement of whites since individual whites do not have to concern themselves with being perceived as racial spokespersons nor be they concerned that their actions will be used to make widespread judgments and evaluations against all whites. Such differences expose the power imbalances that shape the everyday educational experiences of students in institutions implicitly politicized by race.

While speaking out in class or serving on panels is fraught with difficulties, students of color often do so to correct assumptions or inaccuracies that occur all too often in classroom settings. Speaking is a political act, an attempt to subvert overly broad representations that threaten to homogenize racial identity. Each student's story here comes out of a process of constructing, asserting, and validating his or her multidimensional self against powerful reductive categories and boundaries. Viewed primarily as racialized minorities, these students of color affirm racial identities without dismissing other facets that shape their experience. Not merely offering a narrative of family process or psychological or spiritual development, they are concerned also to expose the relations of power that they know shape the social construction of identities. Self-consciously, they question, resist, and disrupt Western conceptions of the other.

The second way in which students of color construct themselves within their stories is as active participants, as protagonists, rather than passive victims. They have no intention of telling stories that portray themselves or their peers as mere victims, which would affix them in an inferior or a pitiable place. At the same time, they do not romanticize their struggles. Instead, students of color point to the structural impediments to educational success even as they reveal their strategies for survival. An example of how students position themselves as protagonists is seen in their stories of racism in educational settings.

In these stories about racism in school, students draw on the basic components of any good story, rendering their specific experience in a familiar and conventional narrative form. As noted by Rosenwald and Ochberg, "a good story presents a coherent plot. The narrative 'now' must grow plausibly out of what has come before and point the way to what might reasonably come next" (1992, 9). As students of color describe their early experiences of racism in school, their words paint a picture of them as small children discovering the pain of stereotypes and the devaluation of racial difference. As they continue their stories, they move from describing themselves as exoticized objects of curiosity, ridicule, or exclusion to describing themselves as active agents challenging the forces of oppression.

Like all stories, their narratives include recognizable characters beyond the main actors, the hero/heroine and the enemy. What is unique in these students' narratives is the complex portrait of the hero/heroine. Rather than identify a single heroine/hero or elevate the self as the explanation for one's survival, the students of color point to a sociocentric ensemble of supporters including the family, community, peers, and student organizations. They see that it is not their individual effort alone that explains their achievements; rather, their success in college comes from a web of relationships that fosters their ability to adapt and resist an oppressive environment. Although the students use a conventional narrative form, they modify it in ways to fit their cultural worldview and experience.

Who then do they construct as the enemy? Using dominant narrative structures, students of color cast individual racists in the role of the enemy. Peers who hurl racist slurs, counselors who discourage students of color from continuing their education, and teachers who do not contest racist stereotypes all fit the image of the enemy. Yet, once again, the stories by students of color expand this conventional narrative style to include institutional racism. Students artfully reveal the oppressive social conditions, largely unseen and unspoken, that move the story of racism to a more complex level.

At the heart of their narratives is a story of personal development and emancipation. Through stories, students construct themselves first as children struggling to understand the painful experiences of racism and then as active social participants with a mission of creative social change. Yet their stories are not complete. Indeed, it was because they wanted their stories presented here that they continue to write the plot of ongoing struggle and empowerment. The growth from being acted upon to acting may be a conventional narrative frame, but here it also serves the purpose of letting the speakers construct effective social action. This then is the third way in which students portrayed themselves—as social activists.

In *Teaching to Transgress: Education as the Practice of Freedom*, bell hooks discusses what is commonly the experience of students of color in coming to college: "Knowledge was suddenly about information only. It had no relation to how one lived, behaved. It was no longer connected to antiracist struggle." For hooks, this conception of knowledge did not fit with her early experience in a predominantly black school with mostly black women teachers. There, students "learned early that our devotion to learning, to a life of the mind, was a counter-hegemonic act, a fundamental way to resist every strategy of white racist colonization." Like hooks and her first teachers, the students of color who eagerly share their stories here do so with the goal of establishing a more liberatory educational experience. Because they see themselves as social activists, they take the risk of exposing their private experiences within an institution that too often rejected their narratives as constituting forms of credible knowledge. Students of color tell their stories with the insistence that it be their story, their history, told under their own name.

While students take advantage of opportunities such as this to speak out in order to educate others and resist stereotypes, they also display resistance when they refuse to engage in this form of representation. Silence is not often recognized as a form of speech, but, in fact, silence and the refusal to engage in dialogue, storytelling, and information sharing constitutes a response and a form of resistance (Trinh 1989). This kind of resistance has its effect when faculty recognize student silence as such. Responding to questions with silence becomes one way that students of color in a classroom can shift responsibility for learning back to faculty and other students. This strategy can backfire, however, if silence is not recognized as a form of communication or resistance. When students of color refuse to engage in dialogue or choose to not correct biases in open contestation, their silence can be misinterpreted as assent. The specific relations of power in the traditional classroom privilege a certain form of knowledge (i.e., empirical as opposed to lived experience) and gives greater validation to knowledge producers (faculty's contribution to knowledge production rather than students). Within this context, the student of color's choice to remain silent in the face of misconceptions has the potential to reinforce unequal power relations and racist assumptions.

While allowing individuals to construct their own identities as social actors, stories also help shape the interpretation and understanding of our larger social worlds. Thus, like Studs Terkel (1992), who has used narratives in a lively way to develop analyses and complex portraits of U.S. society as a whole, students of color commonly use stories to portray U.S. society in ways that whites generally do not see. It is to these tales that we now turn our attention.

STUDENT TALES: DEBUNKING RACIAL FICTIONS

Of the many hegemonic ideas surrounding race, perhaps the most enduring is the belief in meritocracy. Indeed, many students of color have embraced this ideal as a result of years of socialization. Many of these students had high expectations about college life before they came to the university, only to realize later how unaccommodating both the curriculum and college life really are. The promise of higher education comes largely from its own discourse about what it stands for. The university presents itself as an open, tolerant, intellectual home where scholars objectively discover and disseminate knowledge; it characterizes itself as a meritocracy (Feagin, Vera, and Imani 1996, 1). Indeed, it is this story that shapes students' expectations about college life. Only after entering college do students of color usually quickly realize how uncharacteristic this dominant story of college life is.

Using their personal experiences in college, these students narrate a tale that challenges the fiction of meritocracy. In sharing their stories here, they speak to educate the campus at large about racial intolerance, Eurocentric curricula, and their coping techniques. As the university is described through their eyes, they produce a new discourse about education. They understand what Michel Foucault would call the "regime of truth" in the university. But their analyses also imply the possibility of constructing a new curriculum, a new discourse about education, and a new politics of "truth." In their verbal style, the students are authoritative and articulate. As student leaders of ethnic student unions, they are what Antonio Gramsci would call "organic intellectuals." They want to be recognized as part of the process of "making meaning" that goes on in a university.

Central to students' politics of "truth" is the rejection of the fiction of individual merit and two other closely linked fictions: color blindness and equal opportunity. Color blindness, the belief that one does not or should not see color difference, is often erroneously expressed as our contemporary reality in academia or, at minimum, as our goal. The belief that one should not see color presumes that color difference itself is problematic rather than the association of color with character traits. Students of color offer a critical perspective on the goal of color blindness. Rather than embrace the goal of color blindness, the students here point to the viable potential of recognizing difference without naturalizing or hierarchically evaluating it. For example, stories concerning skin color privileges within minority groups are used by students of color to reveal the continuing salience of race and to subvert dominant notions of color difference. In other words, they reveal the possibility of recognizing skin color privilege while simultaneously rejecting the association between skin color and ability. The goal of many dominant group members, color blindness rests on a presumption that equal opportunity already exists. Indeed, the ideology of color blindness rests on the assumption that race no longer shapes anyone's life chances. The narratives shared by students of color require the listener to question this assumption. Stories of continuing stereotypes, differential treatment by teachers, and street harassment by community members and police officers revealed the ongoing salience of race.

Another tale that students of color share through their narratives focuses on knowledge. Through the use of personal experience, students of color reject hegemonic definitions of knowledge, and they embrace lived experience as a valuable source of knowing. The students here articulate a certain analysis about issues that are givens in the students' communities but are not acknowledged by the dominant culture. Such knowledge derives from community wisdom that most white administrators and teachers in a liberal bourgeois university environment rarely acknowledge as daily reality. In fact, the students come from oppressed groups that have already articulated a history, a version of daily life, and a passing on of survival skills. Geo. Ann Baker explains in her narrative that "the oral tradition is valid for me because that's how our history is passed down, by word of mouth. It's not written; we're educated through oral traditions." Geo. Ann tried to use her grandmother's story as a resource when writing a speech for a class but was told it was inappropriate because it was not written. Her grandmother's story, officially repressed, reveals the fictions of race and the alternative knowledge that students and faculty of color have to offer.

Storytelling, lived experience, and community anecdotes, which form the basis for reality building for many students of color, are consistently characterized by dominant authorities as inferior forms of knowledge. Yet students of color do not concede and accept the institutional bias toward a narrow range of knowledge forms. Instead, they continue to value alternative forms of understanding and seek ways to integrate them into their own minds and into the classrooms. Thus the essentialist belief in one truth, accessed through a particular mode that requires one to "be objective" and stand outside and apart from oneself, is challenged by students' alternative story making. The students of color who speak in this volume contest the structures of knowledge proposed in the classroom, the behavior of many of their fellow students, and the reduction of their identity to issues of race. They understand the mechanisms of ideology, and they challenge the general basis of consent in the university.

Consequently, these student narratives emphasize the difference between the way students of color see the university environment and the way that institution sees itself. Any minority culture or oppressed group has to know the ways of thinking and the mores of the dominant culture, but, as students clearly reveal, this does not result in reciprocal understanding. Students of color who read this book may feel empowered at seeing the strength of students who have mastered both ways of thinking; white readers, especially students, teachers, and administrators, may resist the demand that they also conceptualize their educational process in terms of race.

THE POWER OF HEGEMONIC TALES: RACIAL ESSENTIALISM

The "disruptive stories" of students of color reveal the dynamic negotiation of meanings around race, identity, and the educational process and institution (Yeoman 1999). This negotiation occurs between and within many groups, including between institutional elites and students and within student groups. If the students have much in common in their analysis of race as a problem culture, their narratives can also be looked at in terms of the contradictory aspects of how they both embrace and contest aspects of racial essentialism in their own ethnic identity formation.

Many contemporary theorists of race have critiqued the concept of race as founded on unstable or even empty premises that nevertheless have great social force. For example, race is commonly, with legal force, associated with blood quantum, hair type, or skin color, what Gayatri Spivak calls the "criteria of chromatism" (Spivak 1987, 235). Summaries of some of these kinds of essentialism can be found in the writing of Diana Fuss (1989), who defines essentialism as the "belief in true essence—that which is most irreducible, unchanging, and therefore constitutive of a given person or thing," and also in the writings of Joan Ferrante and Prince Brown, who specifically address the workings of racial essentialism (Ferrante and Brown 1998). Racial essentialism assumes that races are real, immutable, and mutually exclusive. And racial essentialism contains its own narrative or implied story that links race, language, physical appearance, and a host of intellectual and emotional competencies (see Smedley 1993 for a thorough history of this practice). The power of racial essentialism as a widely accepted social narrative is that it continues to frame how individuals are positioned in society through the social construction of difference.

The students' stories in this book reveal the legacy of racial essentialism's power in shaping their identities as they continued to be positioned in racial terms using skin color or other markers of difference. For example, the American

Indian students who speak here point out that they are often questioned about their racial status on the basis of their tribal membership. Tribal membership emerges out of colonialist history in which the federal government has long defined "Indianness" on the basis of blood quantum, a reflection of racial essentialism (see Jaimes 1992). In order to qualify as "Indian," one must be able to document a particular "amount" of Indian heritage. Those who cannot are denied access to treaty rights and, just as important, to validation of their identities. In this light, Gretchen Freed-Rowland describes how difficult the process of enrollment was when she entered the university as an adult, even though her birth certificate said she was half "red" and half "white." Similarly, the Chicano/ Latino students talk about confronting essentialist assumptions that they can or should speak Spanish or be dark skinned. And Asian-Pacific Islander graduate student, Sweeter Sachuo, shares similar expectations that he be bilingual.

Essentialist ideas of race have a long history and still pervade how the dominant society views and constructs the other. Today's students of color, like those in earlier periods, face the task of challenging essentialist links made between race and intellectual ability. The assumption of racial inferiority is evident in students' common experience of having counselors trying to dissuade them from attending college as well as in seeing the surprise of many white faculty and peers at their academic ability and performance. It is through discussing these common experiences and protesting against them, if only among themselves, that these students feel unified. They share a common positioning as the racialized other, in which they become reduced to objects, especially through dominant stories. Yet stories are not simply told—they are received, negotiated, accepted, and confirmed. These students' narratives reveal the ways in which they negotiate reality through their own disruptive stories.

The students' stories reveal the different ways they react to narratives of racial essentialism that circulate in the culture at large. The students often simultaneously disrupt, reflect on, and confirm aspects of racial essentialism. Since we are all living in unequally valorized worlds and cultures, we get pulled into others' fictions and into the dominant ideological versions of reality, which are propagated institutionally, legally, discursively, and representationally.

For example, these students' college experiences help them develop disruptive stories to challenge essentialist ideas about behavior and belonging. Their individual biographies and various exposures to communities of color shape the degree to which they feel aligned with others in their racial group. For example, Leyla Farah, who was positioned as a "representative for black people" in her predominantly white high school, discovers in college "black people who had totally different life experiences and lived in a world completely different from mine." Such experiences, made possible by the diverse student body at universities, help students of color challenge monolithic concepts of their ethnic group and also reveal that an individual's own racial identity is shifting and unstable.

Within the student narratives, these disruptive stories challenge other ideas that reflect and confirm racial essentialism. As their stories recount incidents in which other students of color assert essentialist notions of race, they question such assumptions. For example, in student organizations students of color frequently use with each other what Gloria Anzaldua (1990) refers to as "ethnic legitimacy tests," attempts to discern the authentic from the fake. Some of the students discuss how they found their membership in racial groups questioned on the basis of language, tribal membership, skin color, or cultural knowledge. Not surprisingly, those who fail to measure up in the eyes of in-group members as "authentic" discuss this problem in their narratives, and they critically identify the limiting boundary criteria of their racial group's membership. Although their own communities at times reinforce racial essentialism, hooks notes that this is "not nearly as frustrating as confrontation with the white avant-garde in politically charged cultural contexts in which they [liberal whites] seek to appropriate and usurp radical efforts to subvert static notions of black identity" (1990, 21).

An extended example of the complexity of student voices vis-à-vis racial essentialism can be seen in how they agitate politically to have more faculty of color on campus. Some students of color have expectations and politics that utilize racial essentialism, which simply reveals the power of this concept of race. For example, some students base their politics on what Gayatri Spivak calls a "strategic" use of racial essentialism (1987, 206), in that they lobby strongly for more faculty of color using an argument based on identity politics. For such activists, " 'experience' emerges as the essential truth of the individual subject, and personal 'identity' metamorphoses into knowledge" (Fuss 1989, 113). The argument is that personal experience confers on students and faculty of color the ability and right to teach about the subject of racial oppression and collective responses to it.

Such essentialist logic is strongly refuted by some students; other students see the need for more faculty of color but use a different argument. They argue that the university needs more faculty of color not because they are inherently knowledgeable by virtue of their race but because they can serve as important role models and potential mentors. Students articulating such a position do not make the essentialist assumption that lived experience is the only or most appropriate qualification to teach effectively about race relations. Diana Collins-Puente uses both arguments in her narrative when arguing for more faculty of color: "If students are always taught the history of other cultures by Euro Americans, they learn academic knowledge but not the feelings and emotions running behind the different cultures. . . . It's also important for students to see faculty of color as role models." While Diana's comment reveal her assumption that minority faculty would inherently teach, feel, and/or express feeling differently than white faculty, she also identified their potential roles as mentors to students of color.

Still other students tire of continuously having to play the role of teacher; they argue that whites, both faculty and students, should shoulder more responsibility for teaching and learning about race and racism. These last two political positions continue to value experiential knowledge, but, crucially, they do not assume that all persons of color have similar experiences nor do they limit knowledge simply to an intimate participation within a racial subculture. Likewise, the demand that whites take more responsibility for understanding race illuminates the often hidden story that whites too have a racial identity and a racial position. Requiring white academics to play a more active role in education about race transforms the racial dialogue about education in complex ways, perhaps bringing out into the open for the first time the fact that privileged access to resources means that whites in the educational sphere have advantages at the expense of minorities.

Even as some of the students' stories reflect a racial essentialism, they use such concepts of ethnic cultural integrity and cohesiveness to their advantage by creating campus communities. In terms of their day-to-day functioning, student organizations based on race served as primary places to find support and assistance. Students of color serve as mentors to one another, providing important information about which classes to take, which professors to avoid, and where to socialize without fear of exclusion. Often students in this book discuss how their early college experiences of exclusion and heightened visibility led to their search for refuge from such a hostile environment. They often discover refuge in racially based student organizations. There, positioned as other by the dominant institution, students of color use this marginalization to organize along racial lines. While the internal politics of student groups are shaped in part by a cultural racial essentialism, such groups also provide the basis for collective action. These student organizations serve as organizational watchdogs, identifying problematic and exclusionary practices and policies and advocating for change.

It is often through student organizations or classroom participation in courses dealing with race or gender that students learn in a formal way how to articulate contestatory narratives that oppose and negotiate dominant ones, especially around race and power. They learn to create new stories that can reinterpret past experience on the basis of their finding out about larger legal, historical, institutional struggles, both past and present. Both from formal and political education, they learn to weave discourses in new hybrid forms, a sampling of which is offered here.

While students of color often develop new stories with one another, they also understand how this context provides them an avenue to enlarge their audience. Stories such as these are often disseminated through student of color networks, but the students here anticipate that a potentially larger community might be constructed through hearing their stories. At certain moments in history, there is a dialectical process between storytelling and community building. As Plummer argues, "Stories need communities to be heard, but communities themselves are also built through story tellings" (1995, 174). It is now time to turn to the audience to whom these stories are offered.

THE AUDIENCE

If it is through narration that one can construct oneself, the location of one's self at the same time always occurs in relation to others. Usually we only make sense of our experience by telling it to our circle of friends; this reciprocal reflecting on experience is the way we learn to understand ourselves, others, and our milieu. Such ongoing dialogue shapes and reflects back on action, and, in this way, narrative actively constitutes both self and world. In many ways, the students' construction of themselves as multidimensional social activists and subjects here rests on their understanding of an audience. Significantly, these students presume at least two audiences and speak with these groups in mind.

The first group of implied listeners are those who might be "well-meaning" but do not clearly see how these racialized structures and often unspoken experiences and feelings of people of color characterize most institutional settings in the United States, especially workplaces and schools. Even though members of this supportive group of coworkers, peers, and authority figures share a common goal of creating a more inclusive environment, they often fail to do so because of their racial blinders. As students participated in this project, their willingness to expose their painful experiences and detailed biographies was based on an assumption that such information would be listened to. Yet they also presumed, correctly or not, that the potential of this audience to create change was limited by many listeners' belief in what we term the racial fiction of color blindness. Recognizing the political environment of the contemporary era, the students of color were probably accurate in their assumption.

For example, public support for the elimination of affirmative action programs implies the largely held belief that an even playing field exists among racial groups. After all, if such equality in opportunity exists, then there is little need to attend to color. Contesting this problematic assumption underlies student narratives. Their communities' realities belie the myth of equal opportunity. In *Living with Racism: The Black Middle-Class Experience*, Feagin and Sikes (1994) reveal how middle-class blacks continue to experience racial discrimination in public accommodations, neighborhoods, and the workplace despite the protections of their social class. Similarly, students of color reveal how their racial positioning by dominant group members continues to hamper their progress in higher education.

The second audience includes other students of color or other marginalized groups who have had similar experiences and who might be able to use the students' stories and analyses of the educational system to help change this kind of situation wherever they study or work. Many of the student narratives in this book describe anecdotes and situations of overt institutional and individual racism. More important, running alongside these stories, replete with a sense of pain these incidents cause, are the students' own analyses of the incidents they narrate. As these students talk about their schooling, it is clear that their social analysis of racism makes them authorities on the institutional dynamics of oppression within higher education. In one sense, their awareness of and actions to redress racism give them, among themselves, a pan-ethnic bond across ethnic groups. They often identify as people of color marginalized by the institution, as outsiders seeking to create change. In this way, in their ongoing conversations and actions around race, these students forge a unity with other nonwhites culturally, and they often make alliances with or have sympathies for gay/lesbian and feminist struggles.

Such an ongoing discourse and social awareness unites them loosely in what Herbert J. Gans, writing in 1979 about Jews, has called a communally held "problem culture" (Gans 1979). With this in mind, we can read the student narratives in this book as the common knowledge that circulates in a culture of resistance. In fact, the students' experiential knowledge and that of their friends often leads to formal study around issues of oppression because of their shared understanding that they need to learn more about this "problem culture." Thus they may use the curriculum to enhance their sense of ethnic identity by taking ethnic studies courses or courses on race in the social sciences, seeking to understand the larger history of racial oppression and to study how race structures institutions and group privilege. They also may study the arts and literature to encounter original creative work by people of color, often reading works of fiction that deal with some of the issues they currently face. In many ways, students piece together a comprehensive understanding of the nature of oppression that links their personal experience to a historical, political, and structural context.

CONCLUSION

As they are attended to, these stories hopefully can have a transformative potential at the individual level of the reader's consciousness and the social level of the reader's capacity for action (Richardson 1990). On an individual level, new stories encourage people to make sense of their lives anew, especially when the stories challenge limiting, dominant narratives about race and identity historically based on biology and essentialist views of culture. These narratives encourage readers to construct a sense of self that is no longer based on notions of hierarchy with the concomitant requirement that some people be cast as unequal and inferior. In addition, they encourage the construction of more fluid boundaries of belonging that go beyond a particular skin color shade. Students of color here tell new stories of belonging based on a unified experience of exclusion and oppression along many group dimensions, yet one that is characterized by internal diversity. In other words, while all students of color share a common experience of being treated as the other, they differ in terms of how they respond to this positioning, the degree to which they experience othering, and their understanding of this difference.

On a social and cultural level, alternative stories build community, and this connection with others establishes a real foundation for making change. The political potential of these students' "disruptive" stories occurs as listeners respond to such stories by creating a new institutional order, a different institutional community, perhaps informed by the formerly "subversive" view of reality. The relationship between stories and community shapes student organizations and, likewise, shapes the purpose of this book. As we make these stories by students of color available to a wider audience, we view listening to such stories as a necessary ingredient for building broader communities that share the goal of acting together for social change.

REFERENCES

Anzaldua, Gloria. 1990. "En Rapport, In Opposition: Cobrando Cuentas a Las Nuestros." In *Making Face, Making Soul,* edited by Gloria Anzaldua, 142–48. San Francisco: Aunt Lute.

Brown, Alanna Kathleen. 1995. "Pulling Silko's Threads through Time: An Exploration of Storytelling." *American Indian Quarterly* 19, no. 2: 171–80.

Carroll, R. 1992. "The Values and Vision of a Collective Past: An Interview with Anna Lee Walters." *American Indian Quarterly* 16, no. 1: 63–74.

De Danaan, Llyn. 1990. "Center to Margin: Dynamics in a Global Classroom." *Women's Studies Quarterly* 1–2: 135–44.

Feagin, Joe R., Hernan Vera, and Nikitah Imani. 1996. *The Agony of Education: Black Students at White Colleges and Universities.* New York: Routledge.

Feagin, Joe, and Melvin Sikes. 1994. *Living with Racism: The Black Middle Class Experience.* Boston: Beacon 1994.

Ferrante, Joan, and Prince Brown Jr. 1998. *The Social Construction of Race and Ethnicity in the United States.* New York: Longman.

Fuss, Diana. 1989. *Essentially Speaking: Feminism, Nature, and Difference.* New York: Routledge.

Gans, Herbert. 1979. "Symbolic Ethnicity." In *On the Making of Americans: Essays in Honor of David Riesman.* Edited by Herbert J. Gans and David Riesman. Philadelphia: University of Pennsylvania Press.

Griffin, G. B. 1995. *Season of the Witch, Border Lines, Marginal Notes.* Pasadena, Calif.: Trilogy.

hooks, bell. 1990. *Yearning: Race, Gender, and Cultural Politics.* Boston: South End.

———. 1994. *Teaching to Transgress: Education as the Practice of Freedom.* New York: Routledge.

Jaimes, Annette. 1992. *The State of Native America: Genocide, Colonization, and Resistance.* Edited by M. Annette Jaimes. Boston: South End.

McIntosh, Peggy. 1988. "White Privilege: Unpacking the Invisible Knapsack." In *Race, Class, and Gender in the United States: An Integrated Study.* 4th ed. Edited by Paula S. Rothenberg. New York: St. Martin's.

Plummer, Kenneth. 1995. *Telling Sexual Stories: Power, Change, and Social Worlds.* London: Routledge.

Rhoda, Carroll. 1992. "The Values and Vision of a Collective Past: An Interview with Anna Lee Walters." *American Indian Quarterly* 16, no. 1: 63–74.

Richardson, Laurie. 1990. "Narrative and Sociology." *Journal of Contemporary Ethnography* 19, no. 1: 116–35.

Romero, Mary. 1992. "Please Don't Call Me for the Quincentennial." *CSWS Review* 6–9. University of Oregon Center for the Study of Women and Society.

Rosenwald, George, and Richard Ochberg. 1992. "Introduction: Life Stories, Cultural Politics, and Self-Understanding." In *Storied Lives: The Cultural Politics of Self-Understanding.* Edited by George Rosenwald and Richard Ochberg. New Haven: Yale University Press.

Smedley, Audrey. 1993. *Race in North America: Origin and Evolution of a Worldview.* Boulder: Westview.

Spivak, Gayatri. 1986. "Imperialism and Sexual Difference." *Oxford Literary Review* 8, no. 1–2: 225–40.

Spivak, Gayatri. 1987. *In Other Worlds: Essays in Cultural Politics.* New York: Methuen.

Stivers, Camilla. 1993. "Reflections on the Role of Personal Narrative in Social Science." *Signs: Journal of Women in Culture and Society* 18, no. 2: 408-26.

Terkel, Studs. 1992. *Race: How Blacks and Whites Think and Feel about the American Obsession.* New York: New Press 1992.

Trinh, T. Minh-ha. 1989. *Woman, Native, Other: Writing, Postcoloniality, and Feminism.* Bloomington: Indiana University Press.

Yeoman, Elizabeth. 1999. "How Does It Get into My Imagination? Elementary School Children's Intertextual Knowledge and Gendered Storylines." *Gender and Education* 11, no. 4: 427–41.

5

Diversity in Higher Education Nationwide

Donna Wong

Issues and solutions surrounding campus diversity issues remain in continual dynamic tension, reflecting changing racial demographics and competing political philosophies at all levels of U.S. society. That tension permeates all aspects of university life, in particular, the institutional issues of admissions, retention, curriculum, faculty recruitment, affirmative action, research, and workforce preparation.

This chapter offers a broad perspective on diversity in higher education, identifying issues of primary concern to students, parents, administrators, faculty, and the general public. These issues are directly or implicitly addressed in the student narratives in part 1 of this book. This chapter broadens the context by including statistics and the perspectives of educational leaders and faculty across the United States.

Woven into the chapter are brief historical perspectives on diversity issues and initiatives as they developed in higher education nationally. This historical perspective highlights the contrast between today's relatively diverse campus and yesterday's campus, which was racially homogeneous in enrollment and monolithic in values and curriculum. History provides an important context to evaluate how contemporary attitudes, policies, and diversity initiatives have emerged to influence social change.

OBSTACLES AND SOLUTIONS TO ADMISSION: THE IMPACT OF PRIMARY AND SECONDARY SCHOOL DIVERSITY

University admissions officers are faced with the dilemma of bridging the gap between general admissions criteria and the qualifications of the minority youth

113

who fall below admissions criteria because of low standardized test scores and inadequate academic preparation.

For most people in the United States, the American dream of prosperity is predicated on merit, and their dream incorporates a vision of educational opportunity, including college access. Unfortunately, the gap between the dream and reality is greatest for minority youth, since so many of them mature in settings where they have little educational opportunity. Low test scores and inadequate academic preparation are endemic in the neighborhood schools where poor minority youth have spent their primary and secondary years in relative cultural isolation, especially for those in black ghettoes and Hispanic barrios and Native American reservations. The deplorable inequality and continued racial segregation of public schools have been documented by Jonathan Kozol in his books *Death at an Early Age* and *Savage Inequalities*,[1] and also by Harvard researcher Gary Orfield, who has written on dismantling school desegregation. This relative lack of educational opportunity affects high school graduation rates, so that in 1997 the gap between high school completion rates for whites and African Americans was eight percentage points, and between whites and Hispanics more than twenty percentage points. The consequence is that lower high school graduation rates contribute to the underrepresentation of racial minorities in higher education.[2]

Regardless of the underlying reasons for underrepresentation in colleges and universities, concerned admissions officers and university policy makers assume responsibility for developing and nurturing a racially diverse campus community. Heretofore, that meant affirmative action. But those policies are increasingly under fire, with increasing litigation aimed at overturning all forms of affirmative action. Consequently, colleges that understand the need to admit more students of color are exploring alternative ways of meeting their goal. In fact, colleges can do so as long as the same criteria for admission are applied to all racial groups. One method seeks to establish admission criteria—for all racial groups—other than the SAT, since the most salient correlation with the SAT is parental income.

In a current project that began in 1999, nine colleges are using an alternative test to the SAT to predict success in college. Developed at Harvard University, this test, called the Bial-Dale College Adaptability Index, identifies noncognitive skills and involves the assembly of Lego blocks coupled with interviews. The evaluators believe that the advantage to this alternative exam is that it can project which students will be able to persist and seek needed help when they enter a competitive and selective college setting.[3] The pilot experiment tests about seven hundred seniors at public high schools in New York City; many are black and Latino students with average grades and standardized test scores who were selected by their guidance counselors and principals for showing potential. Based on the new test's scores, Pennsylvania State, Rutgers, and the Universities of Delaware and Michigan have committed themselves to accepting twenty students each, and five other liberal arts institutions have agreed to admit four to five students each. The students will be tracked throughout their college careers.

However, the issues of diversity in education that affect students of color at the college level begin far earlier in their education, as evidenced by many of the student narratives. From my work at the University of Oregon and Emory University and my interactions with public school districts in Oregon and Georgia, I have seen firsthand the importance of diversity in elementary and secondary education curricula and in discipline policies reinforcing racial tolerance. Tolerance alone is not enough, since it implies a power relation that "allows" other perspectives. What is needed as well is an attempt to fully understand and embrace alternate perspectives. In this regard, for instance, I have often seen that school districts which routinely enforce a tolerance policy have greater success when they also have an equity officer as well as a diversity planning committee to ensure curricular inclusiveness and diverse student activities that promote the achievements and traditions of racial/ethnic groups. As more immigrant students enter the public schools, each demonstrably tolerant school district has begun a process of developing new bilingual programs or hiring English as a second language teachers to accommodate the special language learning needs of students coming from other countries.

Correspondingly, any standardized testing that places non-English speaking students and students of color at a disadvantage must be reevaluated so that these students do not automatically become separated from the academic paths that lead to postsecondary education. Additionally, elementary and secondary schools may need their districts to develop social service centers to help immigrant parents with a broad range of needs to facilitate their transition to the local community and U.S. society. There are many ways that young people of color can get "frozen out" of higher education so that they never get into college nor are encouraged to go there. These issues must be addressed across their full range by college faculty and administrators seeking to increase the admission of students of color and ensure their retention until graduation.

Since educational opportunity leading to college access has to be fostered well before admission, a number of universities and colleges offer outreach programs and special readiness programs to junior and senior high, low-income/minority students to introduce them to a variety of career fields and to provide them with mentors. These programs provide academic and emotional support that helps young people build academic skills, self-esteem, and a work ethic. But the number of students of color who can be served in these outreach programs is low, especially given the predicted increase in the numbers of Hispanic and black students in the coming years.[4]

Diversity in classrooms and social settings offers tangible educational benefits for *both* majority and minority primary and secondary students. Children growing up and interacting with peers from many different racial/ethnic backgrounds are exposed to multiple languages among their schoolmates, consider ethnic foods and dress as part of the mainstream U.S. diet and lifestyle, and often have day-to-day classroom experiences providing a global perspective. This latter experience is also a stimulus for learning from an increasingly "wired" classroom, which may include computers and cable television. Students learn about "geography" and other countries in an ever more sophisticated way, and through the Internet and e-mail they often write to international pen pals. K–12 schools not only study but commonly celebrate ethnic holidays from diverse parts of the world. Surveys have found the millennial generation to be the most tolerant of all the generations,[5] and this may have happened because they learned at an earlier age to function well in multicultural settings.

POST-ADMISSION: RESEARCH ON THE BENEFITS OF DIVERSITY IN HIGHER EDUCATION

In 1996 the U.S. Fifth Circuit Court of Appeals struck down a University of Texas affirmative action admissions policy that preferred black and Mexican American applicants over better-qualified white applicants.[6] The ruling declared "that student diversity has no educational benefits."[7] The thought process behind the decision, as well as the huge negative impact of such a ruling, underscores the great need for research to concretely evaluate the impact of affirmative action. Historically, diversity studies have focused on the *problems* that minority students experience. The Texas court decision emphasizes the need for data-based research on the educational *benefits* of diversity. The decisions in future challenges to affirmative action in admissions and retention policies will turn on the availability of credible longitudinal data demonstrating diversity's positive effect on students' attitudes, experiences, and behaviors. Furthermore, data that confirms the ways in which a diverse campus climate plays a beneficial role in education influences not only judges but also voters, who make important decisions on the many referenda that appear with regularity on the ballot to denounce affirmative action.

Noteworthy among the existing research addressing the benefits of diversity is a 1996 University of Michigan study, a model for others wishing to examine or gather data on the educational benefits deriving from affirmative action policies.[8] In this study, Patricia Gurin, a professor of psychology, surveyed minority and majority college students over a four-year period, inquiring about how affirmative action shaped their behavior. She concludes, "Diversity fosters active, conscious, effortful thinking, the kind of thinking needed for learning in institutions of higher education."[9] The racial diversity available in large universities exposes students, many who come from segregated communities, to multiple, different, and contradictory perspectives. Gurin found that five years after leaving the college setting, the students who had the most diversity experiences during college continued to have the most cross-racial interactions.[10]

Another important longitudinal study providing information about students admitted under affirmative action policies is found in a book by William G. Bowen and Derek Bok, *The Shape of the River*.[11] The study follows African American students during school and after graduation to gauge their success on their campuses, within their communities, and in their professional work settings. In fact, these students, who had been admitted to select institutions only because of affirmative action, made significant community contributions.

In terms of postgraduate education, a survey conducted by the Gallup Organization under the direction of Dean Whitla, director of the counseling and psychology program at the Harvard University Graduate School of Education, questioned students at two of the most selective law schools, Harvard University law school and the University of Michigan law school. The survey, which contained more than thirty questions about their exposure to racial and ethnic diversity, had an overall positive response from more than 80 percent of the law students, and the two schools had similar responses despite the fact that Harvard is private and Michigan is public. The majority of students indicated that classroom interactions with students from other racial and ethnic backgrounds had a significant impact on their views about the criminal justice system. Some white students, for example, wrote that it was impossible to understand the criminal justice system without hearing the perspectives of minority classmates. Nine out of ten students reported that diversity had a " 'positive' impact on their education experience . . . and that they gained a much broader perspective on a variety of educational and personal matters."[12] Students of all races felt that classes with diverse students were superior to single-race classes and that both white and minority students benefited. Asian American and white students, the so-called victims of affirmative action, had positive attitudes toward diversity. Many students wished for even more far-reaching affirmative action efforts and outcomes.

The expansion of research focusing on the benefits of diversity in higher education is an important mechanism for colleges to inaugurate at this point in time. It can indicate the need for implementing mission statements that set forth diversity as a goal.

COLLEGE DIVERSITY: A PATH TO EQUAL OPPORTUNITIES AND WORKFORCE DIVERSITY

Changes in campus diversity correlate with national workplace trends. Shifts in corporations' educational expectations have occurred over the last several decades as businesses implemented new technologies and expanded to diverse consumer markets. Many occupations now require employees to demonstrate not only specific technical skills but also personal qualities that indicate "team player" potential and multicultural awareness. Similarly, to prepare students for a cooperative workplace, more college courses now require group projects that enable students to exchange ideas, conduct research, and make team or multimedia presentations. In order to prepare students to enter the modern workforce and to serve a diverse society, educational institutions must provide practice in cross-cultural communication and multicultural sensitivity, two keys to effective teamwork. To do this, the college curriculum needs to break racial stereotypes and systematically teach students to collaborate and work effectively together as a group.

Because higher education must prepare minorities for all segments of the workforce, U.S. Bureau of Labor statistics are widely used in career guidance, planning for postsecondary education and job training programs, and figuring long-range employment trends. Those statistics indicate that total employment is projected to increase by 14 percent between 1998 and 2008, but virtually all job growth will occur in the service sector. "Professional specialty occupations," a subcategory of service industries, is projected to increase most quickly and add the most jobs, an estimated 5.3 million. Another subcategory, "service workers," is expected to add 3.9 million jobs. Together service workers and professional specialty jobs are expected to provide 45 percent of the total projected jobs over the 1998–2008 period.[13] *Significantly, these two job categories lie on opposite ends of the educational attainment and earnings spectrum.* The challenge for colleges is to prepare students, including minority students, for both categories.

To prepare students for the higher end of the earnings spectrum, colleges have developed programs to encourage students of color to enter careers from which they might have traditionally been excluded. Such programs typically entail evaluating students' customary "paths" through college, establishing data on how students select their majors and monitoring how balanced access is for students who want to enter different disciplines. In terms of encouraging students of color to enter the sciences, for example, undergraduate science programs specifically aimed at students of color help diversify the racial makeup of those entering medical, scientific, and engineering professions—areas of expertise traditionally dominated by white males.

Because businesses across the nation are taking diversity seriously, in some ways they are taking the lead. For example, many businesses now hire diversity trainers or management consultants at the worksite to assist with communication, build respectful relations and positive morale, and maximize productivity among employees and management. At Emory University, corporate businesses such as Accenture (formerly Andersen Consulting) send diversity recruiters to

Does it seem like people are trying too hard to diversify everything? - could it be negative?

host special functions to attract applicants from diverse cultural backgrounds. It also can be commercially profitable to tap into the convergence of diverse viewpoints and value differences between people, viewing differences as strengths. Business operates from the economic imperative to reach consumers from all groups, so that one of the most obvious commercial values of understanding diverse populations can be seen in the growth of niche marketing to targeted groups. This kind of marketing includes manufacturing and selling products to suit the special needs and tastes of immigrant or multilingual consumers. Working under such a marketing policy, employees who understand those special needs and tastes and are familiar with the traditions and cultural expectations of different ethnic groups are at an advantage. Thus both majority and minority college graduates who have taken courses encompassing multicultural, interdisciplinary perspectives can highlight this background when looking for work.

CHANGING DEMOGRAPHICS BREED CHANGES ON CAMPUS

Following World War II, colleges expanded enrollments to include returning soldiers, which meant that many more working-class students, particularly men, went to school. At that time, only five decades ago, many universities were de facto racially segregated, especially through exclusionary admissions policies and discriminatory practices on campus. Such practices were the basis of widespread student protests and sit-ins in the 1960s and 1970s, in which racial and cultural divides were confronted. The more blatant discriminatory practices were dismantled through effective legislation and the concurrent development of ethnic studies programs. Furthermore, many universities initiated programs to recruit minority students and to retain students from disadvantaged backgrounds, as well as those who became disaffected and dropped out because they experienced college as "outsiders." Consequently, many more racial/ethnic minority and immigrant students—historically denied access due to discrimination—began attending college. More recently, in response to assaults on affirmative action, many colleges and universities have renewed their commitment to mission statements that set time lines and establish strategies to make their historically white institutions more racially and culturally diverse.[14]

Entering college, or staying there, has not always been an easy process for students of color. The civil rights movement and pressure from the NAACP Legal and Educational Defense Fund and the U.S. Department of Education Office of Civil Rights (OCR) set legal mechanisms in place to force colleges to admit students of color. However, this did not produce significant numbers of minority college students. Even after Title VI of the Civil Rights Act was passed, nineteen southern and border states had established dual racially segregated systems of public higher education that continued until legal standards for collegiate desegregation became explored in further legal cases. State governments and university officials did not want to desegregate their campuses and opposed accepting qualified black students until the courts forced change.[15] Other reasons for slow desegregation were the near riots and threats to safety that occurred when black students broke the color lines by enrolling in traditionally white institutions.

Additional support and incentives, such as race-specific scholarships and multicultural offices, were necessary (and are still) to increase college enrollment and graduation rates for students of color. Once this new generation of students was on campus, institutions had to take steps to halt their alarming attrition rate. Measures included constantly evaluating the experience of students of color, often through campus climate surveys and interviews. The goal was to change the "inhospitable" campus climate that these students regularly faced.

Examples of such broadly institutionalized support programs are the federally funded TRIO program and the more recent GEAR UP program. Over the past twenty-five years TRIO has provided students of color and first-generation, low-income secondary and college students coaching to help them with goal setting, positive attitudes, study skills, and survival techniques. The mentors in these programs, as well as group support, encourage students, and the programs have effectively increased retention, graduation rates, and entry into professional and graduate schools.

As a result of TRIO programs and other initiatives, the percentage of minority students who attend college has steadily increased. The percentage breakdown of the college population shows that the enrollment of white students remains steady at about 70 percent of the total enrollment, rising almost 1 percent between 1996 and 1997. During that same one-year period, Hispanic student attendance rose 4.5 percent, black student enrollment increased 3 percent, Asian American students rose 3.7 percent, and American Indians increased 3.6 percent.[16] Minority students now account for more than 26 percent of enrolled U.S. students. This figure is comparable to the general population of color, which now accounts for about 25 percent of the U.S. population according to the 2000 census. Furthermore, in a new study by the Educational Testing Service Network, the number of college and university minority students in the United States will increase by 2 million, making them 37.2 percent of the total undergraduate population by 2015.[17]

In this regard, according to Deborah Wilds, former deputy director of the Office of Minorities in Higher Education at the American Council on Education, "Given the changing demographics in this country and with the increased

If it weren't for athletic scholarships, would universities be as diverse?
Do Athletic scholarships let in the wrong kind of diversity?

representation of people of color, we should be seeing larger gains" by them in college enrollments.[18]

Athletic competition also accelerated integration on college campuses. The pressure to integrate campuses, particularly southern campuses, was fueled by the desire to remain competitive on a national level. Colleges and universities that had black athletes on their sports teams excelled over teams without black athletes. This was important to alumni and administrators because success on the athletic field brings prestige and financial rewards to the athletic department and to the university in general.

The original drive to recruit black athletes was not intended to educate and graduate them but to exploit their athletic talents and create winning teams. Such an exploitative undertone informs the disproportionate use of special admissions to bring black athletes to campuses, although there have been efforts over the years to diminish egregious forms of exploitation. In 1997–1998, 48.7 percent of the athletes in Division I revenue sports (football and men's and women's basketball) were African Americans.[19] The overall graduation rates of all athletes range from 21 percent to 93 percent.[20] At most institutions, the rate differs greatly from other students when the graduation rate of all students is compared with the graduation of student athletes. Furthermore, the *1997 NCAA Division I Graduation-Rates Report* shows that 46 percent of all African American student athletes graduated within six years, as compared to 62 percent of white student athletes.[21] ~ *Relate to above question*

Coaches blithely attribute athletes' leaving college before graduating to an opportunity to pursue professional sports. But, in fact, very few college athletes actually move on to the professional level. Many athletes drop out due to academic failure, which usually begins with lack of college preparation. To satisfy pressure from athletic departments and donors, most major colleges have special admissions programs that have lower standards, including lower SAT scores and lower GPA requirements. In this way, the admissions office reserves a limited number of acceptances to each year's freshman class for talented athletes. Most of these limited spots are filled by black male athletes participating in the revenue-producing sports. Athletes who stay till graduation face another negative outcome of preferential admissions policies for athletes: many faculty and classmates assume that most black male students are in college because of athletics and perform in a substandard way academically.

Beyond the special issues facing black athletes, there is a high attrition rate for many students of color. Over the years, in order to address this attrition rate, researchers have worked to identify retention factors for minority students. Recent statistics show that on four-year campuses, 45 percent of African American and Hispanic students graduate within five years of matriculation, compared with 57 percent of white students. While these studies have established that all students face complex issues related to college retention, two of the strongest barriers for students of color relate to their isolation and adjustment to college life. Even on the graduate level, recent research shows that graduate students of color, especially women, lack mentors and feel more isolated than white students.[22] Intervention programs and individual offices have attempted to address these issues but usually have not operated together in a coordinated and institutionalized campus-wide effort.

To implement a comprehensive, campus-based retention program, Swail and Holmes propose a five-component structure and plan of action.[23] The five components are financial aid, recruitment and admissions, academic services, student services, and curriculum and instruction. Practitioners from these different offices must work together toward common goals focusing on student needs. This research-based model recommends activities, policies, and practices that the five offices can adopt. Ideally, a cross-university retention task force would be formed for this unified effort in reducing attrition. Together, the groups would form linkages to provide a student monitoring system that would capture a snapshot of students so that proactive, individualized advising could occur regularly to catch problems before they occur. This model posits establishing important formal linkages between university programs, namely, student services and academic services. Student services, on-campus housing and residential programming, close counseling relationships, diversity in instruction, and faculty and student interactions are all areas that can be further developed to enhance social integration and make a positive campus climate supportive of diversity. The effect on minority students of institutionalizing these linkages reflects Vincent Tinto's theory of academic and social integration and retention. Tinto's studies and findings established that students' sense of belonging (academic and social) and their expectations impacted on their retention and graduation from college. If the quality of student life and learning are improved through enhancements and additions, positive retention is a by-product of these institutional efforts.[24]

Colleges, then, are seeing a bronzing of the student body. Most university presidents and administrative leaders are initiating a climate of inclusivity and equity, realizing that such a climate builds overall educational excellence. In this vein, President Robert A. Corrigan of San Francisco State University states,

> The urgency of responding to diversity is clear: it is obviously here now, in our communities, and we hope, on our campuses. The business world now echoes and reinforces our commitment to diversity, recognizing its need for a well-educated work force that reflects the range of its customers. . . . Faculty and students are sharing their appreciation of the intellectual richness that diversity adds to the academic experience.[25]

At the level of national leadership, Richard Riley, former U.S. secretary of education, offers a similar perspective:

> Another very valuable part of any college experience is something that a student often takes for granted, and that is the education brought about by diversity. Living and learning with students whose background and experience are different from our own can be just as important as what you learn in the classroom.[26]

DIVERSITY IN THE CURRICULUM, INTERNSHIPS, AND COMMUNITY SERVICE REQUIREMENTS

One of the most frequent issues that the student narratives in this book address is the university curriculum, often the site of the most visible struggle for diversity on a college campus. Arguably, an ongoing effort has to be exerted by many people to build a curriculum that reflects the ethnic makeup of U.S. neighborhoods, schools, and workplaces. If such a curriculum is developed, especially in the social sciences and humanities, all students, including Euro Americans, receive an education allowing them to better function in a pluralistic society. The more successful curricular changes are global and inclusive, teaching immigration and diaspora patterns as well as the history of and contributions by minority people in the United States.

There are tangible benefits to such curricular changes. For example, according to a 1994 study, students whose professors used racial/ethnic materials in their class readings reported getting more satisfaction out of their college experience as a whole.[27] The course material provided improved racial understanding, making a classroom climate more hospitable to students of color while providing white students kinds of knowledge and awareness not otherwise available to them. In terms of a larger social benefit, studies at the University of Michigan found that a program promoting intergroup dialogue effectively decreased prejudice in the student body:

> Students who are given the opportunity to learn about and discuss topics like racial prejudice and anti-Semitism in the controlled environment of a college classroom report that it becomes easier for them to discuss these kinds of issues in mixed student groups outside the classroom.[28]

Including courses on diversity as a general education requirement has been an ongoing fight. As of 2000, 63 percent of U.S. colleges and universities have a diversity requirement or are developing one.[29] The first ethnic studies program began in 1969 after San Francisco State University had a third world strike; students nationwide revolted, protesting for new courses and programs based on the cultures of peoples of color in the United States. By the late 1980s, many existing college courses focused on the issues and concerns of underrepresented groups; now hundreds of undergraduate ethnic studies programs exist.

A particularly successful model, the Curriculum Transformation Project at the University of Maryland–College Park (UMCP), has institutionalized a process for achieving a diverse curriculum in which students must register in a core curriculum that includes one or two mandatory courses grounded in diversity. At UMCP, commitment to diversity is seen as essential to the college's mission, which defines the educated person as learning about non-Western as well as Western cultural traditions. Summing up the university's goals, Ellin Scholnick, associate provost for faculty affairs and psychology professor, states, "Diverse perspectives provide the basis for the creativity and questioning that produce new ideas."[30]

Once established, ethnic studies programs have often faced bitter ongoing struggles. Within many universities, scarce funding has resulted from the failure of academic senates to fully support a specialized ethnic studies curriculum as well as new scholarship on people of color. Even long-standing programs are not immune. For example, in 1998, the University of California–Berkeley ethnic studies program was temporarily downsized, partly because the numbers of African American and Latino students rapidly fell after passage of California's Proposition 209 (1996), which rejected affirmation action policies that gave preferential treatment to minority and women students.

Closely related to an inclusive curriculum, successful campus initiatives include expanding campus–community connections and providing students opportunities to interact with local communities outside of class. Some schools encourage students to earn college credit as they work in various community agencies serving the minority public in internships with local social service agencies; in these service learning internships, college students work in the nonprofit sector, help a needy clientele, and become aware of class, race, and gender issues within various socioeconomic communities. Most universities have established internships with local public school districts so that university students can become volunteer teaching assistants or mentors to both elementary and secondary students. Outside the official university structure, often within each ethnic student organization or ethnic theme residential house, a community service component exists. Student leaders communicate with community leaders within the city to identify volunteer projects based on their common identification with an ethnic community.

On an international level, internships are being formed between universities and corporate sponsors to launch new global partnership programs so that students can study communities of color worldwide. For instance, the Coca-Cola Foundation is working with University of Florida students in a project called

World Citizenship Program. Selected students work in UNICEF and CARE projects in Africa and Latin America. The twelve-week internships have students participating in humanitarian projects that include disease control, farming, forestry, nutrition, and public relations. Other World Citizen Programs will engage other universities and agencies such as the Red Cross, Peace Corps, and International Rescue Committee.[31]

FACULTY OF COLOR RECRUITMENT AND RETENTION

A priority in higher education is to expand the racial profile of the college professoriate. As of 1998, ethnic minorities were underrepresented on college and university faculties: while 29.3 percent of undergraduate students were minorities, the percentage of full-time minority faculty was 12.2 percent.[32] Underrepresentation of faculty of color increases as we move up the tenure track and pay scale. Of associate professors, minorities make up only 11.9 percent nationally, according to a 1997–1998 report from the American Council on Education. "The numbers of faculty of color are just dismal at that level," says Deborah Wilds, former deputy director of the American Council on Education's Office of Minorities in Higher Education.[33] Only 9.2 percent of full professors are people of color.[34]

Aggressive recruitment is necessary to attract qualified minority faculty candidates. However, aggressive recruitment plans for scholars of color often elicit claims of "reverse discrimination" against white men. This perception exists in spite of the data indicating a continuing pattern that white men secure the best jobs in higher education, a job market considered tight. To illustrate, Daryl Smith's study of employment experiences of 393 white men and women and minority Ph.D.s who were recipients of prestigious Ford, Mellon, and Spencer Fellowships showed that "only 11 percent of scholars of color were actively sought after by several institutions simultaneously, which means 89 percent of these scholars were not the subject of competitive bidding wars."[35]

At UC–Berkeley, a reputedly progressive institution, the percentage is actually shrinking as current faculty of color are moving to campuses that embrace and support diversity. Currently nine out of every ten tenured Berkeley faculty are white. Moreover, Berkeley's black and Hispanic student enrollments have dropped over the past two years due to the recent admissions changes and implementation of anti–affirmative action policies. Ethnic studies professor emeritus Carlos Muñoz, who taught there for over thirty years and retired in 1999, criticizing the lack of diversity among students and faculty. He says that the student rebellions of the 1960s—against the Vietnam War, for free speech and third world studies—masked but didn't change Berkeley's essentially conservative nature. Refuting critics of these recent drops, Chancellor Bob Berdahl asserts, "It is true that the impact of Proposition 209 has been felt at Berkeley, but to suggest that Berkeley is no longer a place of diverse viewpoints and multicultural experiences is quite wrong." And the UCB chancellor's office demurs as well: "We are doing everything that can be done within the law to retain and enhance the diversity of our faculty and students."[36] The relation between increasing numbers of faculty of color and the elimination of affirmation action will continue to be conflictual at most institutions.

What can be done to increase minority faculty representation on campuses nationwide? Certain steps can ameliorate this underrepresentation, such as designing initiatives to increase the pool of qualified Ph.D. scholars of color, which will result from increasing educational opportunities throughout the secondary and higher education systems. Once such a pool exists, institutions must implement strategic plans to increase diversity by offering incentives to the best candidates, for example, assigning a lighter teaching load the first year so that the new professor can conduct research for publication; providing senior faculty mentors who will guide the new professor along the tenure track calendar to meet performance benchmarks; and offering spousal hires. Another strategy is to involve local communities of color in the hiring process—a "welcome wagon" into the local community of color. This kind of extended effort is especially necessary when administrators ask candidates of color to consider moving to a predominantly white campus town. These initiatives have a common thread: the institution must identify and remove obstacles that hinder the hiring, retention, and tenuring of more faculty of color.

The more diverse the faculty, the more probable that the academic community will foment and support new directions for scholarly research and gain more recruitment of graduate students of color. Such steps enrich the college itself, especially intellectually, and they also enrich the college experience of all students.

NATIONAL ORGANIZATIONS FOR HIGHER EDUCATION PROFESSIONALS AND STUDENTS ADDRESS DIVERSITY

An encouraging path toward a more diverse, inclusive campus community has been built over the last decade through the formation of national diversity networks for administrators, faculty, and students. Several national organizations of higher education, such as the American Association of Colleges and Universities, have allocated funds to establish a diversity component and staff to create such networks. Through these resources, national and regional conferences regularly occur around the country that gather administrators, faculty scholars, and students to share ideas, research, and strategies; the goal of the conferences is usually to deal with existing diversity issues and tackle new obstacles. These national and regional meetings among diversity-conscious educational leaders have effectively established national consensus on a set of diversity principles and priorities. They have built communication and resource networks, as well as coalitions. Often participants return home with new tools and insights with which to attack local institutional problems, and they gain increased energy from knowing clearly that they are not alone in the struggle. In addition, the emergence of the Internet has facilitated communication among this group of concerned educators, who use it to obtain up-to-date information about national organizations, conferences, diversity initiatives, and publications. (The resource section in this volume identifies Web locations and descriptions of services.)

A comprehensive overview of ongoing national efforts and "lessons learned" has been published in a very useful document, *Diversity Blueprint: A Planning Manual for Colleges and Universities.*[37] This publication describes how the University of Maryland–College Park and other campuses took specific steps to create effective institutional change. According to *Diversity Blueprint*, the five most important institutional-level planning priorities are leadership and systemic change; recruitment, retention, and affirmative action; curriculum transformation; campus-community connections; and, faculty, staff, and student involvement.[38] The *Blueprint* also sets forth principles by which to evaluate the process for change: "These principles are accountability; inclusiveness; shared responsibility; evaluation; and, institutionalization."[39]

The Diversity Blueprint deploys "models" to demonstrate effective ways of fostering greater respect for diversity within institutions. One such model is the Association of American Colleges and Universities (AAC&U) project, Racial Legacies and Learning: An American Dialogue, which is "designed to foster learning and dialogue about America's racial legacies and opportunities."[40] For this project and others, the role of the Ford Foundation has been to offer financial support. In 1998 Ford Foundation's Campus Diversity Initiative (FFCDI) funded more than fifty colleges and universities to develop a campus week of dialogue in the spring as well as a follow-up with campus–community study dialogues in the fall; the goal of the dialogues was to move people to discuss differences and find their commonalties, moving "toward a better understanding of community intersections, of our profound interdependence, and of our continuing need to learn from one another's experiences and contributions."[41]

The FFCDI dialogue on race held at the City College of the City University of New York (CCNY) collaborated with the Center for Mediation and Conflict Resolution to train students in conflict resolution and tolerance training. Similarly, a dialogue project in Los Angeles was initiated by Mount St. Mary's College, whose STAR program (Students Talk About Race) facilitates dialogues about race with middle and high school students at the local high schools. In this effort the students meet weekly for fifty minutes to discuss a wide range of topics, from individual prejudice to media portrayals of race. The goal of these dialogues nationwide was to work with existing community organizations to enhance the public's understanding of race relations and the challenges and possibilities of embracing a diverse cultural heritage. America's campuses are communities within U.S. communities, and they should be committed to advancing public understanding of large societal issues as they prepare students for life after college, including careers and employment.[42]

In addition to these organizations in higher education, faculty in general and faculty of color in particular have formed associations to address recruitment and hiring, mentoring and networking, and specific research and publication interests related to the issue of campus diversity. Noteworthy is the unified effort of the American Association of University Professors, which endorsed affirmative action in faculty hiring in 1973. Many faculty associations by racial and ethnic groups have emerged in the past to meet the need for collegial support on issues such as denial of tenure and promotion, sexual and racial harassment, accent discrimination, glass ceilings, and research.

For example, since 1986, the Midwest Consortium for Latino Research, housed at Michigan State University, consists of members from nine midwestern colleges and universities. Its mission is to provide leadership for Latino research in a variety of disciplines and to carry out projects such as a Latino faculty survey or annual roundtables that focus on faculty development issues. An excellent resource about faculty of color associations and their work is *Faculty of Color in Academe: Bittersweet Success.*[43]

Finally, ethnic student organizations have built nationwide networks that focus on issues specific to their racial or ethnic group, and these are important mechanisms of coalition building. Since the late 1960s, many college organizations such as Black Student Associations, MEChA, Asian American Student Union, and Native American Student Associations have functioned strongly on most college and university campuses. The names vary from campus to campus, but all these clubs actively help with retention, recruiting students of color, sharing cultures on campus, and addressing local political issues. New cultural clubs have proliferated in recent years in response to an increased campus presence of diverse students, such as Hindus, Muslims, Baha'is, Vietnamese, and Caribbeans. Typically, these individual ethnic clubs have membership in larger national, often pan-ethnic organizations that sponsor annual conferences. At these national college conferences, students formally articulate a prioritized agenda of diversity issues, often branching beyond college matters and into community-wide political issues, such as immigration rights, bilingual education, and racial profiling. Importantly, regional and national conferences provide networking for career opportunities, so students of color can gain expanded contacts to use beyond graduation.

National student government organizations also take up diversity issues, sometimes initiating diversity workshops or teach-ins, and in general integrating racial diversity concerns into the running of college student governments on a national scale.

CONCLUSION

Unquestionably, changes in racial demographics have precipitated changes on campuses nationwide. Over time, an awareness of minority students' needs has led to informal diversity committees, whose work and interests eventually has culminated in structured diversity initiatives at most campuses throughout the country. Social networks on campus, often catalyzed by student activism, have bridged the perspectives of students of color and majority students, faculty and administrators. Social networks have also bonded disparate factions within the minority community as they work toward goals of mutual benefit, improving the campus climate for all minority students. The social networks continue to provide opportunities for a new generation of students, faculty, and administrators who need to learn how to become agents of social change on campuses. In particular, students, faculty, and administrators of color, historically excluded from participation, now share in the dialogue and decision-making committees that help build cultural awareness, ethnic studies courses, and race-sensitive scholarships and aid.

In summary, the national scene is moving toward redefining university policies as culturally and racially inclusive, rather than exclusionary. Sometimes the victories seem small. Although recent research indicates a more general agreement that campus diversity benefits all students, faculty, and society, resistance to diversity remains. Legal challenges to affirmative action and increased public scrutiny on race factors, especially in college admissions, continually create tension and instability in the process of building multicultural campuses.

Further legal challenges and shifts in diversity policies can be expected; policies are never fully and permanently protected, especially in light of pending budget cuts for higher education, both locally and nationally. State institutions of higher education across the nation are facing budget decreases. In California, due to the recent slump in the stock market and a stagnant economy, the University of California campuses have faced a $89.8 million proposed cut to the system's core budget. At the beginning of 1990, the state provided nearly half of the university's operating funds; by 1999, state budget cuts reduced that contribution to 32 percent. Typically, such decreased state contributions translate into increased student tuition, which has a negative impact on minority students and low-income families.[44]

Most promising for the future is the existing diversity momentum: more people of diverse backgrounds and at varying levels of power have become educated on race issues and have willingly formed coalitions that advocate and promote racial diversity, justice, and equality within the institutions of higher education.

REFERENCES

Locke, M. 1999. "Berkeley Confronts Issues of Diversity." *Atlanta Journal Constitution*, December 9.

Orfield, G. 1999. "Affirmative Action Works—But Judges and Policy Makers Need to Hear That Verdict." *Chronicle of Higher Education*, December 10.

University of Maryland–College Park and Association of American Colleges and Universities. 1998. *Diversity Blueprint: A Planning Manual for Colleges and Universities.* Washington, D.C. Chapter 3.2, "Leadership Statement."

———. 1998. *Racial Legacies and Learning: An American Dialogue.* Washington, D.C. Brochure.

———. 1998. *Views from the Field, Faculty Recruitment in Higher Education: Research Findings on Diversity and Affirmative Action.* Washington, D.C. Brochure.

NOTES

1. Jonathan Kozol, *Savage Inequalities: Children in America's Schools* (New York: Crown, 1991); Kozol, *Death at an Early Age: The Destruction of the Hearts and Minds of Negro Children in the Boston Public Schools* (Boston: Houghton Mifflin, 1967).

2. American Council on Education, Office of Minorities in Higher Education, *17th Annual Status Report, Minorities in Higher Education, 1999-2000* (Washington D.C.: American Council on Education, Office of Minority Concerns, 2000).

3. B. Gose, "Seeking Diversity, 9 Colleges Try Alternative to Standardized Tests," *Chronicle of Higher Education*, December 3, 1999, A50.

4. U.S. Department of Education, Office of Educational Research and Improvement, *The Condition of Education 1998* (Washington, D.C., June 1998). 377 pages. See http://eric.uoregon.edu/ trends_issues/numbers/index.html (Trends and Issues by the Numbers).

5. R. Zemke, C. Raines, and B. Filipczak, *Generations at Work: Managing the Clash of Veterans, Boomers, Xers, and Nexters in Your Workplace* (New York: AMACOM/American Management Association, 2000), 137.

6. David Savage, "Court Lets Stand Ruling against Race Preference," *Los Angeles Times,* July 2, 1996. Available at http://aad.English.ucsb.edu/docs/Hopwood.html.

7. G. Orfield, "Affirmative Action Works—But Judges and Policy Makers Need to Hear That Verdict," *Chronicle of Higher Education,* December 10, 1999, B7.

8. Patricia Gurin, "New Research on the Benefits of Diversity in College and Beyond: An Empirical Analysis," 1996. Available at http://www.umich.edu/~newsinfo/Admission/Expert/gurintoc.html

9. Quoted in Orfield, "Affirmative Action," B7–8.

10. Available at www.diversityweb.org/Digest/Sp99/benefits.html.

11. W. G. Bowen and D. Bok, with J. L. Shulman, *The Shape of the River: Long-Term Consequences of Considering Race in College and University Admissions* (Princeton: Princeton University Press, 1998).

12. Orfield, "Affirmative Action," B7–8.

13. Bureau of Labor Statistics, U.S. Department of Labor, "Employment Projections 1998–2008," *Monthly Labor Review,* November 1999. All statistics in this section are from this report. Available at http://stats.bls.gov/news.release/ecopro.nr0.htm. Labor projections and relative occupational trends can change 180 degrees with unexpected turns of the economy.

Even before the events of September 11, 2001, the labor market had been weakening; but following the terrorist attacks, mass layoffs occurred involving hundreds of thousands of workers, affecting several industries and local economies. For higher education, this downturn in the economy causes reductions in state support to public institutions that, in turn, affects construction, repairs to facilities, and hiring freezes. For college students, the economic slowdown creates a much more competitive job market upon graduation.

14. See the resources section at end of this book for examples of diversity mission plans and the following Web site: www.diversityweb.org/Leadersguide/IVLSC/isap.html.

15. M. Christopher Brown II, "The Quest to Define Collegiate Desegregation," in *Black Colleges, Title VI Compliance, and Post-Adams Litigation* (Westport, Conn.: Bergin & Garvey, 1999).

16. National Center of Education Statistics, U.S. Department of Education, Tables: *Fall Enrollment in Postsecondary Institutions 1997.* Available at http://nces.ed.gov/pubsearch/pubsinfor.asp?pubid=2000160.

17. Report by Anthony Carnevale and Richard A. Fry, *Crossing the Great Divide: Can We Achieve Equity When Generation Y Goes to College?* Available at www.biztrail.com/minority_student_population_burg.htm.

18. S. Carlson, "Minority Students Posted Slight Increase in College Enrollment in 1997, Report Says," *Chronicle of Higher Education,* December 17, 1999, A50.

19. "1999-00 Race Demographics of NCAA Member Institutions' Athletic Personnel," in *The NCAA Minority Opportunities and Interests Committee's Two Year Study* (Indianapolis: NCAA, 2000).

20. 2000 NCAA Division I, II, III Graduation Rates Summary.

21. National Collegiate Athletic Association (NCAA), *1997 NCAA Division I Graduation-Rates Report* (Overland Park, Kans.: NCAA, 1997), 624.

22. Evelyn M. Ellis, *Diversity Digest,* Fall 2000, 10.

23. W. S. Swail and D. Holmes, "Minority Student Persistence: A Model for Colleges and Universities," in *Academic Achievement of Minority Students: Perspectives, Practices, and Prescriptions,* ed. Sheila T. Gregory (Lanham, Md.: University Press of America, 2000).

24. Vincent Tinto, *Leaving College: Rethinking the Causes and Cures of Student Attrition,*

2d ed. (Chicago: University of Chicago Press, 1993). See Web site on retention information from Vincent Tinto presentation, October 24, 1996: http://intra.montacalm.cc.mi.us/studentservice/st_persistence/Tinto.htm

25. University of Maryland–College Park and Association of American Colleges and Universities, *Diversity Blueprint: A Planning Manual for Colleges and Universities* (Washington, D.C., 1998), chap. 3.2, "Leadership Statement."

26. University of Maryland–College Park and Association of American Colleges and Universities, *Racial Legacies and Learning: An American Dialogue* (1998), 8. Brochure.

27. O. Villalpando, "Comparing the Effects of Multiculturalism and Diversity on Minority and White Students' Satisfaction with College" (paper presented at the annual meeting of the Association for the Study of Higher Education, Tucson, November 1994).

28. X. Zuniga et al., "Speaking the Unspeakable: Student Learning Outcomes in Intergroup Dialogues on a College Campus" (paper presented at the annual meeting of the Association for the Study of Higher Education, Orlando, Fla., November 1995).

29. Deborah Humphreys, *Diversity Digest*, Fall 2000, 1.

30. University of Maryland–College Park and Association of American Colleges and Universities, *Diversity Blueprint*, 6.3.

31. "Coke Offers Third World Internships," *Atlanta Journal Constitution*, December 9, 1999, A8.

32. University of Maryland–College Park and Association of American Colleges and Universities, *Views from the Field, Faculty Recruitment in Higher Education: Research Findings on Diversity and Affirmative Action* (Washington, D.C., 1998), 15. Brochure.

33. M. Locke, "Berkeley Confronts Issues of Diversity," *Atlanta Journal Constitution*, December 9, 1999, A8.

34. University of Maryland–College Park and Association of American Colleges and Universities, *Views from the Field*, 15.

35. *Views from the Field*, 17.

36. Locke, "Berkeley," A8.

37. University of Maryland–College Park and Association of American Colleges and Universities, *Diversity Blueprint: A Planning Manual for Colleges and Universities* (Washington, D.C., 1998). Order at http://www.aacu-edu.org/cgi-bin/cgiwrap/www/aacu/pubs.cgi.

38. *Diversity Blueprint*, v.

39. *Diversity Blueprint*, iv.

40. University of Maryland–College Park and Association of American Colleges and Universities, *Racial Legacies*, 4.

41. *Racial Legacies*, 7.

42. *Racial Legacies*, 9.

43. C. Turner and S. Myers, *Faculty of Color in Academe: Bittersweet Success* (Boston: Allyn & Bacon, 2000).

44. Sources: Ellen Chrismer, "State Budget Cuts Impact UC," http://www.dateline.ucdavid.edu/052501/DL_budget.html; "Facts 1999: Operating Funds," http://coe.berkeley.edu/EPA/Facts/funds.html.

6

A Historical Look at Students of Color at the University of Oregon

Donna Wong

In this chapter I analyze issues of diversity at one institution, the University of Oregon. Focusing on one school permits a precise examination of the connections between changing racial demographics, recognition of minority students' needs, and subsequent institutional changes. The interviews in part 1 of this book present the voices of University of Oregon students. The students discuss the contexts in which change has taken place and make a strong argument for the institutional need to develop a comprehensive mission and plan to address diversity issues. They teach us that institutions cannot just open their doors to underrepresented students of color without considering the adverse as well as the rewarding experiences that lie ahead for them.

Contemporary struggles build on history, and so in this chapter I present a history of minority participation at the University of Oregon. My outline of historical factors can act as a model for others in addressing the historical context of desegregation and diversity achievements at their respective campuses. Here I address Oregon's racial makeup, historical admissions practices and experiences of students of color at the University of Oregon, campus policies, off-campus living conditions, and development of relevant campus structures.

The chapter includes a description of a united effort by students of color at the University of Oregon to support a multicultural curriculum proposal, a policy initiative that ignited arguments among students and faculty about the direction of liberal higher education. The chapter concludes with an assessment of more recent student diversity initiatives that have brought about a more collabo-

133

rative and comprehensive campus effort among students, faculty, and administration.

HISTORY OF MINORITIES IN OREGON

The University of Oregon is the state's flagship university. The university's policies in regard to race—or lack thereof—have generally reflected the state's historic lack of diversity. Vast portions of the state had and continue to have no minority residents. Small logging towns and farming communities, totally white, dot the landscape. Even today, many white students arriving at the University of Oregon have never been in a public classroom with a student of color. Only in the state's few urban centers—and only in the past several decades—have schools taken on an integrated look.

White privilege and sense of entitlement were matters of fact based on critical mass. An overview of the past seventy years of censuses shows that Oregon was and is a predominantly white state. To make a sixty-year contrast, we can note that the 1930 census report described Oregon as 98.2 percent white, 0.2 percent black, and 1.5 percent other races (Mexican, Indian, Chinese, Japanese, Filipino, Hawaiian, Korean, Hindu, Malay, Siamese, and Samoan).[1] To make a seventy-year contrast, the 1990 census reported Oregon as having changed little. The racial demographics are 86.6 percent white, 3.2 percent Asian Pacific Islander Americans, 8 percent Hispanic or Latino, 1.6 percent black, 1.3 percent Native American, and 3.1 percent persons reporting two or more races.[2]

Minorities living in Oregon have faced racial intolerance and hate-motivated violence. Oregon has a long, documented hostility toward people of color. From the 1840s to the 1860s, many exclusionary laws discriminated against its early black settlers, Kanakas (native-born Hawaiians), Indians, and Chinese. These Oregon territorial laws, including an antimiscegenation law that was not repealed until 1959, regulated and restricted the behavior of people of color for decades.[3] Several congressional land acts and ill-fated treaty programs from the 1830s to the 1860s forced Indians off their lands, authorizing the government to give away millions of acres to Euro American settlers.[4] From the 1850s through 1870s, cattlemen, settlers, miners, and the U.S. Army massacred many Indians and compelled survivors to move on. The discovery of gold in 1858 led white miners to drive tribes from their villages, establishing mining towns in their place.[5] Chinese, hired by the white miners as laborers to build the towns, were excluded from mining by discriminatory taxes and exclusionary policies.[6]

Despite the small numbers of people of color, Oregon was a hotbed of Ku Klux Klan activity in the early 1920s. Klan organizers appeared in Medford, Eugene, Salem, and Portland, swiftly making Oregon the center of Klan activity west of the Rockies. The Klan recruited more than fifteen thousand members throughout the state (including ten thousand in Portland in the early 1920s). Klan activities in Oregon included attacks on blacks, Jews, and Roman Catholics. The Klan boycotted minority-owned businesses and published a *100 percent Directory*, listing only white Protestant-run businesses. The Klan successfully lobbied the Oregon legislature in 1923 for a school bill eliminating parochial education. However, in 1925 the U.S. Supreme Court declared the Oregon Compulsory School Measure unconstitutional.

By the 1930s, the Klan disappeared as a formal political force; however, the Klan legacy of hate and violence manifests itself in Oregon today through skinhead groups and radical enclaves that dot Oregon and the Pacific Northwest. Students of color at the University of Oregon today often express concern about directly confronting local skinhead violence. The students' perception is borne out in data. According to the 1993 FBI *Report on Hate Crimes,* Oregon had 279 reported hate crimes. In comparison, California—with ten times Oregon's population—had only one hundred reported hate-motivated incidents.[7]

Individual racist acts and racist official policies created a hostile environment that suppressed the state's minority population well into the twentieth century. The 1930 U.S. census showed only 2,234 African Americans in the entire state, just 0.2 percent of the state's population. Even in the city of Portland, the area with the greatest concentration of blacks, discriminatory housing covenants lasted well into the 1950s. Elsewhere in the state, the relatively few remaining minorities faced de facto segregation so that limitations on property ownership and lack of job opportunities long affected the economic status of minority families in the Pacific Northwest.[8] Limited to low-paying jobs, minority families had limited resources available for education.

HOME OF THE UNIVERSITY OF OREGON:
EUGENE, OREGON

In 1876, the University of Oregon opened its doors in the city of Eugene. Eugene was a white city, located 110 miles south of Portland. Not until the mid-1930s did a few black residents live on Eugene's edges, mainly single men employed by the Southern Pacific railroad who stayed invisible to Eugene community life. The black presence gradually increased in Eugene during the 1940s, but housing for them did not. Real estate agents and city officials prevented black families from living inside Eugene city limits, confining blacks to flood lands on the city's outskirts or in neighboring Glenwood, an unincorporated area between Eugene and Springfield.[9] Jobs for blacks consisted mostly of domestic work for both women and men. Briefly, during World War II, blacks gained jobs in lumber and railroad work, and by the 1950s the black population of Eugene had grown to 140.

In conjunction with, and under pressure from, the 1960s civil rights movement, biracial committees formed to build public pressure for changing housing and employment opportunities in Eugene. According to the 1990 U.S. census, minorities made up few of the city's 112,669 residents; 1,410 blacks (1.3 percent of the total population), 1,004 Native Americans (or 0.9 percent), 3,896 Asian Pacific Islanders (or 3.5 percent), and 3,051 Hispanics (or 2.7 percent). Except for the recent influx of out-of-state and international students, trends around race/ethnicity at the university paralleled trends in the city of Eugene and in the state. At the University of Oregon, racial diversity gradually developed into a visible issue as the slow but gradual entry of minorities into the previously all-white flagship university pushed demands for change. Some of that change came by way of voluntary consensus, but other changes happened only in response to federal legislative pressure, student and community protest, and the university's institutional economic interest.

According to the University of Oregon archives, the first student of color, a student of Japanese descent, Paul Gotow, enrolled in 1876. The first African American student, Mabel Byrd, enrolled in 1916. (Accurate information on Hispanic and Native American students is not available.) Later, just as black railroad workers cracked the restrictions against minority presence in the workforce, black athletes helped expand the numbers of minorities at the university. In 1926 the first black athletes were recruited from Portland high schools to play on the University of Oregon football team. In that year, the university signed two black players, Bobby Robinson and Charles Williams, as quarterback and fullback, respectively.[10]

Indicative of the second-class status imposed on all minorities at the time, including minorities in the Eugene community, football players Robinson and Williams were not allowed to live in the university dormitories because previous Filipino students had "caused a problem" living there. The truth was that all students of color were required to rent off-campus housing. Significantly, Ellen Law, an African American student, attempted to live in the dorms but was blocked in 1941. The exact date when on-campus housing became racially integrated is unknown, but the civil rights legislation of the 1960s established equal access in fact if not spirit. The spirit of civil rights also produced institutional introspection in the form of a statewide AAUP Research Council report entitled *The Negro and Higher Education in Oregon* (May 1964). It referred to a special study group that investigated the reasons for the relative absence of Negroes in the faculty and among students.[11] This report was the first manifestation of official interest by the University of Oregon in the education of minority students.

PRE-ADMISSIONS: OBSTACLES FROM SECONDARY
EDUCATION TO COLLEGE

In Oregon's high school system, the "pipeline" to college, minority students have suffered from unequal educational opportunity, which occurs both in educational policy and in expectations placed on the students, both in and out of the classroom. For example, minority students historically faced exclusionary policies preventing their participation in extracurricular activities (i.e., sports and clubs); thus Oregon high schools had a quota system in which only one black athlete at a time could participate on a sports team.

In the classroom, unintended bias and racism in teaching has often hindered minorities' academic achievement and college preparation. Educational research shows that teachers form expectations of their students on the basis of race/ethnicity and socioeconomic status.[12] In this regard, Shirley Minor of Portland, a 1971 University of Oregon black alumna, recalls, "I had high school counselors who said I didn't have any business going to college."[13] Lower expectations on the part of teachers and counselors become self-fulfilling prophecies; minority students respond by not performing up to their abilities. These lowered academic expectations correlate with minority and working-class high school students not having access to college information. In fact, as Minor stated, the minority student can be explicitly guided away from college. On a regular basis, minority students were discouraged from receiving financial aid information and applications to four-year college institutions.

Impact of Financial Aid on Enrollment of Students
of Color at the University of Oregon

A major obstacle to higher education for minorities was and is family income. This is especially true for those coming from Portland, which has the largest population of minorities, but is 110 miles from the University of Oregon campus. The university is a residential institution, and thus students are not able to commute and live at home. Since many minority families in Oregon have encountered employment discrimination and have lower family incomes, parents simply have not had the money to pay for college tuition and living expenses, especially away from home. However, enrollment of students of color has slowly increased in Oregon's colleges due to new student financial aid programs that offer loans and scholarships.

Issues of attendance and graduation, and how they are affected by the availability of financial aid, are impacted by inadequate data, since it limits institutions' ability to remedy past inequities. In this case, official records and analyses of the correlation between financial ability and minority enrollment and retention are nonexistent. Even with this inadequate data, some numbers stand out. There are records of students receiving financial aid at University of Oregon between 1969 and 1973 who also participated in the university's Special Services Programs. These records show the following retention rates: forty-two of sixty-seven African Americans persisted, which is a 62.7 percent retention rate; four of twenty-five American Indians, a retention rate of 16.0 percent; six of twenty-one Spanish-surnamed U.S. students, a retention rate of 28.6 percent. In contrast, low-income white students had a total retention rate of 78.5 percent, and the three Asian American students documented had a 100 percent retention rate.[14] Note that this data applies only to students in the Special Services Program; to be eligible for the SSP, students' income, parents' educational levels, and academic needs were assessed. Although data for the university as a whole is missing, extrapolating across the campus, we can see that retention rates for minority students have been much lower than for whites, even low-income whites.

Institutional scholarships that help reduce a family's financial burden are typically bound to high academic achievement, and work-study jobs—part of the typical financial aid package—reduce the number of hours a student can devote to academics. Disadvantaged minority students, often coming with less competitive academic records and no managerial job skills, have had to rely heavily on loans and have received more loans and fewer scholarships than whites.[15]

The difficulty in finding data at the University of Oregon highlights a common situation: historically, universities did not differentiate the needs or issues of students of color. However, it is now clear that an institution of higher learning committed to retaining students must adequately record and track data such as graduation rates to evaluate the performance of students who have been successfully educated; it must do this also for advanced degrees, tracking how students move through the educational system and go on to professional and graduate schools. The problem of inadequate data was not limited to the University of Oregon. Higher education enrollment figures by race and ethnicity were not systematically collected on a national level until fall of 1976, when the National Center for Education Statistics, U.S. Department of Education, began to record them. Much of the data prior to 1976 were estimates derived from institutions' underreporting or not reporting racial/ethnic data. Now the U.S Department of Education's enrollment tables categorize minority students by five race/ethnic groups: black non-Hispanic, white non-Hispanic, Hispanic, Asian or Pacific Islander, and American Indian/Alaskan Native.[16] Before 1976, U.S. statistics were both indirect and institutionally nonspecific; the national statistics that we have on minorities in postsecondary schools came from national census survey samples of households collected on African Americans starting in 1961 and were not broadened to include a Hispanic category until 1972.

The Beginning and End of Minority Scholarships

At the University of Oregon, the growth rates, enrollment patterns, and retention rates of *all* University of Oregon students first came under close examination in 1980. This was when the Carnegie Council on Policy Studies in Higher Education predicted that the most dramatic feature of the next twenty years would be a substantial decline in overall enrollment.[17] This enrollment drop was predicated on a nationally projected drop in numbers of eighteen-year-olds from 4,211,000 in 1980 to 3,426,000 in 1990. The University of Oregon projected a corresponding enrollment decline, which would mean a significant decrease in state funding. Given such a potential drop in revenue, in the early 1980s the University of Oregon began a strategic action program to aggressively retain all students.

The strategic action program led to a policy of "enrollment management" to keep institutional funding stable, predictable, and growing.[18] As a result, in 1979–1982, the registrar's office began "trying to understand why students leave, to actively converting our University into a caring institution, with increased emphasis on academic quality and service."[19] Hence economic interests propelled the compilation and examination of statistics on freshman persistence, graduation rates for entering classes, and enrollment and retention rates by race/ethnicity/gender. At the University of Oregon in the early 1980s, the projected drop in general enrollment, coupled with the potential loss of institutional revenue, coincided with the first step to actively recruit high school minority students.

In 1985 the Oregon State Board of Higher Education set a diversity goal that a cultural, ethnic, and racial mix on campuses be achieved "to expose all students to an academic environment that reflects the global community they will join" upon graduation.[20] The board realized that the state's colleges needed a focused recruitment and retention effort; otherwise, they faced a possible decrease in minority student participation. Following this mandate, with minority participation in mind, in 1987 Oregon developed a scholarship program, the Underrepresented Minority Achievement Scholarship Program (UMASP) to recruit African American, Native American, and Chicano/Latino high school seniors into Oregon higher education. (Asian Americans were not a targeted group.) In 1990 the program for minority scholarships was extended to college juniors and transfer students of color. Despite cuts in state aid to higher education institutions in the mid-1990s, the Oregon State Board of Higher Education remained committed to minority scholarship programs. Approximately sixty UMASP scholarships were granted to students of color each academic year, and additional Target of Opportunity Laurel Awards provided merit-based tuition scholarships to students from an ethnic minority community to enhance the university's racial diversity. Such attention to minority recruitment and retention has made a difference. University of Oregon enrollment ratios of major ethnic groups for the fall term, from 1982 through the mid-1990s, showed a continuous upward trend for students of color in admissions as a whole.

Those successful admissions and retention policies have come under fire, since affirmative action admissions policies were recently overturned in California with Proposition 209 (1997) and in Texas with the *Hopwood* ruling (1996). Like other institutions across the country, the University of Oregon is faced with revising the criteria of the UMASP minority targeted scholarships to eliminate race as a qualifying characteristic. Consequently, the UMASP has been renamed the Diversity Building Scholarship Program, making grants to "students who enhance the educational experience of all students by sharing diverse cultural experiences."[21] What patterns will emerge in the enrollment of students of color in the University of Oregon in the next decades? Will the University of Oregon face a decline in students of color without the allowance of race as a factor in scholarship awards? Answers to these questions remain to be seen.

ENROLLMENT: NEW TRENDS AND IMPLICATIONS

The University of Oregon's dilemma mirrors national projections for the next century: shrinking public and private resources for higher education, accompanied by a rise in demand for college degrees. The cost of college in Oregon continues to increase, federal financial aid is down, and race-based scholarships are under challenge. If finances are a factor for a student choosing a college, the enrollment and retention of students of color at the University of Oregon will be adversely affected by the loss of federal student aid, the loss of race-based scholarships, and University of Oregon budget cuts. Tuition at the University of Oregon has skyrocketed: the impact of legislated property tax limits has forced the university to supplement fewer tax dollars by raising tuition nearly 40 percent from fall 1990 to fall 1991.[22] Unfortunately, the availability of federal Pell grants has been reduced. Caught between higher tuition and less federal aid, low-income students turn to loans for their education.[23]

System-wide budget cuts caused streamlining and downsizing of costs and services, as well as reductions in student services personnel. The cuts also precipitated the university's deemphasis of activities originally implemented to attract students of color. For instance, the university shifted priorities from in-state recruitment, which often targeted minority students, to heavy out-of-state and international recruitment campaigns. The objective is clear: out-of-state and international students pay triple the tuition fees of Oregon residents. Underscoring the effect of the redistribution of recruitment resources, in 1993 the University of Oregon fall admissions figures indicated smaller numbers of Native American students and in 1994 fewer African American students.[24]

In 1998 the state raised high school graduation requirements, which in turn raised admission requirements for University of Oregon students. Coupled with rising tuition, these changes disproportionately impact large numbers of moderate- to low-income students, a category containing the largest pool of minority students. Projected trends at the University of Oregon for the first decade of the twenty-first century indicate that motivated students of color, financially strapped and less academically prepared, unable and unwilling to meet the economic sacrifices for the sake of education, will drop out or be relegated to and perhaps ghettoized in less selective and cheaper community colleges. This projection correlates with recent research that shows students of color who depend on loans are more likely to drop out due to growing debt.[25]

THE EMERGENCE OF STUDENT SERVICES AND CAMPUS CLIMATE ISSUES

Campus climate consists of all the elements in the daily environment of higher education. Climate is a crucial consideration in evaluations of the "comfort factor" that students of color experience on campus. In short, climate refers to how minorities perceive their "belonging" to the larger group of enrolled students. Too often, they perceive of themselves as outsiders.

The collective percentage of "students of color" at the University of Oregon has steadily increased from 5.78 percent (1981) to 11.7 percent (1999) of total university enrollment.[26] But these statistics are misleading in regard to the comfort factor of individual groups. To illustrate, in 1999, African Americans accounted for 1.6 percent (264) of the total enrollment of 16,716 students; Asian, Pacific Islanders 6.1 percent; Hispanic 2.9 percent; and Native American 1.2 percent. Given the small minority student population and the correspondingly low minority population in Eugene, the four underrepresented groups of students attending the University of Oregon are culturally separated from family, church, and friendly community. If the minority students also feel unwelcome or ostracized from mainstream campus life, they face painful day-to-day struggles in addition to fulfilling academic demands.

All the student interviews in part 1 of this volume agree on one thing: Students of color perceive the ivory tower image of academia as carefully cultivated and based on white, European American traditions, values, and attitudes. Since the students' perception is not shared by the larger campus population, changing the campus climate often meets with resistance. Yet many people are working within the institution to create such a change, an effort which shows students that cultural diversity is valued and respected. Over the years, for example, some steps have been taken at the University of Oregon to improve campus climate.

Barriers have been overcome. Whereas in 1941 students of color were barred from the University of Oregon dorms, in 1986 a multicultural residence hall was created to house and welcome undergraduate students of color interested in cross-cultural awareness and sharing. Today this multicultural housing option accommodates more than fifty students and employs two university resident assistants of color who plan cultural and ethnic activities for dorm residents. For many of the students interviewed in this book, living in a multicultural dorm is crucial to their survival on campus.

Research on students of color who graduate reveals that involvement in ethnic student organizations improves their chances of getting a degree.[27] The social and cultural activities organized by ethnic clubs create a living community for students and help raise awareness of cultural differences on predominantly white campuses. At the University of Oregon, ethnic student unions and clubs have existed since the late 1960s. These student unions and clubs function as advocacy organizations and sites for meeting people and for support. New Student Week activities recruit incoming students of color to these ethnic student unions and thus promote early friendships and peer mentoring. The associations made within these clubs help students of color survive challenging academic experiences and make a transition into the university's generally chilly social climate.[28]

The history behind the ethnic clubs demonstrates both a response to racist exclusion from mainstream groups and a perceived need among minority students to bond with peers. Armando Laguardia, a 1970 University of Oregon graduate, states,

> The university was an alien environment to non-white, middle-class students. We weren't allowed in the fraternities or sororities. We had to create our own things, our own environment. We stuck out like a sore thumb.[29]

Fraternities were another milieu in which students of color faced both racial discrimination and slow acceptance. In 1964 an African American student, Herb Sanders, rushed but was not selected. An investigation into this incident culminated with University of Oregon president Fleming finding no discrimination.[30] Progress was slow: Greek organizations were marginally integrated during the late 1980s. In 1990, the dean of student affairs specifically addressed racial issues in the University of Oregon Greek fraternity/sorority system in a special program entitled Colors. During a time of slow progress in integrating existing fraternities, University of Oregon black students set up links with the eight national, historically black Greek fraternities and sororities, and they organized local affiliate chapters in the late 1980s. Today several black fraternities and sororities are on campus, such as Alpha Kappa Alpha sorority and Kappa Alpha Psi fraternity.

The ethnic group with the longest history at the University of Oregon campus is Asian Pacific Islanders, some sharing a common bond of growing up in Hawaii. Hawaiian students are multiracial—including Chinese, Japanese, Korean, Filipino, native Hawaiian, and mixes of these groups. Even before Hawaii attained statehood in 1959, the University of Oregon was a popular mainland campus for Hawaiians. In 1941 the Hawaiian students formed a student organization called Hui-o-Kamaaina, translated as Club of Old Times. The organization aimed to (1) encourage cooperation and unity among Hawaiian students and (2) spread and develop knowledge and appreciation of Hawaiian culture. Today it continues as the Hawaii Club.

Another early cultural appreciation organization, the Cosmopolitan Club, was formed in 1960. With over eighty international and U.S. students, this club aimed to create "an informal, multicultural atmosphere" for members interested in learning about different cultures and socializing.

Four major ethnic student organizations at the University of Oregon were formed in the late 1960s in response to cultural pride movements: the Black Student Union (BSU), Movimiento Estudiantil Chicano de Aztlan (MEChA), the Asian/Pacific American Student Union (APASU), and the Native American Student Union (NASU). In addition to promoting social goals, the four function as advocacy groups. They sometimes collaborate on a national level, acting in coalition as political special interest groups in demanding curricular changes, funding for multicultural programs, and policy changes that affect working-class students and faculty of color.

The group activities sponsored by the ethnic student unions vary. Some are traditional cultural events such as the Native American Powwow, in its thirtieth year, and the Martin Luther King Jr. Celebration. Other activities deal with survival issues. For example, the African American male support group branched out from Black Student Union members in 1992 to focus specifically on helping and motivating new black male students. A common objective of ethnic organization is building community relationships between university students and the local ethnic communities. For instance, MEChA students sponsor fund-raising dances and cultural events in order to make connections with local migrant and immigrant families and to assist Eugene-based Chicano/Latino social service agencies. APASU brings important Asian American leaders to speak at Eugene events during Asian Heritage Month. Other student organizations sponsor similar activities to connect students of color to their heritage.

Campus–community cooperation can be far-reaching. In the case of MEChA, the organization extends to six Oregon campuses, holding yearly statewide meetings to identify common political and economic issues facing Chicano/Latino student scholars. At the statewide meeting, representatives are selected to travel to a national conference that provides a forum to establish common goals and a matrix of political action. These conferences give student leaders unique political leadership opportunities, sometimes influencing them to pursue careers in politics and law.

In addition to the student-formed associations, the university administration established a special office to provide student services and academic programs to minority students. First named the Committee for Minority Education in 1983, the office now exists as the Office of Multicultural Affairs (OMA) with the goal of enhancing retention among underrepresented minority students. OMA, staffed by counselors of color, provides academic advising, mentoring, tutoring, computer support, course selection, and advocacy for students of color and scholarship recipients. OMA sponsors fall orientation retreats to help incoming students adjust to a predominantly white campus and to introduce them to other students of color, providing them with bonds to their peers early in college. OMA-sponsored activities and support of student clubs have proven essential in helping improve the success of students of color attending college.

In addition to OMA, a grassroots effort by students, faculty, and staff formed a race task force (RTF) in 1987 to support students of color and address specific acts of racism or racial intimidation. The RTF included students, administrative staff, faculty, the university public safety office, the Counseling Center, and the student conduct office. Given the impetus of that grassroots effort, a newly organized body, the bias response team, replaced the unofficial race task force in 1999 and now is a formal appendage of the Office of Student Life.

In essence, as the interviews of University of Oregon students reveal, building a positive campus climate means eliminating racism. Racism has serious effects, causing students emotional harm, self-doubt, and low grades. A research report found that exposure to racism "did appear to be debilitating and seemed to have retarded the college adjustment of most students of color."[31] Moreover, many students of color now enter college with high expectations for their college experience and fewer expectations of racism; such students, especially Asian Americans and Latinos, are shaken academically and socially when they are the target of racist acts. As a consequence of overt and institutionally embedded racism, students suffer, feeling removed from their original commitment to college, and often withdraw because they feel marginalized and "pushed out" when living and going to school in a racially charged environment.

When an institution has instituted practices and policies that work toward respecting diversity and promoting a safe, inclusive learning environment, that institution openly demonstrates that it considers students of color valued members. A college with a formal plan of action to increase diversity by recruiting more students and faculty of color acknowledges the need for a "critical mass" to facilitate attracting and enlarging these communities of color. In sum, what constitutes the normative behaviors and beliefs of an institution reveals its prevailing warm or cold climate. (See the checklist in the appendix to identify both positive and negative aspects of a specific institutional culture.)

THE MULTICULTURAL CURRICULUM PROPOSAL

The quest for multicultural curricular requirements for graduation at the University of Oregon entailed a decade-long struggle. In the early 1990s, the ethnic student unions proposed that the number of available ethnic studies courses be increased and that ethnic studies courses be a university-wide graduation requirement. The proposal met resistance from all corners of the university. This kind of resistance toward developing new multicultural curricula and programs was implied in a Ford Foundation study of national trends in multiculturalism and the curriculum in 1992. According to the report, the Northwest region has not been as quick as the rest of the nation to incorporate multicultural general education requirements. More than a third (34 percent) of all colleges and universities have a multicultural general education requirement and more than half (54 percent) of all colleges and universities have introduced multiculturalism into their departmental course offerings.[32] However, only twelve of the more than three thousand classes listed in the University of Oregon catalog dealt with the history or experience of people of color in the United States. Of the twelve or so listed courses, some had not been taught for years. One student of color states in the narratives in this book, "We can't take the class and learn about our history or culture if it is never taught."[33] Nor could the white majority take classes to learn of the minority experience in U.S. society.

The early 1990s proposal by the ethnic student unions was not the first proposal dealing with race: a "race, gender, or non-European-American" course requirement had been approved at the University of Oregon in 1988–1989. It was intended to educate students about the social diseases of sexism and racism in the United States (and the global community) to prepare students for a pluralistic society.[34] However, the requirement was strongly criticized by the ethnic student unions because it did not emphasize the minority experience in the United States. For example, courses such as Ancient Chinese Art or Primitive Man, an anthropology class taught from a European perspective, satisfied the requirement.

In 1992 students presented a resolution to revise the requirement so that only courses teaching the "major conceptual issues relevant to understanding ethnicity, culture, race, and pluralism in a rapidly changing U.S. context" could fulfill the requirement.[35] The issue remained a top priority for students of color. Consequently, in 1992–1993, a multicultural curriculum committee of students and faculty met, researched, and presented a proposal to expand graduation requirements to include two courses—one course on gender, race, or non-European cultures, and a second course on race in U.S. society focusing on the specific experiences of African Americans, Asian Americans, Latinos, or Native Americans.

The proposal by the multicultural curriculum committee to expand the requirement was defeated by a vote of the full faculty assembly. Detractors argued that the requirement threatened the "academic freedom" of faculty and that the university should not add required courses "in response to contemporary social and political issues, however important." Underlying the debate was money—a lack of additional resources to hire new faculty to teach the new courses. Also, there was resistance to shifting funds from existing academic departments to fund a new ethnic studies department.

In 1993, Students of Color Building Bridges (SCBB), a coalition of five minority student associations, escalated the debate by threatening to discourage minorities from attending the University of Oregon if the university administration did not improve campus conditions for minorities by hiring and supporting minority faculty, creating a more tolerant campus environment, and improving the multicultural aspects of the curriculum.[36] Additionally, the group threatened to ask minority alumni to withhold donations until the "unfriendly environment" improved. The SCBB threat precipitated the creation of yet another special faculty committee appointed by the vice provost of academic affairs during the 1993–1994 academic year; the mission of that faculty committee was to craft a workable compromise on a multicultural curriculum requirement. In February, the Associated Student Union Organization withdrew its lone student representative from this committee, saying the panel lacked good faith. The revised requirements were as follows: undergraduates must take two courses from the following three categories: American cultures (race and ethnicity in the United States, *including* European American as an ethnic group); identity, pluralism, and tolerance (the study of issues addressing classes, genders, religions, sexual orientations, or other groups that contribute to cultural pluralism); and international cultures (the study of world cultures in view of race and ethnicity, prejudice and tolerance, and pluralism and monoculturalism). The final vote on this revised proposal came before the faculty assembly in April 1994; it passed without much debate in a substantially less well-attended assembly. During this assembly, a statement from the four student ethnic unions was read, explaining these organizations' "desire not to support or condone the legislation.

Our heritages are very valuable and it is not in our interests to force a reluctant populace to learn to appreciate them."[37]

On the whole, students of color felt that the newly adopted multicultural requirement had been "watered down" by white traditionalists. Andres Montoya, a member of MEChA, stated that the requirement "will give the university an excuse for not doing what it should be doing for students of color."[38] Although budget cuts and lack of resources to hire new faculty were obstacles to expanding course offerings and requirements, students of color felt that money became an easy issue to hide behind and a reason to sidestep multicultural curricular reform. The curriculum battle continued through the 1990s. Students who began the multicultural curriculum fight in 1991 graduated and moved on, new students took up the banner, and the focus changed. The multicultural requirement that would have exposed all students to a minority perspective was abandoned, and momentum shifted toward establishing an ethnic studies major. That major was finally approved in October 1997 by the Oregon State System of Higher Education, and in fall 1999 a new Native American history professor was hired to direct and hire faculty for the ethnic studies major.

Although the students of color did not get everything they originally envisioned, their demands led to an examination of the curricular content of courses and the political act of teaching and learning: who is and who is not included, who is valued and legitimated by present relations and conditions. The opportunities and obligations of a university to provide new and recovered knowledge of peoples of color and to promote multicultural understanding have finally begun to be realized at the University of Oregon.

CONTINUING DEMANDS:
CATALYSTS FOR CHANGE

The student activists who advocated for the multicultural curriculum requirement also proposed that the University of Oregon establish a multicultural center in the Student Union building where all students would be welcome to meet, plan, and help with educating the community about diversity. The student-funded Multicultural Center (MCC) was approved in the mid-1990s, and it became the catalyst for a series of changes. The MCC is *the* hub of activism, connecting students of all races and backgrounds, especially by listserv and computer bulletin boards, to collaborate on diversity programming. The MCC's "primary goal is to promote personal growth, cultural pluralism, community education, positive social change, and the ending of human oppression by examining issues of gender, sexual orientation, and culture with primary focus on race and ethnicity" (http://gladstone.uoregon.edu/~multictr). In the past three years, the MCC has sponsored annual conferences on diversity, featuring renowned keynote speakers. Its floor space was dramatically expanded in 1997, enabling it to accommodate meetings of ethnic student unions, workshops, guest speakers, art displays, a resource library of books and videos, and a computer lab for students. The MCC coalesces disparate groups into one physical location, encouraging dialogue and cooperation toward achieving common goals.

Consequently, in the spring of 1999, when an incident of intolerance and racism occurred in a UO class, involving racial stereotyping and threats of sexual violence to women through a class listserv, a coalition of students at the Multicultural Center quickly organized and publicized a protest at the president's office. The coalition of students, including the ethnic student unions, the women's and GLBT (gay/lesbian/ bisexual/transsexual) organizations, organized an overnight sit-in addressing their concerns to one another, the president, and administrators. Students allowed themselves to be arrested, knowing that their act of civil disobedience would help promote outrage at the ignorance and racism going unchecked within the university. Although charges against the students were not dropped, the administration acceded to many of their demands. A major accomplishment was the hiring of ten student interns who spent the summer researching and formulating a new diversity initiative plan.

The diversity interns defined the concept of diversity in a broad way, combining gender and ethnic constituents' demands:

> It means . . . recognizing our individual differences. These can be along the dimensions of race, ethnicity, gender, sexual organization, socio-economic status, age, physical abilities, religious beliefs, political beliefs, or other ideologies. It is the exploration of these differences in a safe, positive, and nurturing environment . . . moving beyond simple tolerance to embracing and celebrating the rich dimensions of diversity contained in each individual.[39]

Over the summer of 1999, the student interns each analyzed a specific aspect of university structure, policy, and governance, making charts that detail decision-making flows within the administration. Students not only consulted Internet sites of universities that had undertaken major diversity initiatives but also developed an ongoing interface with concerned University of Oregon faculty and members of the administration, mostly among the student affairs staff. Together, a diversity steering committee and an administrative team for diversity continue to work through meetings open to anyone in the university community willing to contribute. Two concrete goals were achieved. First, a bias response team was formally established, through which the university could better respond to incidents of racism, homophobia, and threat on campus and, more importantly, could act productively to promote respect for diversity in all aspects of campus life. Second, a policy statement, the University of Oregon Affirmation of Community Values, was approved by the university senate, and it was molded after the language that the diversity interns proposed for a pledge of respect. The following diversity concerns are still being discussed: that faculty be required to take diversity training; that more faculty and students of color be recruited; that a new vice provost be hired to take responsibility for diversity issues; and that a diversity institute be established.

Close study of the work of previous diversity task forces and protests over the years shows that students have become very astute as how they can best organize, do research, and analyze possibilities in order to initiate change. They have been very specific about allocation of resources, identifying what steps must be taken to foster diversity and affect university structures. In this effort, the process of change has entailed a collaborative effort among many groups—including students, faculty, staff, possibly outside funding agencies, and certainly the administration. Students are willing to pressure the administration but want to work with it and not against it. In this effort, they have chosen not to work as outsiders but to try to reshape institutional structures from the inside out.

In response, the university president has learned to value close communication with students in order to understand their college experiences from their perspective as students of color on a predominantly white campus. The president has shown more responsiveness to the school's diverse student body and faculty by institutionalizing committees that regularly address race relations and improving campus climate. While not all student suggestions are taken up, students continue to be vocal. They are confident that gradually strategies and compromises can be worked out within the new social networks.

During 1999–2000, a Web site on the University of Oregon's diversity issues was designed by students to focus on the university's comprehensive diversity goals (http://diversity.uoregon.edu). The Web site is a place where the university mission statement and strategic plans are spelled out, with the goal of energizing faculty and departments working on these issues and of holding the administration accountable. The same Web site informs students and staff about structures to which they have access to redress inequity and harassment, and it lists resources available to all (i.e., scholarships), including links to other sites and pedagogical tools.

In conclusion, University of Oregon students are currently taking steps to make the diversity mission plan a reality. University of Oregon classes, once composed of mostly white, upper-middle-class students, are slowly changing to accommodate the needs of a more diverse student population and a more diverse workplace. Financial aid remains a problem, and continuing recruitment efforts to communities of color must be made. In the next millennium, the University of Oregon will continue to change. Students of color have become agents of change, altering educational policies, changing the direction of curriculum, and calling attention to an unfriendly campus climate that tolerates racism. Working together in coalitions as well as in separate ethnic groups, students of color are instrumental in pressing for progress. By questioning the university's academic and social life, they have advocated for improvements that build a safe and culturally pluralistic learning environment.

NOTES

1. U.S. Department of Commerce, Bureau of the Census, *Abstract of the Census: Table 29: Color or Race by Divisions and States: 1930* (Washington, D. C.: Government Printing Office, 1930).

2. U.S. Department of Commerce, Bureau of the Census, *State and County Quick Facts: Oregon* (Washington, D.C.: Government Printing Office, 2000). Available at http://quickfacts.census.gov/qfd/states/41000.html.

3. Q. Taylor, "Slaves and Free Men: Blacks in Oregon Country, 1840-1860," *Oregon Historical Quarterly* 83, no. 2 (1982): 153–70. Professor Quintard Taylor was the chair of the history department at University of Oregon from 1997-1999 and taught African American history from 1990 to 1999. Since fall 1999, Dr. Taylor is the Scott and Dorothy Bullitt Chair of American History in the Department of History at the University of Washington. He is an award-winning author of several works about African Americans in the American West. Dr. Taylor was a key mentor to students of color and also the chair of the faculty and staff of color committee at the University of Oregon in the 1990s.

4. C. Buan and R. Lewis, eds., *The First Oregonians: An Illustrated Collection of Essays on Traditional Lifeways, Federal-Indian Relations, and the State's Native People Today* (Portland: Oregon Council for the Humanities, 1991), 1–128.

5. Buan and Lewis, *First Oregonians.*

6. S. Lowenstein, *The Jews of Oregon 1850-1950* (Portland: Jewish Historical Society of Oregon, 1987), 1–236.

7. "FBI Says Most Hate Crimes Linked to Racial Bias," *Eugene Register Guard*, June 29, 1994, 8A.

8. Q. Taylor, "A History of Blacks in the Pacific Northwest: 1788–1970" (Ph.D. diss., University of Minnesota, 1977).

9. M. Thoele, "Black Island in a Sea of White," *Eugene Register Guard*, January 31, 1993, 1A.

10. "Bobby Robinson and Charles Williams: First Black Athletes in the University's History," *Eugene Register Guard*, December 1, 1974, 3EE.

11. R. Agger, G. B. Johnson, and B. Siegel, "The Negro and Higher Education in Oregon," *AAUP Research Council Report*, 1964, 1.

12. T. Good, "Teacher Expectations and Student Perceptions: A Decade of Research," *Educational Leadership*, February 1981, 417–22.

13. L. Strycker, "We Stuck Out Like . . . Black UO Alums Remember Racism, Say It's Still Here," *Eugene Register Guard*, August 29, 1982, 1B.

14. E. Williams, "A Comparative Analysis of the Attrition and Retention Rate of Students Who Received the Educational Opportunity Grant at the University of Oregon for the Academic Years 1969–70, 70–71, 71–72, and 72–73" (Ph.D. diss, University of Oregon, 1975), 1–164.

15. Williams, "Comparative Analysis."

16. National Center for Education Statistics, U.S. Department of Education, *Table 12, College Enrollment of Students by Race and Ethnicity in Mini-Digest of Education Statistics 1997* (Washington, D.C.: Government Printing Office, 1998).

17. Carnegie Council on Policy Studies in Higher Education, "Three Thousand Futures: The Next Twenty Years for Higher Education: January 1980," *Carnegie Council on Policy Studies in Higher Education: A Summary of Reports and Recommendations* (San Francisco: Jossey-Bass, 1980), 195.

18. University of Oregon, Office of Student Affairs, *University of Oregon Annual Report for Retention, 1984–1985* (Eugene: University of Oregon, 1985).

19. *University of Oregon Annual Report for Retention, 1984-1985*, 1.

20. Office of Academic Affairs, Oregon State System of Higher Education, *Minority Student Enrollment and Graduation Trends* (1989). Report for the Oregon State Board of Higher Education by J. Payne, assistant vice chancellor for curricular affairs.

21. Office of Financial Aid, University of Oregon Web site: http://financialaid.uoregon.edu/SCG-dbsinfo.htm.

22. OSSHE Institutional Research Services. 2000. "Changes in Tuition Compared to Changes in Enrollment. Table of Fee Rates." www.ous.edu/irs/factbook96/student/tuienrl.htm.

23. L. Steven, "Federal Focus: Pell Grant Funds Cut," *The Board Bulletin: News Summary of the Oregon State System of Higher Education*, June 24, 1994, 3.

24. *Fourth Week Statistical File and Profile of Students, 1990–1998*, Fall 1999, table 1.12, "Comparative Enrollment by Ethnic Background Admitted Students."

25. J. Carmona, "Minority Students Who Depend on Loans Found More Likely to Drop Out," *Chronicle of Higher Education*, May 25, 1994, A28.

26. OUS Institutional Research Services, *Fourth Week Enrollment Reports*, Report ERDD-03, Fall 1981, Fall 1998. http://www.ous.irs/factbook/WEBstudent/hcethnic.txt.

27. L. C. Attinasi Jr., "Getting In: Mexican Americans' Perceptions of University Attendance and the Implications for Freshman Year Persistence," *Journal of Higher Education* 60 (1989): 247–77.

28. J. Fleming, *Blacks in College* (San Francisco: Jossey-Bass, 1984).

29. Strycker, "We Stuck Out," 1B.

30. "UO Discrimination, Pt. 1," *Eugene Register Guard*, February 4, 1964, 8A; "UO Discrimination, Pt. 2," *Eugene Register Guard*, February 25, 1964, 1A.

31. G. LeSure, "Research Report: Ethnic Differences and the Effects of Racism on College Adjustment, Described in Racism on Campus May Affect Asian, Latino Students Most," *Campus Crime*, March 1994, 22.

32. B. Schmitz, "Cultural Pluralism in the Academy," *University of Washington Center News*, Fall 1992, 8.

33. University of Oregon, Office of Multicultural Affairs, *Office of Multicultural Affairs (OMA) Newsletter*, Winter 1992, 1–6.

34. University Assembly Minutes for Senate Assembly held on March 2, 1988. University of Oregon, *Notebook of Assembly Multicultural Curriculum Committee Minutes 1988-1994*.

35. University assembly minutes for senate assembly held on May 27, 1992. University of Oregon, *Notebook of Assembly Multicultural Curriculum Committee Minutes, 1988–1994.*

36. J. James, "Minorities Present List of Demands," *Eugene Register Guard,* March 2, 1993, 1C.

37. University assembly minutes for senate assembly held on May 25, 1994. University of Oregon, *Notebook of Assembly Multicultural Curriculum Committee Minutes, 1988–1994.*

38. University assembly minutes, May 25, 1994.

39. University of Oregon diversity internship Web site: http://darkwing.uoregon.edu/ ~diverse/index.html. See also http://diversity.uoregon.edu.

7

Hate Crimes, White Backlash, and Teaching about Whiteness

Abby L. Ferber

An African American student in Washington discovered threatening hate notes in his gym locker, which had been covered in graffiti. The note warned of impending lynching and death ("Black Student Receives Death Threat" 2000). At historically black Florida A&M University in Tallahassee, two pipe bombs went off, followed by a call to a local radio station revealing that the bombers' goal was to "get rid of some of them niggers." A second call charged that blacks "got no business having a college where there ain't nobody . . . smart enough to get a degree" ("Hate Goes to School" 2000, 8). At the University of Kentucky, two students, one black and one white, were attacked by a group of ten white men who choked the black student while calling out a deluge of racial slurs and broke the white student's nose and wrist while yelling "nigger lover." In fact, such hate crimes on college campuses are increasingly commonplace, as indicated in a frightening report released by the Southern Poverty Law Center:

> At SUNY Maritime College in the Bronx, 21 Arab students flee after a series of assaults and incidents of racist harassment. At Brown University in Rhode Island, a black senior is beaten by three white students who tell her she is a "quota" who doesn't belong. At the State University of New York at Binghamton, three students are charged in a racially motivated assault that left an Asian-American student with a fractured skull. A Harvard resident tutor quits after being subjected to homophobic vandalism. E-mail threats and slurs are sent to 30,000 students and faculty at Stanford University, along with others at many other schools. Holocaust deniers publish their screeds in campus

newspapers and, in a few cases, are backed up ideologically by professors. ("Hate Goes to School" 2000, 8)

In 1998 alone, 250 incidents of these kinds of campus hate crimes were reported from all geographic regions, according to the FBI's state hate crimes statistics, and experts agree that these crimes remain vastly underreported, for reasons ranging from fear of retaliation to the assumption that authorities would not or could not do anything (Pincus and Ehrlich, cited in Fenske and Gordon 1998). Nevertheless, schools are the third most common site for hate crimes in the United States, garnering 9 percent of the total number of incidents reported.

Far more pervasive than hate crimes, bias incidents have become frequent occurrences on campus. A recent report estimates that there are 1 million bias incidents each year on campus. According to campus hate crimes expert Howard Ehrlich, only 20 percent of bias and hate crimes are reported to campus officials, and according to the U.S. General Accounting Office, many incidents are then never reported to the federal government, despite laws requiring schools to do so. This happens because institutions of higher education want to protect their image, which affects both recruitment and revenue (Fenske and Gordon 1998). When these acts of hate and bias do occur in a college setting, as Ehrlich has found, they elicit a "keen awareness of such incidents by minority students, and a contrasting lack of awareness by majority students" (Fenske and Gordon 1998, 32). Consequently, Ehrlich has advanced the notion of co-victimization to account for the experiences of those who "may have directly *witnessed* an eth-noviolent attack on another person, or they may have *heard* about it from the victim or from others. For co-victims, attacks on peers are seen as threats not only to the entire group but also to their own personal well-being" (Pincus and Ehrlich, cited in Fenske and Gordon 1998, 133). Thus when hate crimes and bias incidents occur, they shape the broader environment that students of color must negotiate, and such incidents potentially impact all students of color.

As one scholar observes, "The politics of racial hate, fear, and anger is significantly increasing on U.S. college and university campuses. Hate literature, graffiti in public places, name-calling, denigrating epithets, and violence continue to disrupt the lives of racial minorities attempting to get a college education" (Kent 1998, 189). In fact, incidents of racial harassment have increased sharply since the 1980s (Kent 1998, 190). According to Noel Jacob Kent, "Part of the answer is that life on campus closely mirrors the dominant patterns and attitudes of the larger society. In both, racial structures and meanings are in flux and hotly contested" (1998, 190). For this reason, and this is one of the major themes of this book, focusing on education provides us with a microcosm of race relations in the United States and an antidote to the distorted picture painted by many.

Let's consider one example: I was recently asked to write a book review of

Race Pride and the American Identity, by Joseph Tilden Rhea. He argues that "the great triumph of the civil rights movement of the 1960s was to end legal segregation in the United States." This movement was followed by a second movement for racial equality, aimed primarily at changing cultural attitudes by promoting an alternative vision of the past. Rhea provides a case study focusing on battles waged and won at four national, historic sites that demonstrate the politics over cultural memory and the battles people of color have fought to rewrite history and challenge their exclusion. He demonstrates that the "race pride movement" has provided people of color with a stronger sense of identity, heritage, and pride while at the same time improving their national status. He writes, "Recognition of the role of minorities in American History has increased not because of a general drift toward cultural pluralism, as is often believed, but because of concrete actions which can be documented" (Rhea 1997, 7).

This important lesson needs to be endlessly repeated. Each semester my students are utterly amazed to learn that the suffrage movement struggled to gain women the right to vote for over seventy years. Most students never thought about how the vote was won, and once asked to consider it, they guess that as soon as women organized and demanded that right, it was simply granted. Our students often assume that greater racial and gender equality will come with the slow march of progress, and consequently, achieving equity does not require their effort. They wonder why there is so much fuss over inequality today: "Give it time," they say, and "progress will come." However, as Kent points out, "Rather than the steady decline of discrimination and maturing of the 'color-blind society' envisioned by integrationists, 'racial meaning' [has] remained bitterly contested. The battle for full participation continue[s] as 'trench warfare' " (Kent 1998, 191).

Underlying the assumption that progress is inevitable is the belief that racial inequality is no longer a significant problem. In fact, Rhea seemingly embraces this view: "Many in our country believe that it is the lack of national recognition of minority cultures which explains the persistence of gross inequalities in our society. . . . They fail to recognize the degree to which the Race Pride movement has already triumphed in public discourse. Its images are now established in our minds and in our historical landscape. Those who hope for a more just society will have to look beyond Race Pride" (Rhea 1997, 127). While acknowledging that "gross inequalities" still exist, Rhea suggests that equality has been gained in the realm of culture, but his conclusions are unsupported by the evidence.

The narratives of students of color in this book seriously problematize such a contention that people of color now have the institutional power to define their own past and have significantly redefined the national conscience once and for all. They also highlight the very different experiences and perceptions of white students and students of color.

Focusing on the battles being waged within our schools provides perhaps a more realistic account. As Elizabeth Minnich argues, "Our educational institutions . . . are, not alone but preeminently, the shapers and guardians of cultural memory and hence of cultural meanings. Here too, then, we must do our work of critique, re-membering, creation" (Minnich 1990, 12). The integration of a multicultural curriculum has been uneven and in many places is still largely absent. The battle over U.S. history, memory, and identity is continuous, and success is never secure. With each victory, the backlash grows (Ferber 1998).

WHITE BACKLASH

As one white student observes, "There is a growing realization by white males that they no longer have their privileged advantages, who feel they may not do as well as their fathers, and they are looking for scapegoats" (Kent 1998, 195). Today's young people are perhaps the first generation to face the realization that in all likelihood they will be worse off economically than their parents. As James William Gibson argues, "The post-World War II American Dream—which promised a combination of technological progress and social reforms, together with high employment rates, rising wages, widespread home ownership, and ever increasing consumer options—no longer seem[s] a likely prospect for the great majority" (Gibson 1994, 11). Instead, corporate downsizing, declining real wages, changing technology, the steady decline in manufacturing jobs replaced by lower paying jobs in the service sector, and the increasing gap between the wealthy and everyone else has left many people in the United States feeling vulnerable and betrayed. In this situation, minorities often serve as easy scapegoats for those seeking simple solutions. Economic dislocations easily become rearticulated and explained as resulting from changing race relations. As another student put it, "Being white means that you're less likely to get financial aid. It means that there are all sorts of tutoring groups and special programs that you can't get into, because you're not a minority" (Kent 1998, 195).

Gallagher discovered a similar phenomenon in studying backlash among white college students. He concludes, "The perception that a racial double standard exists on campus is commonplace . . . [and] provide[s] the foundation for a white identity based on the belief that whites are now under siege" (Gallagher 1995, 176–77). Research by the Southern Poverty Law Center confirms this. One student says, "My college is black dominated. . . . It just sickens me how the media, the government, and academia will bend over backwards to pave the roads with gold for these simpletons," while another states, "I, and many of my fellow students are becoming increasingly concerned about the rapidly increasing minority enrollment" ("Hate Goes to School" 2000, 11). Another student argues, "There is a new Ethnic Studies requirement. . . . Not all students are buying into this multicultural garbage that is being forced down our throats" ("Hate Goes to School" 2000, 11). Similarly, in my research on white supremacist groups, I found as a popular lament of the white supremacist movement the following kind of argument: "The white people of America have become an oppressed majority. Our people suffer from discrimination in the awarding of employment, promotions, scholarships, and college entrances." Thus, in the current climate, it is not only organized hate groups but also large numbers of mainstream whites who believe that they have lost their privileged status and instead have become victims of racial discrimination; they embrace a strategy of rearticulating whiteness to reclaim privilege.

Research on affirmative action confirms this perspective. When asked whether African Americans or whites were at greater risk of discrimination at work, respondents named whites twice as often. Between two-thirds and four-fifths of whites surveyed thought it likely that less qualified African Americans won jobs or promotions over more qualified whites, despite the reality that only a tiny number of whites experience discrimination. Of the 451,442 discrimination complaints filed with the EEOC between 1987 and 1994, only 4 percent charged reverse discrimination (and only a tiny number of the cases were found credible upon investigation). Less than 2 percent of cases reaching the courts charge reverse discrimination (and almost all of these were dismissed by the courts for lack of merit) (Reskin 1998).

Underlying these diverse manifestations of the contemporary backlash— including charges of "reverse discrimination," battles in higher education over curriculum transformations, and the organized white supremacist movement— lies the common assumption that racial inequality has been remedied. It is from this perspective that neoconservatives assume that race-based policies end up discriminating against white males. These arguments for color-blind policy assume that racism has become a thing of the past. Based on his interviews with white students, Gallagher concludes,

> Much of the anger white students expressed stems from their belief that in a "color-blind" society . . . race-based organizations are racist and "discriminatory" toward whites. . . . The majority of white students believe affirmative action is unfair today because issues of overt racism, discrimination, and equal opportunity were addressed by their parents' generation in the 1960s. (Gallagher 1995, 175)

The Southern Poverty Law Center report concludes that expressions of diversity often spark white students' resentment and actually precipitate incidents of hate and bias. As colleges and universities make efforts to educate students about diversity and to foster an inclusive atmosphere, many white students will be hav-

ing their first protracted living and working experience outside of a homogeneous white culture. While many white students will be receptive, others
"dealing with diversity up close for the very first time . . . dig in and react against
it" ("Hate Goes to School" 2000, 10).

Researchers studying campus ethnoviolence have found an expanded Contact
Theory useful as a tool for understanding the increase in hate and bias. This
theory argues that increased contact between majority and minority groups is
potentially positive if certain conditions are met, and it is especially important
that the groups meet in a situation where they have equal status. If groups do
not meet on equal grounds, conflict may increase. Other factors are also important—specifically that the contact enables members to undo negative stereotypes
and that they work together actively toward mutual goals. This kind of research
emphasizes the crucial role played by the university in creating an environment
that prevents ethnoviolence because the broader social context can either foster
or discourage hate crime and bias. Hurtado, Dey, and Trevino have examined
the relationship between increased campus diversity and racial climate and con-
clude that "the structural diversity of an institution is significantly related to
students' perceptions of racial tensions and experiences of discrimination on
campus" (cited in Fenske and Gordon 1998, 136).

Such research is useful as we interrogate our educational system. The students' narratives in this book abound with examples which demonstrate that
students of color do not have equal status in academia. The low numbers of
minority faculty in conjunction with a lack of curriculum on people of color and
women announces the low status accorded these groups, and thus universities'
reluctance to change contributes to the national climate of white backlash and
the myth of meritocracy.

Americans are not taught the realities of the history and continuing foundations of racism in the United States, and they find it hard to redress a problem
they know nothing about. As a result, many white people do not embrace the
addition of multicultural curriculum. As one student writes, "There are all kinds
of groups here: a gay organization, a black student organization . . . but if someone wanted to create an organization for Whites . . . I am sure that would be
drummed out" ("Hate Goes to School" 2000, 10). These sentiments reveal that
whiteness remains unexamined and white privilege invisible in the curriculum.
Courses in history, literature, and politics still present the experiences of white
men as the neutral norm, so that white students do not see that the curriculum
and normative organizations already overrepresent the experiences of white men.
In this way, as educational institutions perpetuate a largely canonical course of
study, new generations continue to grow up ignorant of white privilege and the
oppression of people of color and women.

"White Americans resist relinquishing the sense of entitlement skin color has given them throughout our history." Seldom, however, does the college experience cause students to question whether such entitlement exists. Neither do they find their own, nor their society's, racial biases seriously challenged by the curriculum they study or the associations they make. Few institutions mandate study of cultural identities and values. Only infrequently do white undergraduates investigate the framework in which African Americans (among others) are marginalized by both university and larger society. (Kent 1998, 197)

CURRICULUM CONTRADICTIONS?

When we look at U.S. history, we find a central paradox. What we discover is a society that "preached inclusiveness and equality while vigorously practicing an ever more pernicious and ultimately destructive discrimination that disadvantaged all those not affiliated closely with mainstream, upper-class whiteness" (Bell 1993, ix).

This is what Derrick Bell refers to as the *constitutional contradiction*, and Gunnar Myrdal the *American dilemma*: While our founding fathers wrote that all men are created equal, at the same time they developed exclusionary procedures limiting equality to property-holding white men. Indeed, U.S. history is filled with such contradictions, and they continue. Rather than teach about the constitutional contradiction, our curriculum often continues to keep this history hidden.

In contrast, one of the goals of multiculturalism, argues Hu-DeHart, is "to correct the omissions and distortions of the work and perspectives of generations of 'triumphalist' scholars and teachers. Triumphalists are conservative, neoconservative, and even liberal historians, writers, high government officials, and opinion makers who champion a traditionalist view of American history as an unbroken string of successes, who willingly ignore inconvenient inconsistencies" (1993, 7). The triumphalist view is currently evident in works by conservative scholars like Dinesh D'Souza, Allan Bloom, John Leo, Charles J. Sykes, and Roger Kimball. The problem with their versions of U.S. social history

is that the images of the people who built America and benefited from it are overwhelmingly and almost exclusively those of European immigrants and their descendants. . . . The fact of the matter is "our" in "our national identity" and "our national culture" and the "we" in "we the people" historically have been exclusive. (Hu-DeHart 1993, 9)

As a result, when white history is taught as our nation's history, its "one true story" is advanced at the expense of Americans of color, since a false unity is assumed whenever white experience is advanced as the neutral, universal norm.

New research on whiteness, however, takes these arguments even further. In *Whiteness of a Different Color: European Immigrants and the Alchemy of Race*, Matthew Fry Jacobson argues that "racism [is not] anomalous to the working of American democracy, but fundamental to it" (Jacobson 1998, 12). In his analysis of the construction of whiteness in U.S. history, Jacobson finds that the notion of contradictions and hypocrisy is

> too simple a frame to do justice to the historical conjunction of racialism and American democracy. Exclusions based upon race and gender did not represent mere lacunae in an otherwise liberal philosophy of political standing; nor were the nation's exclusions simply contradictions of the democratic creed. Rather, in the eighteenth and nineteenth centuries these inclusions and exclusions formed an inseparable, interdependent figure and ground in the same ideological tapestry. (Jacobson 1998, 23)

Central to the multicultural agenda, then, should be a focus on whiteness. Multiculturalism not only brings in the voices of those who have been excluded but must cast a critical eye on what has traditionally passed as neutral and universal—the experiences of white men. Examining whiteness critically means analyzing how it is constructed and experienced. In this way the curriculum deliberately incorporates that knowledge and experience which has been excluded, and it also reconsiders what has been accepted as the center. "Knowledge that is claimed to be inclusive . . . but that is in fact exclusive must be transformed, not just corrected or supplemented. . . . Curriculum transformation puts the emphasis not on joining what is but on changing it" (Minnich 1998, 31, 13).

Racism and privilege go hand in hand, and racism should not be reduced to simply individual acts but instead seen as an institutionalized system that oppresses some and privileges others. Key to the experience of whiteness, then, is that white people do not recognize nor experience it as privilege. This foundational misrecognition undergirds the current white backlash. Because white privilege seems the norm, any threat or loss of that privilege becomes defined as an attack and an attempt to give minorities special privileges. For this reason, a growing field of whiteness studies expands multiculturalism to explore white experience as shaped by racial privilege.

Multiculturalism and critical whiteness studies have been attacked by those defending the triumphalist versions of U.S. identity and history and defending white privilege as the deserved norm. "We are being told by those fundamentally opposed to the democratization of society and of the academy that multicultural education 'dilutes the national identity,' 'weakens the canon,' and 'fragments a common Americanness,' or as Arthur Schlesinger Jr. put it, leads to the 'disuniting of America,' " (Thompson and Tyagi 1993, xiv, xvii). Conservatives depict multiculturalists as "having taken over the academy as they insinuate doctrinaire policies and political perspectives into the 'vulnerable' minds of 'innocent' students" (Thompson and Tyagi 1993, xv).

Yet most of us who are educators have "trouble recognizing [our] own experiences in these descriptions of university classrooms" (Thompson and Tyagi 1993, xv). The student narratives that form the core of this book document and testify to the preposterousness of such claims. These students set the record straight: they give voice to the real silencing that has occurred. The multiculturalists and feminists labeled "thought police" and accused of having taken over the universities are instead fighting daily and tirelessly for a little piece of the pie, for modest goals like the creation of ethnic and women's studies programs, one-course diversity requirements, curriculum integration workshops, funding to hire faculty of color, and mentoring programs for women and faculty of color struggling to survive.

While our classrooms are becoming increasingly multiracial, "changes in the ranks of professors are not keeping pace with student demographics" (Williams et al. 1999, 249). Thompson and Tyagi note that "most colleges and university faculties in the United States still include less than five percent people of color," and there has been little progress over the past few decades (Thompson and Tyagi 1993, xvi). Clearly, there has been no hostile takeover. Yet the distorted myth propagated by the conservative backlash and embraced by the mainstream media is far too familiar and passes for reality far too often. For example, men's movement author Aaron Kipnis rails,

> At last count there were over 600 academic women's studies programs, yet not a single one examining . . . men in our society. There are about 15,000 courses devoted to women's studies, yet only 91 courses on men's studies . . . in this increasingly antimale academic environment. In many instances, male-affirming voices on campus are actually repressed by feminists. . . . indoctrination still takes precedent. (Kipnis 1995, 282–83)

Kipnis here describes a conspiratorial academic environment where feminists are in control and gender inequality is a relic of the past. Similarly, conservative columnist John Leo argues in a recent issue of *U.S. News and World Report,*

> The American campus has become a chilly place for males. The American campus is very different from what it was 15 or 20 years ago—heavily politicized, doctrinaire, obsessed with race and gender, contemptuous of all things white and Western [taken over by] the West-bashing multiculturalists and male-bashing campus feminists. (Leo 1999, 19)

When I read these quotations in professional conferences, my colleagues often respond with laughter, and we wonder where this school is that these authors describe. Certainly no one I know has ever found it. What accounts for this dramatic difference in perception? As Johnson suggests,

> In systems of privilege, the focus is on dominant groups all the time as a matter of course, so much that it's never recognized as something special. Thus the slightest deviation can be perceived as a profound loss of privilege. (Johnson 2001, 111)

For example, research on classroom participation documents that when men dominate the discussion, gender participation is perceived as equitable. However, if women are responsible for as little as one-quarter to one-third of the interaction, "men perceive that women have taken over" (Johnson 2001, 111).

We find here a reversal of the reality of inequality. If gender bias were a thing of the past, then any attempts to aid women or minorities would seem to give them unfair advantages and attack white males. Both affirmative action and women's studies programs become depicted as attempts to privilege women and minorities. Whenever it is assumed that white men receive no special power or privilege from the structures of contemporary society, the balance of power becomes reversed, and all attempts to remedy inequality get redefined as attacks against white men, instances of "reverse discrimination."

The narratives in this book reveal the disturbingly dangerous consequences of this narrowly defined education for students. The above debates are by "no means only conceptual; they reveal and perpetuate the articulated hierarchy in intrapsychic, educational, social, historical, and political relations that have very serious consequences indeed" (Minnich 1990, 160). Simply denying that race matters any longer and trying to erase our racist past from history will not get the country far in eliminating racism. Yet, as we saw earlier, for white students, an introduction to diversity and increased interracial contacts may lead to different paths. For many students this may precipitate a journey to explore race and ethnicity as it structures our lives and experiences. Yet the direction of that journey is not guaranteed. Some white people may take the opportunity to work for social justice while others may experience a profound threat to their sense of privilege and entitlement that leads to reactionary behavior.

Perhaps the most overt obstacle we face in promoting social change is the resistance of white people. If dominant groups really saw privilege and oppression as a problem, it would be much easier to combat. Excluding those white people who can only be described as prejudiced, the remaining whites do not see privilege as a problem for the following reasons: they don't know it exists; they don't have to; they see racism as purely an individual problem; they do not want to relinquish their privilege; or they are afraid (Johnson 2001).

How do we get increasing numbers of white people—in the workplace or in an educational setting—first to "see" whiteness and then to help construct a multicultural environment? Organizational diversity consultant Daniel Distelhorst addresses this issue in the following section, "A Problem Seeing."

A PROBLEM SEEING
by Daniel Distelhorst

Why is it so difficult for most white people to accept as real the effects of personal and institutional racism laid out so clearly in this book? The problem is their inability to see.

While I cannot speak for all white people, I can speak from my own experience and from my place in society. As a tall, white, educated, upper-socioeconomic, heterosexual male, I am situated in a very different place than most of the students of color who speak in this book. I do not experience what they experience. I do receive unearned privilege relative to them. Until just a few years ago, it was very difficult for me to see and accept their experience as real or to acknowledge my privilege. I too denied racism and defended what I thought to be an overall fair and equitable system of meritocracy. I assumed that everything I accomplished was based solely on my own efforts and that I was competing fairly. It wasn't that I saw unfairness and then consciously chose to deny it; like most white people, I literally didn't *see* it.

Ironically, most white people deeply believe in the values of fairness and equality and would take action to correct situations of inequity—if they "saw" them. The problem is that most white people do not experience the things described in this book; it doesn't happen to them. They do not experience the effects of personal and institutional racism directly so they usually remain unaware of the unearned privilege that racist systems confer on them. They also do not usually understand the negative effects racism has on them. They have rarely given any thought at all to what it means to be white in this society.

It is hard to underestimate the strength of white denial and defensiveness around the issue of racism. David Wellman (1993) suggests that this is because most white Americans subconsciously realize that the racial advantages they have traditionally enjoyed are now threatened. If they accept racism as real, then they are compelled to level the playing field in order to preserve their sense of fairness, but to their relative disadvantage. They resolve this dilemma by minimizing racism in various ways, since if racism is minimal, then they as whites don't have to make basic changes in lifestyle, power, or prestige. Even a relatively unprejudiced white person can hold this perspective, and it sets up a difficult barrier to breach.

In my work, as I deal with white resistance to seeing racial privilege, I also face a deeper question: How can I get through to white people about why they *personally* should engage with diversity issues and be willing to change them-selves? It's a question I have considered with my diversity colleagues; I have scanned the literature for answers and reflected on in my own journey. For me, some of the best explanations come from Janet Helms (1992), who provides a model that is a useful map of that journey. Although real life is never as linear and predictable as any stage theory, Helms's model resonates well with my own, and many other white people's, experience. Here is a summary of the process of development—white racial identity development—that she describes:

Contact. Whites pay little attention to their racial identity. They perceive themselves as color-blind and completely free of prejudice. They are unaware of their own assumptions about other racial groups and think of racism as the prejudiced behaviors of individuals.

Disintegration. With a growing awareness of racism and white privilege, whites feel the discomfort of guilt, shame, and anger. They now notice societal inequities that contradict their idea of U.S. meritocracy, and, once aware, they become zealous in wanting to work against racism.

Reintegration. They face social pressure from friends to not notice racism, and they may become angry at people of color; because they grow frus-trated at being characterized as part of a group, whites often respond to others who point out white privilege by stating, "I'm an individual."

Pseudo-Independent. having gained an intellectual understanding of racism as a system of advantage, white people may commit themselves to unlearn their racism. The feeling of "guilty white liberal" may come upon people who do not know what to do about racism, or they escape guilt about whiteness by associating with people of color.

Immersion/Emersion. At this stage of the process, individuals recognize the need for a more positive self-definition as a white person. In working for social change, they may see the need to work with other whites less further along in the process, to become allies with people of color and speak up against systems of oppression, and to challenge other whites to do the same.

Autonomy. These people have incorporated a newly defined positive white identity into their personal identity, learned how to act with increased effectiveness in a multiracial setting, and pursue an increasingly multiracial and multicultural existence.

Most of us who are white start out in Janet Helms's first stage, contact: we don't think much at all about what it means to be white. We perceive ourselves as color-blind and without much prejudice. We tend to define racism as the vicious acts of individuals, not a system of unearned privilege that directly advantages us personally. By defining racism that way, we are able to distance ourselves from it.

Moving into stage 2, disintegration, is the most difficult and important step for most white people, going from denial to awareness. In the disintegration stage white people become aware of racism and white privilege, and they begin to notice inequities that stand in stark contrast to the system of meritocracy they have always taken for granted and considered fair and impartial. Some event or experience usually triggers moving out of denial into seeing, so this is rarely just an intellectual exercise. I literally moved out of my previously white male organizational culture, going from a computer firm to a health care firm and beginning studying for a Ph.D. For the first time my organizational cultures were 70–80 percent female and had different unwritten rules. In my Ph.D. program, the females I now interacted with were not deferential to males. All of a sudden, my previously unconscious male way of being wasn't always appreciated or deferred to. It was both a shock and a wakeup call and started me on Helms's journey toward white racial identity development, here starting with gender. The awareness I gradually acquired about gender dynamics and inequities became a leverage point for my learning about the other isms.

Even though most white people now work side by side with people of color, they still have difficulty seeing the systems in their organizations that confer privilege on white employees, and the same dynamics of denial are in place. In most organizations in the United States, white people need to do deep personal diversity work. Otherwise they will never truly see the racist processes in their institution and begin to strive for an organizational culture that works for all and in which all can work effectively together. (By "deep personal diversity work" I mean engaging with these issues in depth, over time, and very personally, not just intellectually.) Unless white people personally "get it," they will never support the creation of cultural and organizational diversity. Instead, they may support the all-too-frequent backlash that comes as an aftershock to much diversity work. So we have a catch-22 situation. Without deep personal diversity work, white people can't see why they should engage in personal change in regard to diversity. Yet without clear and compelling motivation, they won't engage in deep personal diversity work.

The question becomes, What can motivate white people to make the journey worth the painful personal change? Somehow they must come to believe that the pain of not changing is worse than the pain of changing.

Will explaining the "business case" for diversity be enough? In my experience, white people who buy into the business case for diversity will begin to give rhetorical support for diversity efforts and may even begin to require diversity work by others under them in the organization, but that rarely seems to be enough motivation for them to personally engage in deep diversity work. Will appealing to their basic sense of fairness work? Perhaps for some, but it's hard for them to see the unfairness and inequities until they've undergone personal change in their grasp of racism and understanding of white privilege. In my experience, when white people do finally *see* the inequities, they do begin the journey, but it's very hard to *see* white privilege and racial imbalance initially.

A week is a bare minimum for deep personal diversity work. The challenge here is getting people to devote an entire week to a single purpose. One colleague of mine reports success with white people by immersing them in an intense three-day workshop, but the people who attend are already some of the more committed. There are some white people in organizations who, for whatever personal reasons, have engaged in personal diversity work and do get it. They can look for "leverage point" people. Some might be employers in the most pain from employee complaints; perhaps they have faced lawsuits from people of color and women because of their harmful, albeit unintentional, actions. They may become open to change, but they may also become even more defensive.

What is the best way to get white people to engage in diversity work? There is no simple answer. Looking for any and all entry points that might work seems to be the only feasible strategy.

Who should work with these white people to encourage them to begin their diversity journey? I argue that the primary responsibility for such work rests on other white people, not people of color, who are often expected to explain the unequal distribution of privilege to whites, only to be told they are oversensitive when they try. It's time for white people to educate other white people directly or in partnership with people of color. It's time for white people to be seen and heard speaking out, standing alone or beside people of color as allies and partners. It's time for aware white people to help, encourage, support, and even persuade unaware whites to raise their consciousness about a reality different from their own.

Once whites have become aware of a very different reality, most will experience some pain before they move on to stages 3–6. Discovering that you, personally, have unearned privilege relative to others is a very painful realization and violates two fundamental lifelong assumptions: that you have earned everything strictly on your merits and talents alone and that you have had no unfair advantage but have been competing fairly. This new version of reality bothers you, since your sense of fairness has been violated. As you begin to engage with others different from you in new ways, you encounter their rage for the first time. Because you seem to be one of the few white people willing to listen and learn, people of color risk telling you their stories, and with those stories can come a great deal of previously unexpressed rage.

You begin to feel very guilty about the inequities you now see. You feel bad about being a white person and thus bad about yourself. (In my case, I felt very bad about being a white male and remember thinking at one point that we should be banished to some place where we could do no further harm to so many others, including white females.) On a more positive note, you now engage in the difficult, always painful work of changing yourself. You reexamine your ways of being and make changes for the better, and conversely sometimes you relax and revert to old behaviors. The whole process is an exhausting one. But it begins to move you through stages 3–6 of Janet Helms's model.

Books such as this one offer white readers insight into a reality different from their own. Through the stories of these students of color, they can see, in ways they normally could not, personal and institutional racism through the eyes of the people directly affected by it. Since the book offers this analysis in the non-threatening form of personal stories, white readers who are ready and willing to learn may put aside their defenses more easily to find answers to a question that people at stage 2 often have: How can I learn about all this if people of color won't educate me? Raising their awareness of the realities of both personal and institutional racism might lead white readers to grasp that the playing field is not level, that people in the United States are not treated fairly and equitably. This realization may engage their deeply held values of fairness and equality; the cognitive dissonance created by this conflict between the newly seen reality and the deeply held values will move most white readers to change and action. "Seeing" will begin a journey away from racism toward embracing diversity.

SEEING WHITENESS IN THE CLASSROOM

At the college level, how do we raise white students' racial awareness in the classroom? Various approaches have proven successful, and they all attempt to have students grasp some of the points Distelhorst raised: (1) we have never had a level playing field, not even now, and (2) white people's lives are shaped by their racial privilege.

With useful advice for teachers, Beverly Daniel Tatum identifies the most common sources of resistance among students in her courses:

> 1. Race is considered a taboo topic for discussion, especially in racially mixed settings. 2. Many students, regardless of racial-group membership, have been socialized to think of the United States as a just society. 3. Many students, particularly White students, initially deny any personal prejudice, recognizing the impact of racism on other people's lives, but failing to acknowledge its impact on their own. (Tatum 1992, 5)

Tatum suggests that instructors consider teaching students models of how racial identity is formed (she discusses mainly the racial identity formation of whites and blacks). Despite the limitations and over-generalizations inherent in any such model, such a pedagogical approach may provide students with ways to understand themselves in relation to their classmates, family, and friends. Tatum provides an overview of racial identity development for blacks and whites in "Talking about Race, Learning about Racism: The Application of Racial Identity Development Theory in the Classroom." She outlines four strategies to reduce student resistance and foster an inclusive learning environment:

The creation of a safe classroom atmosphere by establishing clear guidelines for discussion

The creation of opportunities for self-generated knowledge

The provision of an appropriate developmental model that students can use as a framework for understanding their own process

The exploration of strategies to empower students as change agents

Sociology professor Mia Tuan, who teaches about race at the University of Oregon, has found, like Tatum, that learning to see whiteness can be very difficult for many white students. In her classes, she aims to get students to "step outside their comfort zone, with the instructor providing safety. They are required to turn in a weekly memo with their reaction to whatever has come up in class, their take on it, their personal hit on the readings, class discussions, ideas that they can relate to all this" (Tuan 2000). Tuan also uses a mandatory weekly discussion group, with trained facilitators studying to be counselors; here students are encouraged to talk openly about race, including what they feel about the issues raised in class, in a safe environment with mediators. Tuan began using these discussion groups after her first year of teaching, when there was an explosion in class and she realized she needed to turn that into a learning experience, both for herself and her students.

Tuan's theory in doing this is that race is a contentious issue, and pain and emotion are part of the process of really learning about race, not just an academic topic. She feels that teachers have to normalize the experience of heavy emotion that often emerges in courses on race, offering safeguards and a way to diffuse it: "You have to deal with emotional issues because they are not very far under the surface in terms of the process of race in the US, and people have certain emotional investments in taking on the knowledge of how race works, or protecting themselves from that knowledge" (Tuan 2000). Her experience supports the theory of racial identity development; she finds that many students seek to return to the safety of ignorance.

Tuan warns students upon entering class that they will move out of their comfort zones fast. She has found it useful to teach Beverly Tatum's *Why Are All the Black Kids Sitting Together in the Cafeteria? And Other Conversations about Race*, based on the developmental process that majority and minority students go through in developing their racial identity. Tuan addresses whiteness up front and at the beginning. She tells the class that most students are starting from a culture shaped by a predominantly white perspective and set of experiences, which will inevitably shape students' expectations and reactions to the class. In her course syllabus for the class Toward Understanding Contemporary Race Relations, she provides a list of the course's operating assumptions:

1. There is no such thing as a "pure" race. All racial categories are socially constructed ones whose boundaries have less to do with biology than one might think— Social and political and economic factors are amazingly salient in determining the permeability and configuration of these boundaries. Rather than fixed or static, then, racial categories are dynamic.

2. We learn how to "do" race. That is, we learn the rules surrounding race, the meanings associated with each race, what boundaries are salient, etc.

3. Whites and people of color typically undergo very different processes in leaning how to "do" race.

4. While ethnocentric tendencies are natural, racism and racial prejudice are not. The latter are *perversions* of this natural tendency that serve a useful *function* in justifying the domination of some groups for material and/or psychological advantage.

5. Racism is a *system* involving both individual and institutional acts, can be both intentional as well as unintended, and is pernicious because it develops a life of its own even beyond the group who first established the power dynamic.

6. Our race relations can best be described as involving both progress and setbacks: "Two steps forward, one step back. Three steps forward, two back." It is not either/or however. A balanced perspective is the hardest to maintain but most necessary for long-term racial healing.

7. Race matters. It mattered in the past, matters today, and most likely will matter in our future.

8. Colorblind-ness is not the ultimate goal but rather color "relativeness." Henry Louis Gates Jr. put it best with this reflection: How would it be "to experience a humanity that is neither colorless nor reducible to color. Bach and James Brown. Sushi and fried catfish?" (Tuan 2000)

Courses on race are always potentially volatile. If an explosion occurs in class, Tuan asks students to sit and write for a few minutes describing their reaction. If she receives a hostile response in class or in one of the weekly memos, she raises the issue respectfully and anonymously to the class: "What is the context that this is coming from? Don't dismiss this. We all know this kind of idea is in the air around us. What do you all think of this?" (Tuan 2000). The identity of the students who write the responses are protected, yet this strategy enables the class to deal with those members' reactions. Tuan does not treat the deliverer of the message as the problem, but the message itself. She employs other techniques as well: she asks what a specific author the class has read might say to this; how many in the room have had a similar experience; how to deal with and reach your relatives or others who say racist things, and so on. Because she is interested in developmental models and stages of racial identity formation, she sometimes asks students about a narrative: Where does this character fit into the structure that Tatum describes? Or, if a white person at this stage is talking to a person of color at another very different stage in the developmental model that Tatum describes, how might they each respond to a certain issue or statement?

Professor Charles Gallagher, who specializes in the study of whiteness, broaches these issues a bit differently in his classes at Georgia State University. He has used his research on white college students to develop an approach for discussing race in the classroom. He points out that while whites usually view whiteness as normative and universal, when he interviewed "whites about what their race and ethnic identity meant to them, respondents got defensive about racial inequality: they suddenly became ethnic by drawing on their ancestors' immigration experience" (Gallagher 2000). By raising the history of white ethnic groups, these students construct a version of history in which white experience is equivalent to that of peoples of color. In this way, racism and discrimination become defined as a part of (just about) *everyone's* past, and white ethnic groups are defined as having "made it" due to their hard work and strong values alone. As Gallagher puts it, this "off-the-boat and up-to-the-suburbs success story provided some whites with a safe rhetorical space to champion a philosophy of color-blind universalism, rather then the racial particularism many whites associate with identity politics" (Gallagher 2000).

This perspective champions the view of America as a meritocracy—anyone who tries hard can achieve the American dream—and ends up blaming the victims for their own failure to succeed. This argument often supports the anti–affirmative action narrative, in which white ethnics succeed without any government support, and people of color are inherently deficient and responsible for their own lack of mobility. Gallagher explores this deployment of the "ethnic card" by whites as an attempt "to maintain racial privilege" without appearing racist. This historical revisionism attempts to equate "the real discrimination white ethnics were temporarily subjected to upon arrival to the United States" and the "three centuries of slavery, Jim Crow, legal segregation and state sanctioned 'benign neglect.' Within this perspective, reconstructed as the social equivalent of being black or Asian, whites are able to maintain the fiction that every group, regardless of color, has been equally victimized by racial and ethnic prejudice" (Gallagher 2000).

How does Gallagher work through these "ethnic myths" with his students? He "takes a walk down history lane." Gallagher covers the history of specific white ethnic and minority racial groups, with which most students are unfamiliar. After acquiring a firm foundation in history, including the conditions of voluntary and forced immigration, as well as forced removal from ancestral lands, students are better equipped to honestly compare the histories, living conditions, and experiences of different race and ethnic groups. Although various white ethnic groups, such as the Irish and Jews, faced discrimination and exclusionary practices, their experiences differed qualitatively and quantitatively from those of African Americans, Native Americans, Chicanos/Chicanas and Latinos/Latinas, and Asian Americans.

"I'm able to demonstrate that everyone did start at the bottom when they 'came' to the United States," explains Gallagher, "but the bottom was not the same for everyone. This follows with a discussion of when a group was able to get a foot on the first rung of the mobility ladder—for the Irish it was almost immediate" (Gallagher 2000). His class explores the occupational segregation of race and ethnic groups at various points in U.S. history, and the consequences this had for each group's upward mobility: "For example, what did it mean for blacks to be excluded from union jobs until the 1950s? What did it mean that the Irish in Boston, NYC, and Philadelphia controlled the unions? In short, I try to get students to see that inequality today reflects how the rules of the game were set up yesterday" (Gallagher 2000).

In my own classes, I utilize an approach similar to aspects of both Tuan's and Gallagher's. I spend time teaching the idea that race is a social construction, since this is usually a new concept for students. We explore examples of historical and cross-cultural variation in the construction of racial classifications, as well as the problems these classifications lead to. For example, many of my students are multiracial, and so they particularly enjoy reading about the experiences of other multiracial Americans who find they do not fit into our classification system.

As we move to an explicit focus on whiteness, I begin by having students compile a list of white privileges that white people experience. This exercise is adapted from Peggy McIntosh's important article on white privilege about unpacking the "invisible knapsack," which students read after the exercise (McIntosh 1998). The majority of my students are white, and they are always quite amazed to discover the ways in which race shapes white people's lives. This is usually a very enlightening experience for them and leads into a discussion of Gallagher's point, that even white ethnics have always been privileged relative to nonwhites. There is a wide variety of readings that may be employed to address these issues (see appendix), and I have found one particularly helpful: "How Did Jews Become White Folks?" by Karen Brodkin Sacks. In this succinct article, Sacks explores the changing racial identity of Jews and highlights the tremendous government assistance white ethnics received, for example, as a result of the GI Bill and other policies, which benefited white servicemen but excluded others. This history is unfamiliar to most of us, but it helps combat the myth of white ethnics' pulling themselves up by their bootstraps. It can also contribute to a discussion of affirmative action by reflecting on special government assistance to white people. In short, there are many resources available for teaching about racial identity and whiteness, and teachers have begun to learn from each other what works and what doesn't. Additionally, scholars are bridging the gap between research and teaching, using the insights of recent research on whiteness and white identity to develop more successful teaching methodologies.

CONCLUSION

This book provides the reader with a microcosm of the debates and issues shaping U.S. society today. It deals with not just education but, more broadly, the politics of U.S. identity. Other debates over bilingual education, affirmative action, immigration and immigrant rights, and equal rights for gays and lesbians must engage the same core issues.

As Henry Giroux points out, race shapes the lives of everyone. The narratives in this book not only provide a powerful glimpse into the daily experiences of college students of color but reveal much about whiteness as well. Giroux argues that we must "make problematic how 'whiteness' as a racial identity and social construction is taught, learned, experienced, and identified in certain forms of knowledge, values, and privileges" (Giroux 1997, 296). A great deal of contemporary scholarship on whiteness has highlighted the ways in which whiteness masquerades as neutral, universal, and unmarked: "both invisible to itself and at the same time the norm by which everything else is measured" (Giroux 1997, 305). For this reason, much can be learned about whiteness from the experiences and insights of people of color. While the recent explosion of scholarship on whiteness largely focuses on white people, people of color can provide a different perspective on whiteness as an institution, a culture, a set of values, and a social construction.

The student narratives in part 1 provide a case study of the ways in which Euro American values and knowledge are privileged and maintained within U.S. culture and schooling. The students' voices also provide us with some understanding of why the backlash has been so immediate and harsh: white backlash is partly a response to the "marking" of whiteness (Ferber 1998). The multicultural movement and the increased presence of students of color on campuses has had the effect of decentering and calling into question the assumptions of whiteness as invisible and neutral. Even very small victories toward increased diversity are perceived as profoundly threatening and destabilizing, and thus they have the potential to propel white people in different directions, toward formulating very different kinds of response.

As the sociological research demonstrates, the broader academic environment is key to promoting either interracial hostility or harmony. Hu-DeHart argues that "if we are not to repeat the sad history of excluding nonwhite Americans from the Jeffersonian pursuit of happiness, then we educators have a crucial role to play, and multicultural education is part of the solution" (1993, 7).

We can learn from one another the kinds of programming and teaching methods that can help achieve an inclusive environment. For example, Arizona State University took a proactive position following a hate crime and near riot in 1989 (for a full discussion, see Fenske and Gordon 1998; Gordon 1991). Research has demonstrated that no single response is adequate, so various programs were proposed and implemented, including a cultural diversity requirement, the bolstering and further development of ethnic studies and women's studies programs (including degrees in Chicano/a studies, women's studies, and soon African American studies), accompanied by interdisciplinary curriculum development, African American–themed campus housing, the creation of racial and ethnic minority student associations and organizations, faculty development workshops and initiatives, a newly created Social Justice Award, increased resources for minority student and faculty recruitment, an annual racial climate survey, and grants allocated for the development of campus programs and activities to decrease racial tension and support improved intergroup relations (Fenske and Gordon 1998; Gordon 1991). These programs require a significant commitment of funds from the university. While these programs at Arizona State met with resistance from some segments of the campus community, they have already shown signs of success: the number of minority students has risen and incidents of racial tension have decreased. This example demonstrates that universities need not resort to limiting academic freedom or free speech. The goals of Arizona State's policy strategy was to increase both academic freedom and cultural diversity at the same time. On the other hand, this example also demonstrates that there is no simple solution: to create an inclusive university climate that fosters positive intergroup relations requires real, ongoing university commitment and support (Fenske and Gordon 1998).

This chapter has highlighted the difficulty of directing white attention to racism and sustaining white commitment to antiracist practice. Although the business case for diversity may provide motivation, sociologist Allan G. Johnson argues that for those whites who undertake the journey to become aware of white privilege and institutional racism,

what can sustain them is a sense of ownership, that the trouble is truly their trouble and not someone else's, because this means that their responsibility to do something no longer feels like an option. . . . It is, quite simply, one of the terms of their participation in the world they live in." (Johnson 2001, 79)

How we go about creating an institutional climate that fosters this responsibility of all people to create a just social environment is the focus of the next chapter.

REFERENCES

Bell, Derrick. 1993. "Foreword: The Power of Prophet." In *Beyond a Dream Deferred: Multicultural Education and the Politics of Excellence,* edited by Thompson and Tyagi, ix–x. Cincinnati: Anderson.

"Black Student Receives Death Threat, Swastikas on Locker." 2000. *Northwest Update,* February 1.

Coppock, V., D. Haydon, and I. Richter. 1995. *The Illusions of "Postfeminism": New Women, Old Myths.* London: Taylor & Francis.

Duke, David. 1999. *My Awakening.* Covington, La.: Free Speech Press.

Fenske, Robert H., and Leonard Gordon. 1998. "Reducing Racial and Ethnic Hate Crimes on Campus: The Need for Community." In A. Hoffman, J. Schuh, and R. Fenske, eds., *Violence on Campus: Defining the Problems, Strategies for Action.* Gaithersburg, Md.: Aspen.

Ferber, Abby L. 1998. *White Man Falling: Race, Gender, and White Supremacy.* Lanham, Md.: Rowman & Littlefield.

Gallagher, Charles. 1995. "White Reconstruction in the University." *Socialist Review* 24, no. 1–2: 165–87.

Gallagher, Charles. 2000. Personal e-mail correspondence with Abby Ferber, August.

Gibson, James William. 1994. *Warrior Dreams: Violence and Manhood in Post-Vietnam America.* New York: Hill & Wang.

Giroux, Henry A. 1997. "Racial Politics and the Pedagogy of Whiteness." In Mike Hall, ed., *Whiteness: A Critical Reader.* New York: New York University Press.

Gordon, Leonard. 1991. "Race Relations and Attitudes at Arizona State University." In Phillip G. Altbach and Kofi Lomotey, eds., *The Racial Crisis in American Higher Education.* Albany: State University of New York Press.

"Hate Goes to School." *Intelligence Report.* 2000. Spring. Published by the Southern Poverty Law Center.

Helms, Janet E. 1992. *A Race Is a Nice Thing to Have.* Topeka: Content Communications.

Hu-DeHart, Evelyn. 1993. "Rethinking America: The Practice and Politics of Multiculturalism in Higher Education." In Thompson and Tyagi, eds., *Beyond a Dream Deferred: Multicultural Education and the Politics of Excellence.* Minneapolis: University of Minnesota Press.

Jacobson, Matthew Frye. 1998. *Whiteness of a Different Color: European Immigrants and the Alchemy of Race.* Cambridge: Harvard University Press.

Johnson, Allen G. 2001. *Privilege, Power, and Difference.* Mountain View, Calif.: Mayfield.

Kent, Noel Jacob. 1998. "The New Campus Racism: What's Going On?" In Adalberto Aguirre Jr. and David Baker, eds., *Notable Selections on Race and Ethnicity.* 2d ed. New York: McGraw-Hill.

Kipnis, Aaron. 1995. "The Postfeminist Men's Movement. In M. S. Kimmel, ed., *The Politics of Manhood.* Philadelphia: Temple University Press.

Leo, John. 1999. "Empty College Syndrome." *U.S. News and World Report.* April 19, 19.

McIntosh, Peggy. 1998. "White Privilege and Male Privilege: A Personal Account of Coming to See Correspondences through Work in Women's Studies." In *Race, Class, and Gender: An Anthology.* Edited by Margaret L. Anderson and Patricia Hill Collins. Belmont, Calif.: Wadsworth.

Minnich, Elizabeth Kamarck. 1990. *Transforming Knowledge*. Philadelphia: Temple University Press.

Myrdal, Gunnar. 1944. *An American Dilemma: The Negro Problem and Modern Democracy*. New York: Harper.

Reskin, Barbara. 1998. *The Realities of Affirmative Action in Employment*. Washington, D.C.: American Sociological Association.

Rhea, Joseph Tilden. 1997. *Race Pride and the American Identity*. Cambridge: Harvard University Press, 1997.

Sacks, Karen Brodkin, 1994. "How Did Jews Become White Folks?" In Steven Gregory and Roger Sanjek, eds., *Race*, 78–102. Rutgers University Press.

Schaeffer, Richard T. 2000. *Racial and Ethnic Groups*. 8th ed. New Jersey: Prentice Hall.

Tatum, Beverly Daniel. 1992. "Talking about Race, Learning about Racism: The Application of Racial Identity Development Theory in the Classroom." *Harvard Educational Review* 62, no. 1: 1–24.

Tatum, Beverly Daniel. 1999. *"Why Are All the Black Kids Sitting Together in the Cafeteria?" and Other Conversations about Race*. New York: Basic.

Thompson, Becky W., and Sangeeta Tyagi, eds. 1993. *Beyond a Dream Deferred: Multicultural Education and the Politics of Excellence*. Minneapolis: University of Minnesota Press.

Tuan, Mia. 2000. Interview by Julia Lesage, September.

Wellman, David 1993. Portraits of White Racism. Cambridge: Cambridge University Press.

Williams, Joyce E., Lisa Garza, Amitra A. Hodge, and Anissa Breaux. 1999. "The Color of Teachers, the Color of Students: The Multicultural Classroom Experience." *Teaching Sociology*, July, 233–51.

Williams, Patricia. 1997. *Seeing a Colorblind Future: The Paradox of Race*. New York: Noonday.

Conclusion: This Is Only the Beginning

Abby L. Ferber and Donna Wong

Making a Difference seeks to provide universities and workplaces with the insider perspective that only people of color can provide. At the same time, we argue that white people must accept responsibility for educating themselves. All people must become involved, accepting responsibility for improving the racial climate of the work environment and social setting of the places in which they study and work. Our institutions cannot expect people of color to continue to educate white people, setting aside their own lives and making themselves more vulnerable and at risk. We hope this book will serve as a tool for classrooms, student groups, faculty committees, administrators, community organizations, and workplaces to begin exploring the experiences of people of color, investigating their own racial climate, and formulating a more equitable environment. We have more resources, ideas, and models than ever before, and the horizon is full of possibilities.

In this concluding chapter we explore the most pressing obstacles confronting us in creating multicultural environments. We also discuss workable strategies that can be implemented to help create inclusive environments. Previous chapters highlighted pertinent areas needing change and identified the kinds of problems that persist as roadblocks to an inclusive learning environment in higher education. The problems can certainly seem monstrous and overwhelming at times, and may leave individuals feeling helpless in trying to reshape their institutions. However, as scholars and activists familiar with research, new programs, and policy development around equity issues, we see the future as hopeful.

Although individuals working for change may feel isolated, there is a huge network of academicians and diversity workers that can be accessed for support. Furthermore, we have a plethora of research about and models for effective practices that have already been implemented and tested and can guide our ongoing efforts. Next we describe a number of models and examples that can assist readers in creating necessary change in their own workplaces, as well as provide further direction and resources to guide this process.

COLLABORATIVE STRATEGIES

Successful diversity initiatives and strategies have been established in numerous colleges and workplaces over the past decade. Here we will highlight some of the most successful strategies and participatory standards that are helping to transform traditional higher educational institutions into multicultural campuses. To transform a traditional environment into a multicultural environment is labor intensive and requires long-term maintenance and commitment. According to research by Sergiovanni and Starratt, an innovation may take fifty years to become institutionalized in an educational setting. Another study by K. Manning and P. Coleman-Boatwright argues:

> The all pervasive presence of the dominant culture in the organizational structure works against progress toward multiculturalism. The realities are not causes for discouragement but, rather, sources of understanding about the need for empowerment, policy making, and goal advancement. The process must be rooted in long-term organizational development to achieve multiculturalism. (367–74)

While attitudes in higher education have clearly progressed to embrace diversity in light of our growing multicultural workplace and global society, resistance still persists. To counter such resistance, the social capital of cultural change agents must be strengthened in number and momentum to achieve long-term diversity goals. Unfortunately the vocal minority who resist such change often frame the issue as a debate between two equal sides, which is not the case.

As we have argued throughout this book, crafting an inclusive environment is both necessary and beneficial. To counter the negative voices that resist taking the steps to create such an environment, it is especially important to point out that a variety of scholars have documented the ways multiculturalism is overwhelmingly supported by most people in an institution *and* has positive effects. For example, recent research has documented the following results (*Diversity Digest* Spring 2000):

- The great majority of faculty favor and value racial/ethnic diversity on campus.

- The majority of faculty and students in multiracial classes believe that the new range of perspectives and experience offered generates more critical and complex thinking skills among all students, and it has a positive effect on their cognitive and personal growth.
- Completion of a diversity course requirement toward graduation significantly reduces student prejudice.
- Diverse student populations have a direct, positive effect on white students' educational experience.
- Socializing across racial and ethnic lines and engaging in constructive, open discussions about race produce widespread positive effects on all students' academic and personal development.

In *The Multicultural Campus: Strategies for Transforming Higher Education*, Valverde and Castenell argue that the process of change must involve many participants. They compile the insights of administrators, faculty, and student affairs professionals recommending what is necessary for campus transformation to occur. The preponderance of responsibility lies with an institution's staff, faculty, and administration. While students have a great influence on diversity efforts, their relatively short stay at any given campus (approximately four years) limits their involvement in long-term action. Since staff, faculty, and administration are employed on campus and have more participation and networking, greater access to resources and institutional power, and a greater investment in the university, they are the ones who must actively carry out strategies to generate positive change in policy and climate. Indeed, an institution that depends on students for diversity efforts, especially if it only reacts at the moment of crisis and student process, will fail.

Leonard Valverde, who has served as professor, director of research, college dean, and academic vice president, suggests three connecting strategies for creating blueprints for social change: *mentoring, networking,* and *ad hoc relationships*. These strategies target three levels of governance and policy construction: the executive and procedural level, the faculty level, and the curricular level.

Mentoring must occur within and across the hierarchical levels in higher education, beginning top-down from governing board members to chancellors and presidents to department chairs to senior faculty to junior faculty to instructors/lecturers to students. Mentoring offers support by openly sharing information and advising others about one's job and responsibilities. In building a more diverse executive team, administrative leaders must mentor people of racially and culturally diverse backgrounds to give them an opportunity to learn and gain access to advancement and peer networks. Through mentoring, the pool for qualified, diverse candidates can be enlarged to fill open or new administrative and faculty positions. The establishment of mentoring networks specifically for people of color can help build a supportive environment for them, so that they wish to stay and participate in shaping the institution over the long term. This is important because a multicultural faculty and staff must be present to accommodate a multicultural student body. In particular, as the student narratives in *Making a Difference* demonstrate, faculty of color especially take on the role of mentoring students of color.

The second connecting strategy is *networking* among people of different ranks and levels of responsibility who come together to work on joint projects. Information sharing and collaborations occur through a wide exchange of perspectives, from students to regents to faculty on one campus and beyond. For example, committees formed on enrollment management often bring students, admissions officers, and financial aid staff together with local school district representatives to discuss outreach and admissions issues. Networking also helps counter isolation that minority faculty may experience in an academic setting. Faculty of color often build contacts with other faculty of color and other departments to produce new courses as well as gather funding to bring key diversity speakers to campus. This kind of collaboration plays a significant role in helping achieve diversity goals.

The third connecting strategy is the development of *ad hoc relationships* among various groups to form alliances on issues of common concern. For example, students frequently form coalitions, bringing together people of color with feminists, gays and lesbians, and local elected representatives to speak out on affirmative action issues. By bonding together and sharing resources, the larger group exerts greater influence and gains an enhanced credibility.

These three connecting strategies—mentoring, networking, and ad hoc relationships—play a role in the development and implementation of a unique, comprehensive, institution-wide recruitment and retention plan. There are many instructive models that can inform institution-wide strategizing, but ideally an institution should develop its own diversity recruitment/retention plan. To do this, it brings into the dialogue its own set of complexities—such as racial demographics, social history, student activism, and faculty resistance. Forming a campus committee with broad representation from students, departments, and other constituencies can produce a strategy that includes specific diversity missions, objectives, tasks, and timelines. But the goal must always be to ensure the greatest possible consensus. For this reason, these kinds of institutional planning committees should involve people from all corners of the campus, top-down, horizontally, and diagonally. Leadership on the committees must be shared among campus constituents so that all parties feel their input is valued.

One example of a model for achieving campus diversity is the Minority Student Persistence Model (Swail and Holmes 2000), based on an extensive review of current literature about retention and activities that have a direct impact on students of color. This research-based, five-component retention framework provides both collaborative and practical activities and suggests effective policies for enhancing student diversity. The goal is to overcome compartmentalized thinking in planning for a multicultural campus. For example, in the past, student affairs administrators and practitioners tended to think within their own boxes (i.e., offices, programs, departments) and specialization. They tended not to address the wider comprehensive approach that is necessary to achieving and maintaining diversity.

The Persistence Model provides a series of concrete objectives for each campus to consider in developing its own institutional diversity plan. It calls for planning and action in relation to the following five components—financial aid office, admissions office, academic services, curriculum and instruction leaders (faculty), and student affairs services; the model points out how those working at these institutional levels can best collaborate to achieve common goals. Briefly summarized below, the Persistence Model's menu of collaborative and cooperative practices center on access issues, as well as campus and curriculum modifications that enhance the academic and social environment.

First, the financial aid office must disseminate information to minority high school and transfer students, increase availability of need-based aid, and be creative and sensitive in offering financial aid packages to freshman students.

Second, the admissions office must establish precollege "bridge" programs, alternative assessment methods (a revision of selection criteria), high school/alma mater visitations, on-campus living orientation, and freshman orientation courses.

Third, academic services must develop proactive academic advising, bridging programs for high school seniors, a variety of precollege programs to create an educational pipeline from elementary school to college, and mentoring programs between faculty and students. Diversity in instruction, supplementary instruction, or academic support would be part of the collaborative focus at the beginning of the student of color's college stay, as would career counseling for juniors and seniors.

The fourth branch of the framework involves a committee on curriculum and instruction, on which faculty critique both instructional practices and course curricula in terms of being current, global, and inclusive; they should also acknowledge different learning styles. Incentives and resources must be provided to faculty for transforming the curriculum and mentoring students. As the student narratives in this book demonstrate, the importance of a comprehensive curriculum that integrates the study of women and people of color cannot be underestimated.

Finally, student services must develop diversity programming and activities addressing the needs of both traditional and nontraditional students. Housing issues such as affordability, a sense of comfort and security, cross-cultural matching of roommates, and food service should also be considered in this comprehensive retention model. Also, faculty-in-residence programs have proved a successful way to bridge student life concerns with academic mentoring.

This is one example of the kind of institutional plan for student diversity that universities need to adopt. A comprehensive plan needs to move beyond a focus on student diversity, however, to include recruitment and retention of faculty of color. From the highest levels of the administration must come a comprehensive strategic initiative, including a widely diffused mission statement, for creating an inclusive and equitable institution. In order to do so, leadership from the president's or chancellor's office is required. The formation of a cross-campus task force necessitates funding priorities, a faculty reward system to increase diversification of curriculum and instructional methods, and ultimately increased student–faculty interaction to meet student needs for academic and social integration.

The University of Arizona's Millennium Project provides us with yet another mode. The product of joint effort by the university president, Peter Likins, and faculty, the University of Arizona designed an ambitious project to evaluate campus climate and culture. According to the study's executive summary, "the aim of the Millennium Project is to enhance the development of an institutional culture at the University of Arizona that fosters productivity, creativity, and academic excellence." The yearlong qualitative and quantitative study identified campus strengths, as well as "aspects of the campus climate that must change to further the university's goal of achieving an academic environment that will allow all faculty, staff, and students to be productive and unhindered by any impediments due to considerations of gender, race/ethnicity, rank, or any other reason." Phase 1 of the study focused on faculty and phase 2, currently in process, focuses on staff. Women's faculty committees have conceived this comprehensive study, with the goal of expanding on the recent studies of women faculty at MIT and elsewhere, which found tremendous gender inequities. Since the MIT study, many university presidents across the nation have publicly committed themselves to addressing inequities on their campuses. The University of Arizona project built on this momentum and provides a unique model in its focus on campus culture for all faculty, as well as the widespread support and buy-in that was garnered from the administration, faculty, and broader community. The results of the study were released along with a series of creative proposals to address the inequities uncovered. Both the study itself and the innovative responses can serve as a model for other campuses. (For more information, see the Millennium Project Web site at ww.u.arizona.edu/~millen/index.html.)

KEEPING UP THE MOMENTUM: STUDENT RESOURCES

Institutionalized diversity committees need leadership to establish goals and program deadlines, and to maintain positive and frequent communication among members. Students have argued that accountability exists primarily if one person at the highest administrative level spearheads diversity initiatives and monitors progress toward goals. In response to their suggestions, some universities are establishing or reorganizing administrative positions, such as appointing a vice provost for diversity, as well as establishing faculty oversight committees, to take on this key role of directing diversity planning and increasing the university's commitment, visibility, and accountability around these issues. In addition, given the increased litigation over affirmative action in college admissions, some universities are appointing an admissions enrollment manager who is accountable for admissions numbers by race and ethnicity and for developing clear application standards for student admission. Another new leadership position is multicultural teaching and learning services coordinator. This person plans programs to enhance university teaching and workshops for faculty development, so that classroom teaching becomes both more inclusive content-wise and more responsive to the wide-ranging values, perspectives, and styles of a culturally diverse student body.

Without this kind of specifically designated leadership and clearly identified responsibilities, institutional mission statements can become empty rhetoric without leading to long-term action. Complacency, skepticism, and dysfunction can easily set in, draining creativity and driving away new participants in the change process. This is where students play a key role in effecting social change. Students are outspoken about "walking the talk." While student inclusion in diversity committees ensures expression of student perspectives and experiences, students are also establishing their own organizations to further diversity efforts. Through student-run initiatives, such as multicultural councils, students can collaborate with peers to propose suggestions, analyze existing policies and practices, and conduct their own action planning. For instance, by creating their own system of electing representatives within their ethnic organizations or student governments to serve as diversity recruiters and multicultural programming coordinators, students can institutionalize continued efforts on diversity matters. Organizational delegates to these student positions will then continue to work with admissions offices to reach out to minority communities and to develop events focusing on race and cultural programming. In this way, students of color and interested participants carry out diversity goals by passing on responsibilities and continuing projects from year to year. Furthermore, students have learned to cooperate and collaborate with their peers and faculty to question administrative policies, or nonaction on crucial issues, and to insist that student voices be attended to seriously.

The same "connecting" strategies mentioned earlier apply equally to student efforts along these lines. Students also mentor, network, and develop ad hoc relationships to achieve diversity goals. Mentoring among seniors and juniors and incoming first-year students of color already occurs at predominantly white campuses, contributing to new leadership and student retention. Furthermore, this kind of networking and developing ad hoc relations also leads many student associations across different college campuses to share ideas, resources, and strategies in accomplishing their mutual goals. In particular, many of these organizations see themselves as having a resistance function on campus and have become ever more organized and sophisticated in programming multicultural events as well as protests. For instance, students can easily turn to nonprofit organizations, such as Berkeley's Ruckus Society or Boston's Center for Campus Organizing, to gain nonviolence training, media campaign strategies, legal training, and action planning guidance. Many organizations, including specific ethnic coalition groups, have established Internet Web sites to promote diversity issues and build new communities among young people. At any point in time, e-mail announcements of local conferences as well as the organizing of protests can be publicized to all its members and to the media to gather support and numbers.

Higher education administrators should respect students' abilities and their high motivation to transform campuses into places that serve their academic and social goals, and to utilize it rather than begin short-lived initiatives to "put out the fire" that has elicited a student protest. In fact, as a campus student body becomes more diverse, there are bound to be more students enrolling with an activist background. It may be in human rights issues or environmental justice movements or gay and lesbian protests, but all these students bring high organizational skills that they can use, in coordination with students of color, to escalate pressure and, if necessary, employ civil disobedience tactics to mount protests.

On campuses that aim to foster amicable working relations to achieve goals that benefit the entire campus, students feel valued. On a much more mundane level of financial need, administrators know that students are increasingly identifying with their role as consumers, understanding their purchasing power in higher education. For whatever reason, administrators need to acknowledge that students appreciate the opportunity to sit at the table and face administrators on issues of policy decision making. As student Eric Ward argues in part 1 of this book, "We people of color are the ones who have answers for racism, yet the administration doesn't want us to do anything. If they did, they would support us more and make our struggle easier." Clearly many students of color do not feel that their input and experience is currently valued, yet the creativity and unique insight that students can bring to the planning process can have an important impact.

LEARNING FROM ONE ANOTHER

Those of us involved in this process of trying to create a more welcoming and diverse environment have learned one important lesson—we must learn from each other's experience. In this section, each of us offers some insights gained while struggling with these issues in higher education. As our individual stories demonstrate, networking has proven to be the key to avoiding some of the pitfalls and obstacles that invariably occur and to developing more successful strategies. As a multicultural affairs administrator, Donna's experience differs dramatically from Abby's faculty perspective, yet both of us can shed light on some methods used on campuses struggling with diversity issues. Donna's experience working in campus efforts for social change reveal some of the barriers she has encountered as well as programs that have been particularly successful. In particular, she has seen the importance of the following: the contribution of faculty/administrators of color, mentoring relationships and burnout, the role of multicultural offices, appointing specific offices and administrators with the responsibility for initiating and assessing diversity efforts across campus, the dilemmas they often confront, and the role of students in creating social change. Abby's experience within two disciplines, sociology and women's studies, reveals how curriculum can best be transformed to include diverse cultural perspectives. From a faculty point of view, she pinpoints the ongoing efforts needed to create and implement new multicultural courses, including the dilemmas, pressures, and obstacles faculty face while teaching full course loads and working toward tenure and promotion.

Donna Wong

I have been a college instructor and an academic counselor for the past thirteen years. I am currently an administrative professional in multicultural student affairs at Emory University in Atlanta, Georgia. My knowledge of my racial and ethnic identity and of the issues within the community of students of color has made me a more effective student affairs professional and has enriched my personal relations. As a person of color who assists students of color navigating through the college experience, I don't have special social antennae that tune into students of color. But I do *relate* to students of color by focusing on their situation from their perspective. I understand the barriers and obstacles that may put them at risk, make their college experience uncomfortable, and threaten their chances for graduation. I step in to help support them as they solve their issues and to advocate for them when necessary.

Reaching out and relating to students draws on my own awareness of racial identity and my pride in identifying as a person of color. In this era, considering this country's history, race is always an issue for people of color. Drawing on my personal experiences, I openly discuss with students the barriers and challenges as well as the opportunities that exist. I remember struggling through college, often feeling discouraged and directionless without anyone to turn to for guidance. In particular, any brushes of prejudice in school brought about mixed feelings of anger, shame, inferiority, and loss of dignity. It took me many years of life experience after college to form a stronger sense of self and to see where I could make a positive contribution to other people's lives. Consequently, in the role I play in student affairs at a level of power and authority, I view students of color as capable and stellar. But I know that my perception is not shared among all faculty, staff, and students. I use my role to provide encouragement and validation, especially by treating all students with respect, dignity, and trust, and by recognizing them as unique individuals. I see my main function as listening and providing the assistance necessary for them to overcome barriers and advance to the next stage.

What is also compelling in terms of my job is that I have experienced a dual cultural identity, which means I have ties to my Chinese heritage, traditions, and values yet am also heavily influenced by mainstream U.S. culture and values. Such diverse cultural "pushes and pulls" that students of color experience may not be recognized by a Euro American administrator, and in fact needed support is not usually provided to help students address these kinds of issues and conflicts. Whereas mainstream majority students may encounter parental disagreements, what may be labeled as *generational* gaps in values and perspectives, students of color typically experience pressure with parents over lifestyle and goals as a result of *cultural* differences. For example, a student wanting to participate in a study abroad program may face resistance from parents who require their children to live at home to help out with the family business and also language translation around the clock. What is viewed as an enriching college activity from one perspective may be viewed negatively by parents as an attempt to break away from cultural roots and family. These complex factors and points of emotional tension create great distractions and stresses that affect both the academic and personal development of students of color. Having academic advisers and counselors on a college campus who are sensitive to such issues and can help find solutions with students of color in their relation to their families is important to their retention and future achievements.

While acknowledging these tensions that students of color experience, I also can underscore the richness of being bicultural and bilingual and celebrate those differences. I have specific experiences to draw on in discussing Chinese traditions and sharing stories of what it's like living a dual cultural identity in the United States. Sharing some of my own personal history with students of color helps me build a bond with them, and in return they appreciate an opportunity to share their background with me as a peer, without having to *teach* me. As an adviser or mentor, I can support students who need to resolve issues that have a cross-cultural context. Additionally, being situated in an institution of higher learning and research, I often point to new ways of producing knowledge within their academic major that addresses their bicultural identity or the needs of their community. I encourage students to fully participate in college life, develop new skills, and take advantage of different kinds of activities to enrich their own experiences and contribute to the greater community.

I often offer the support that first-generation college students need which most other mainstream students get through generations of parents, uncles, and aunts who graduated and survived the higher education system. Thus I teach these students about financial aid, research grants, scholarships, building mentorships with faculty, and applying for internships. This kind of institutional understanding precedes systematic steps to success, and those steps are often not obvious to first-generation students.

As a woman of color in student affairs, I have a special interest in reaching out to women students of color. Having personally encountered the societal expectations of a woman's role in a Chinese patriarchal family, I have firsthand experience with the sexism that exists within my ethnic culture. Having grown up in a patriarchal upbringing, I understand that many other young women currently face similar parental judgments and constraints. They often need to share their stories and seek encouragement, validation, and guidance to forge their own personal and professional direction. I realize my presence on campus is to serve in multiple positions as a role model, mentor, and advocate to students in addition to my current job description.

I have witnessed the degree to which burnout occurs among faculty and staff of color who are burdened with multiple roles. Trying to make tenure or completing one's own job well can be jeopardized by overcommitting to activities. Usually personnel of color feel morally obligated to help out the younger generation of students of color. Working with students of color and guiding their student organizations is a rewarding and necessary role, especially in light of the fact there are not enough faculty of color to be placed in these pivotal advisory roles. Sometimes an advocate must step in administratively for students of color, yet "speaking out" may also be considered unfavorably by administration and academic chairs. Moreover, these "extracurricular" activities such as advising student organizations do not count in tenure review or job evaluations. So time management, prioritizing commitments, and balancing roles (including parenting and volunteering in the community) regularly cause stress for faculty of color and professionals in higher education.

A college campus that is predominantly white often has one specific office delegated to serve the special needs of students of color. This compartmentalization has its benefits in that a fully staffed office focuses on the students of color and the mission of diversity. A multicultural office has an especially important role in recruitment and retention. In recruiting new students of color to the campus, the staff does outreach and provides bilingual material to parents in outlying areas to encourage their children to attend the university. In retaining the students of color once they are admitted, the multicultural office develops special programs that advise students of color on academic issues. The office staff organizes and provides social activities that celebrate different ethnic traditions for the education of the entire college community, and they often involve students in programming these events so the students can develop leadership skills and learn about their own cultural heritage.

While the multicultural affairs office plays an essential role, the downside of a separate office is that the campus administration then steps away from its responsibility of having to engage with its minority student population. Executive administrators may not feel they have to deal with or confront those student issues because the multicultural office is taking care of them. What I have seen and experienced is that often the multicultural office staff comes to be regarded as a substandard, minor branch of campus life. In reality, diversity is everybody's business, yet that philosophical viewpoint is discussed but not followed up on. For this reason, I agree with the Minority Persistence Model's emphasis that the commitment to diversity must be campus-wide.

The multicultural office is usually overburdened with responsibilities ranging from recruitment, retention, programming, fund-raising, mediation, advocacy—and whistleblowing. Because the office has such a broad range of goals and objectives, it may present a confusing face to the outsider or new student. The office may even have an ambiguous image and seem inefficient because it has so many tasks to accomplish. However, until other university offices become more responsive to the needs of all students, the multicultural office is the natural place where students of color go when a problem or crisis arises.

For instance, acts of hate are often reported to the multicultural office because students of color feel safe in revealing the incidents to the staff there. Regrettably, when students have gone to the campus police to report such incidents, they often have faced a negative response, even to the point where the victim is questioned and/or the act of hate is dismissed; sometimes a police report is not even written up. Students of color also face frustration and fear in dealing with other university offices, so the multicultural office takes on the responsibility of communicating with the proper channels to raise awareness, elicit a proper investigation, and advocate for victim support.

In general, when other campus offices are insensitive or neglectful in serving students, especially students of color, the multicultural office has to initiate change and serve as the voice speaking on behalf of students. From the perspective of students of color, as the multicultural office advocates for them, it should bring about instantaneous change in the institutional policies and procedures that offend or neglect them. Consequently, this office faces pressures from above and below, from students and administration alike. Yet, to create a mutual resolution to problems that are often deeply rooted and barely acknowledged requires additional funds for implementing new policies, time for planning effective strategies and collecting funding, and setting up special projects or programs. All this has to be done to institutionalize change. Meanwhile, students become impatient, realizing that the problem will continue until graduation. Others on campus may express resentment as ad hoc spending from the top occurs in response to crisis because in times of scarce resources, special funding of minority programs is often viewed as ill-conceived and undeserved.

Recently on a campus an explosive racist comment was made in a class, and the professors did not handle the situation well. Word of the incident spread throughout campus, which then led to a student demonstration. After the protest, students demanded that all faculty be required to enroll in a multicultural diversity training workshop before being allowed to teach. The multicultural office supported the students as they presented their proposal. However, faculty were divided on the issue, some considering it a valid proposal and others rejecting the very idea of mandatory training. Many faculty resented the multicultural office for supporting what they saw as a curtailment of academic freedom, arguing that shaping their teaching to deal with diversity issues does not improve their teaching ability or contribute significantly to all disciplinary fields.

Another constraint faced by those in multicultural offices comes when we choose to work actively for change. It is hard to be effective when there are few people of color in higher administration. When committees are formed to decide on policy, we may be appointed—invited to the table, as it were—but we do not have a majority vote or power to execute decisions. In fact, our representation at the table often symbolizes that the minority voice is being elicited and heard, yet our views are not always understood or taken seriously. Nevertheless, the overall image when administration asks us to serve on these committees is that students of color are then being well represented.

We face other obstacles as well. In my experience, the functions and objectives of the various committees dealing with diversity issues are often unclear. For example, most universities have a committee on diversity or a race advisory board, an institutionalized group that meets regularly for people to exchange information. But we rarely move forward on any action plans or influence policy changes unless there is a crisis or student demonstration. Offices and committees need clear mandates and assessment procedures, which the higher administration then assiduously follows up on.

The lack of full university commitment and the other obstacles I have encountered lead me sometimes to question my administrative role and participation in committees. My continued presence symbolizes that I'm a happy camper; yet without my presence the group will surely continue on. I continue to attend these meetings because I feel responsible and might even be the squeaky wheel if necessary. I know that often university leaders want to implement change but are hesitant to move forward without input from faculty and staff of color. I also persist because these issues are dear to my heart and students of color depend on our representation at the table of power. In addition, I can make important networking contacts through this committee work, knowing such contacts will often help students in need of assistance.

Unfortunately our access to the administration and its decision-making process may lead students to view us as sellouts. It is true that many decisions are made through compromise, so the outcome of a committee or task force may reflect some progress but not as dramatic as that expected by students. In this way, we experience the frustration of being judged poorly by both students (as doing too little) and administration (as doing too much).

In terms of adverse judgment against us by the administration, our support roles to students of color may be scrutinized by executive administrators as inappropriate mentoring. When we are asked by student groups about how to address a specific issue and initiate change, we (placed in the adviser's role) freely give our advice to students, based on our years of experience navigating the system and engaging the administration's attention. By sharing this privileged information with students, we know that the students may take action and come up with a strategy to promote change. In our position, we understand the power dynamics in which students do indeed have the capacity and grassroots power to call for change. They are the university's paying "customers," and as such their voices count, surely more than ours do. However, our associations with student groups often lead those in higher administration to think that we are the catalysts behind students who rebel and hold the administration accountable. In some cases, I have seen colleagues fear for their careers since, as we are placed in these vulnerable situations of working closely with ethnic student unions and serving as the link to administration, we stand to face criticism from every direction. To endure this stress of feeling vulnerable when working for change, staff and faculty need to demonstrate openly their willingness to support one another and help with problem solving, both in a crisis situation and in working for long-term change. In the worst scenario, a person speaking out can be "pushed out" by the top, confronted with either cooling down and keeping their job or going elsewhere. Again, progress toward gaining a critical mass of faculty and staff of color in an institution can help with devising more effective diversity initiatives, but a strong commitment from the administration is also necessary.

Abby Ferber

As a faculty member in the Department of Sociology at the University of Colorado in Colorado Springs, I have the privilege of choosing whether or not to be involved in campus diversity efforts. Because my own research focuses on race and gender issues and I teach courses on race and gender, I am committed to these issues in the academy. I work in a department incredibly supportive and encouraging of diversity efforts. In fact, the sociology department received the system-wide diversity award for its efforts (one positive attempt by the central administration to recognize and reward diversity work). So I find myself in a department that values and nurtures my concern for these issues.

Within my first few years as a faculty member here, I attended the University of Memphis curriculum integration workshop, an incredible learning experience that inspired the development and implementation of new diversity efforts on my campus. It gave me the opportunity to discuss with other faculty those issues I was addressing in the classroom. In this way, I learned many new techniques for coping with student resistance, breaking down the barriers between students in the classroom, and gaining new resources for classroom teaching. Most important, I left with a new network of contacts whom I continue to turn to when I need to discuss obstacles that I face.

Over the next few years, I invited a number of the speakers at that conference to come speak at my campus. We have a few in-house grant programs through which faculty can apply for funding to bring in guest speakers. Although women's studies and ethnic minority studies can offer limited support, alternative sources such as the President's Fund for the Humanities and the President's Fund for Recruitment and Retention of Minority and Women Faculty have underwritten the visits of these guest speakers. Consequently, every year, we have been able to bring in visiting speakers to address race and gender issues. These visitors usually give a public lecture about their research and offer a workshop for faculty focused on curriculum transformation and teaching issues.

Eventually I and a core group of women faculty associated with women's studies decided to take our diversity programming further. We applied for a grant, and then we requested and received matching funds from our campus to offer a curriculum transformation workshop for faculty members to integrate race and gender into an existing course or to develop a new course focused on race and gender. This summer workshop boosted morale and created invaluable networking among the faculty members involved. Faculty felt that their efforts were valued because we could pay them summer stipends to participate. Out of that workshop an array of exciting new courses evolved, including Race, Gender and the Bible; Shakespeare and Race; and Autobiography and the Construction of the Self. Faculty developed teaching strategies to integrate the study of race and gender issues into existing courses such as abnormal psychology, art history, and the sociology of adolescence.

In this way, we have accomplished a great deal on my campus, due to the extraordinary efforts and devotion of a small group of faculty. This year we have again received funding to offer the summertime curriculum workshop to another group of faculty, and we have also instituted a new film series on race and gender issues. These programs are collaborations between the women's studies and ethnic studies programs, the women's faculty committee, and the faculty minority affairs committee. Our experience highlights just how much can be done through existing channels. It also illustrates, however, the limits of such an approach. Our experience, successful as it was, also demonstrates the importance, as emphasized in the models presented earlier, of a campus-wide commitment to diversity, supported by resources. In order to accomplish the activities I described, individual faculty members must devote their time and energy to writing numerous grant proposals each year. The grant-writing process is time-consuming, and administration of the grant and all of the work involved in organizing numerous speakers' visits to multiple campuses is also time-consuming. Sadly, these efforts are often valued very little when it comes time for merit and promotion review. While the events themselves are rewarding for the opportunities they afford us and others, lack of support from the administration makes faculty members feel that their efforts are neither appreciated nor recognized, which over time contributes to burnout.

Other obstacles we face include limited support from other departments for these activities. For example, participants in the curriculum integration workshops were asked to provide assurance from their department chairs that the newly developed courses would be offered within the following academic year. Despite assurances, a number of departments did not offer the new courses. The greatest obstacle we have faced is the lack of a permanent director for women's studies, although since that program was founded over a decade ago, faculty have fought for and received assurances that a permanent director would be hired. We were recently very fortunate to hire a permanent and highly qualified director for our ethnic studies program, yet no funds were made available to search for a director of women's studies. Women's studies has been run by women faculty in their spare time, with either no or very little funding. Fearing that ethnic studies and women's studies were being pitted against each other, faculty responded by working together to seek a women's studies director. Such a situation is common. While many programs are initiated by volunteers, faculty cannot be expected to carry the burden of administering academic programs as an overload (on my campus, the programs offer a minor). These kinds of programs, so essential to the functioning of a college in the twenty-first century, must become institutionalized.

In short, volunteer faculty efforts cannot last indefinitely. They can serve as an important source of momentum to build support for diversity work on campus, raise awareness of race and gender issues faced by students, faculty and employees, and provide a means of networking, mentoring, and support for those involved. However, the time and energy required cannot be sustained over the long term. Such initiatives must culminate in a campus-wide commitment to diversity, enacted at all levels. Without eventual commitment, support, and resources from the administration, the efforts of the most committed people will diminish over time, leading to resentment among both students and faculty. When these kinds of imaginative efforts are not rewarded or institutionalized, the university is once again perceived as built on empty rhetoric, especially by students of color. I have seen many progressive and well-intentioned faculty members withdraw from university life, feeling as though they have been sucked dry. Their volunteer strategies provide an excellent starting point for building interest, awareness, and momentum, but the development of diversity efforts eventually will reach a peak where they must become institutionalized for their continuation. A campus or workplace can depend on the efforts of its employees to improve it for only so long, before the administration is faced with the critical decision of whether or not to make an extended effort to embrace inclusivity.

On many campuses, faculty members have accomplished great strides in advancing diversity efforts but are at a point where administrative commitment, backed up by funding and resources, must follow. Understanding this all-too-common trajectory is essential for campus administrators, who must learn to recognize this process of development and be prepared to respond. If they give no response, that absence of leadership seems a lack of support and often leads to increased resentment and diminished faculty effort. At my own campus last year, faculty members adopted the stance that if a position for the director of women's studies was not stipulated in this year's budget, we would refuse to run the program any longer. Given our college's limited budget, we agreed to accept either an external or internal search. We gained permission to conduct an internal search for a director who would be given one course off her course load and a stipend comparable to that provided to the director of ethnic studies. Thus I am now the director of women's studies.

The creation of this permanent position represented a major improvement. Our former dean has also agreed to move half of the FTE of the directors into the programs themselves. Women's studies and ethnic minority studies had no

FTE until this year, which meant that if a director resigned, the program would have no guarantee she would be replaced. Creating FTE in the programs helps institutionalize these programs, so their existence does not depend on the goodwill of a given administrator. However, we still seek institutionalization of the curriculum workshop, sufficient instructor funds, and a position for a diversity curriculum coordinator. Universities must recognize that the services provided by such programs benefit and extend to the entire campus. These programs provide cultural and entertainment programming, diversify curriculum, help students fulfill diversity requirements, provide resources and expertise for faculty across all disciplines, and contribute to the recruitment and retention of women and minority students and faculty. Thus they play a much different role than traditional departments. Furthermore, these programs cannot shoulder alone the burden of creating an inclusive, diverse environment.

The contemporary diversity movement provides administrators with a wonderful opportunity. We know that these plans and programs are necessary for the education of students, and they are essential to keeping a campus competitive in this century. We also know that there is overwhelming support for these efforts from students, faculty, and the public. There are many sources of grants, external funding, and private giving available to campuses willing to make a commitment to create an inclusive environment to prepare students for future multicultural workplaces. In short, a firm commitment on the part of administrators, who agree to allocate a modest amount of resources, will produce good returns. With such support, the faculty already working toward this end will continue their efforts, feel appreciated and rewarded, and continue the search for external dollars.

On my campus, we have learned that there is no straight trajectory toward progress and change, and we must be ever vigilant against backsliding and losing what we have gained. Once we finally institutionalized women's studies and ethnic studies, the campus women's center was closed. This student center provided resources and referrals for students dealing with rape, sexual harassment, day care needs, domestic violence, and so on. It was only when students began asking faculty members where the center was located that we discovered it had been quietly closed. Just as we make progress in one battle, another battle arises.

If a campus is to move beyond endless battles such as these, it must embrace a *comprehensive* institutional plan. Such a plan makes sense economically, and it is also important to the changing image of the university in the next century. A look at campus catalogs or publicity materials, which usually display a multicultural assemblage of students and faculty on their covers, tells us that even the most conservative administration knows on some level that commitment to diversity makes sense.

FOCUS ON ONE ARENA: THE CLASSROOM

A great deal of research, in addition to the models presented above, emphasizes that change is complex, requires commitment and resources, and must be part of a broad campus diversity initiative. Attempting to effect positive social change by concentrating efforts in only one area usually leads to short-term, limited improvement. A lack of overall structural change can eventually cause burnout and frustration among those involved. To demonstrate the complexity of change required at each level of the institution, in this section we briefly explore some of the complex issues involved in one realm: curriculum change. For faculty members seeking to begin with change in the classroom, an area they feel they can control, Phyllis Betts, professor of sociology at the University of Memphis, highlights a number of important considerations that may reach beyond an individual teacher's courses:

Collegiality: Diversity asks that we broaden our criteria for faculty appointments to take into account the strengths that faculty with different backgrounds and experiences may bring to the discipline, the department, the students, and the institution as a whole.

The new scholarship and curriculum integration: Diversity asks that we rethink our disciplines and our curriculum, even our epistemology, to question how certain common aspects of our disciplines and pedagogy truncate or distort our knowledge, interpretation, and understanding of humanity, social order, and even the natural world. Some of these assumptions and procedures include omitting the experiences of marginalized peoples and overgeneralizing based on the majority experience, stereotyping that is embedded in established paradigms, and rendering in an idealized way majority group behaviors, attitudes, and values. In fact, curriculum "integration" is hard work. It stretches our disciplinary training and raises issues as to how best to incorporate material with which we may be unfamiliar or even uncomfortable.

Teaching and learning: Diversity asks that we consider how different kinds of students relate to and can best learn in our discipline, taking into account the full range of students' experiences and frames of reference, differences in "styles of learning," and, yes, level of preparation. Diversity means gaining more understanding about how students learn and how we best teach to enable all students to learn to their highest potential.

Classroom dynamics: Diversity asks that we be attuned to classroom dynamics since privilege and marginalization are sometimes replicated in the classroom. Both majority and minority groups may be uncomfortable with a diverse classroom and content that explores unfamiliar group experiences or raises troubling questions about intergroup relations. This may mean juggling freedom of expression and civility in the classroom while engaging students who might sometimes simply prefer to withdraw from discussion. (See Betts 1996)

Engaging this range of issues may be difficult given the lack of preparation most faculty receive for teaching in the first place, the lack of funding and value attributed to professional development at most universities, the limited role models most faculty have been exposed to, and the unspoken assumptions most of carry with us as we become new faculty members. Faculty need strong support networks as they grapple with these issues, or they will experience isolation and alienation in spite of their commitment to learning how to teach in a more equitable manner. As the student persistence model argues, change in one area is insufficient and must be accompanied and supported by widespread change across the institution.

Faculty must also be prepared and equipped to face student resistance. In spite of the discomfort conflict in the classroom causes, resources are available to help faculty on this pedagogical journey. The work of sociology professor Elizabeth Higginbotham, for example, has explored and developed strategies for confronting and minimizing student resistance. Higginbotham observes that "discussions with my graduate students opened my eyes to how we as faculty often focus on vocal resistance and may not recognize other forms" (Higginbotham 1996, 207). She points out that silence, avoidance, and absence from class may also signal resistance. Resistance should be anticipated and can be avoided to some extent by careful attention to pedagogy. For example, Higginbotham offers a number of useful strategies:

Include works that "balance discussions of oppression with careful attention to resistance [and] how individuals can challenge the imbalance of power and overcome apparent barriers to their achievement" (210).

Present materials that view race and gender as "sources of social stratification and dimensions of analysis that speak to us all, rather than concepts reserved for discussion of disadvantaged groups" (204). This approach also helps us avoid focusing on "exceptions" and shifts our discussion to broader social structures.

Certain strategies may help establish a trusting climate. For example, faculty may find it profitable to utilize ground rules; ask each student to present a personal letter of introduction to the class at the beginning of the term; open up discussions of teaching methodology; and have the students work together on cooperative group projects.

On many campuses, faculty are forming discussion groups, reading groups, and pedagogy workshops focused on teaching about diversity. They do this in order to provide each other with a supportive group of peers who wish to learn from each other's experience, share ideas and strategies, and discuss readings and research on these issues. With available funding, excellent specialists in the field can be brought in as guest lecturers and workshop leaders. Once again, administrative support is key to provide the necessary funding, time release, incentive, and reward structure to allow faculty to devote the necessary time and energy to such transformation of their classroom practice.

POSITIVE CHANGES, NEGATIVE OBSTACLES: IDENTIFYING YOUR PRIORITIES

Promising diversity work has been done and many alliances within higher education have been established. Signs of collective, networked, nonhierarchical leadership have emerged. Together, we are crossing institutional boundaries and struggling to transcend the divisions of power that permeate U.S. society. These struggles are leading to greater justice through reform and change.

Below we highlight some of the positive changes that have been made and negative obstacles that still persist. We offer this as a list of benchmarks to evaluate your own institution, and also as a historical statement of what the situation is nationally. In the appendix, we reproduce this section of the essay as a checklist that people in various institutions can use in developing their own ongoing strategies for change.

POSITIVE PROGRESSIVE ACTIONS IN HIGHER EDUCATION: SMALL AND LARGE VICTORIES

There is a large body of research documenting the impact of diversity in higher education, and a growing body of that research provides overwhelming evidence to oppose resistant members of the campus and public and also to provide support in legal challenges against diversity efforts.

An Internet search or a day's work in a library reference room consulting college catalogues will reveal a growing list of multidisciplinary courses being taught at most institutions. Such courses often explicitly treat in an extended way racial/ethnic, gender, and sexual inequality; ethnic communities and cultures; the social construction of race; intergroup dynamics; the ideology and history of race and gender as formative constructs in U.S. and international history; gay and lesbian studies; and the creative work of previously underconsidered groups.

Most campuses now have ethnic studies and women's studies programs, usually offering at least an academic minor, often a major, and occasionally a master's or doctorate.

Some colleges that have made a major commitment to diversity initiatives have created research institutes. They expand the focus of academic research on campus and off, by inviting visiting scholars to incorporate race, ethnicity, and gender in new ways into their research; by developing the study and implementation of new methods of intergroup dynamics on campus; by promoting a greater recognition of the legitimacy of nontraditional, often interdisciplinary research and teaching; and by publishing new academic journals focusing on race, ethnicity, gender, and sexuality.

Faculty, staff, administrators, and students who want to work on diversity initiatives often take advantage of expanded national/regional networks that promote diversity initiatives and serve as resources to other institutions. They do this through the Internet and e-mail, and through attendance at regional and national conferences.

Improved methods of gathering data and an increasing number of models from other universities can be used to assess diversity efforts on campus and identify needs. Many campuses obtain quality information from student focus groups, ethnic/racial groups, and campus climate surveys that explore race relations, levels of tolerance, and campus diversity plans (for recruitment, retention, presence of faculty of color, and curriculum transformation).

Institutions use media and published materials to reflect and promote diversity directly and indirectly. Sensitive to their image, increasingly institutions include diversity as a goal in their mission statements. Two statements that commonly appear are that the college seeks to prepare students for a diverse society, and that, as an implied or explicitly structured goal, it will strive to increase the enrollment of currently underrepresented student populations, which de facto means students of color. To this end, most institutions now have a multicultural admissions director to ensure outreach, recruitment, and enrollment of undergraduate and graduate students of color. In the same vein, there is usually a point person in the financial aid office to collaborate with admissions to form affordable financial aid packages to attract promising students of color. At a higher level, many campuses have made it a priority to increase diverse representation in top management and administration in order to demonstrate the institution's commitment to multiculturalism.

Most institutions currently have training workshops on diversity and multiculturalism for students, as well as faculty and staff. There are numerous excellent models of curriculum transformation that can be incorporated on any campus. In the summer, curriculum integration workshops are offered on many campuses. Less commonly but in a highly effective way, campuses are beginning to create faculty committees, offices, or positions responsible for overseeing the integration of race and gender into the curriculum, improving teaching effectiveness, and improving teaching methodology to serve a pluralistic student body and society.

Many universities and departments have a recruitment/hiring policy and process, using incentives to bring in new faculty of color and, at a later stage, setting up mentoring networks for them to enhance their stay at the institution. In addition, faculty women's committees or committees of faculty of color also deal with retention and climate, and their work could have a greater impact if the committees were funded and their work more seriously attended to and valued by the administration.

Given the legal challenges, many campuses are creatively redefining diversity in order to save scholarships and bridge programs. Some of these strategies include establishing partnerships with in-state school districts that serve diverse populations (starting as early as elementary school visitations or summer programs and developing a well-organized pipeline). They also include asking people of color to play an active role in fund-raising efforts and setting up alumni associations, especially to assist students of color.

Additionally, most administrators have implemented a structured system for interacting with students and staff of color to access their range of experience for advice. In this way, campus community members of color can draw attention to important issues that may otherwise be overlooked, increase interracial understanding and improve social relations, and guide social change. Provosts, deans, and directors are increasingly being held accountable for fostering diversity, and increasing numbers of administrators are taking a proactive approach to creating inclusive campuses.

PERSISTENT NEGATIVE ATTITUDES AND INSTITUTIONAL BARRIERS

Antidiversity sentiment comes from a small, persistent, and often vocal minority. They promote, for example, a "color-blind" argument that race and ethnicity do not or should not matter. Following the same color-blind logic, diversity initiatives are seen as causing resentment and stigmatization or promoting balkanization. Others, using a "reverse-racism" argument, say that diversity initiatives are antimerit, racist, and antiassimilationist. Such sentiments reveal the strength of racial stereotyping that is so common in our country. For example, myths circulate that minority students are underprepared and thus unqualified for admission. This presumably means that colleges lower their standards to achieve diversity in admissions and curriculum.

Even more dangerous for students, faculty, and staff of color is the increased presence of hate groups and hate speech on campuses and on Internet sites; frequently e-mail is used to deliver racial insults and violent threats. Thus all campuses must deal with pressing safety issues. Colleges see a regular occurrence of acts of intolerance, including hate and bias crimes, and, more regularly, discrimination. There is a lack of widespread knowledge of these activities since they are often kept quiet by the administration. This cover-up contributes to the false impression among many whites on campus and in town that racism no longer exists or no longer poses a threat to students.

Campuses continue to perpetuate the gross underrepresentation of people of color in faculty and administrative leadership positions. When faculty of color are recruited, they have a poor retention rate, partly due to the lack of critical mass of faculty and administrators of color on campus and also a generally unsupportive environment. To correct that, the newly recruited faculty need networking opportunities and mentoring programs. Administrators of color need to be promoted to higher levels rather than remain marginalized in positions dealing with EO/AA or multicultural affairs. When the majority of faculty fail to integrate race and gender into their courses, this also contributes to an inhospitable environment.

Financially, there is a lack of resources and funding to implement necessary change. While scholarships and programs once designated for students of color are being eliminated, new scholarship programs based on criteria like financial need or giving access to underrepresented groups have not kept pace. The faculty face a lack of incentives and rewards to revise their curriculum, get involved in diversity efforts on campus such as mentoring, or generate other activities to assist students of color. Most acutely, administrations and state boards of education often fail to be accountable for long-range planning, implementation, and assessment of diversity strategies.

On most campuses, we still find more words than action. Looking at the list of positive changes, we see that diversity initiatives have made significant progress in recent decades. Reviewing persistent barriers and obstacles should not dishearten us. As we have seen, change is possible. And with commitment all of the problems identified above can be addressed and solved. The plethora of research now available and the models and programs already developed make this process of change easier. Universities and workplaces can learn from each other, and there are many places to turn to once institutions begin to look for successful models and programs to implement. For example, the *Diversity Digest*, published by the Association of American Colleges and Universities (AACU), and its Web site, www.diversityweb.org, are excellent resources detailing what kinds of programs work. These sources continually update research references and provide models from campuses across the nation to deal with the full gamut of diversity issues; they analyze and inform readers about the effectiveness of curriculum diversity requirements, diversity's impact on teaching and learning practices, best practices for diversifying the faculty, outcomes of diversity in education, achieving student diversity after affirmative action, designing and conducting a campus climate survey, improving faculty attitudes toward diversity, assessing diversity's impact on student life, and developing models of collaboration with K–12.

ONLY THE BEGINNING

We have provided a list of further resources at the end of this book. Fortunately we have reached a stage where we now have enough research, knowledge, and models to guide us as we strive to develop programs that will work for our own campuses and workplaces. Because we have the resources and guidance available to create positive social change, it is now up to each university and workplace to decide if it is willing to make this commitment. The ball is in our court!

The list of positive steps and negative barriers can help you to begin this process or assess your institution's progress. The list can be used as a checklist to evaluate your own workplace (see appendix). Go through the list and try to evaluate to what extent each positive step has been implemented on your campus. Then go through the list of barriers and assess to what extent these barriers exist on your campus. This will provide you with a starting point for assessing your own campus. Many apply to nonacademic settings as well. Additionally, you might consider developing and implementing a comprehensive campus culture and climate survey, like the University of Arizona's, or a racial climate survey, as well as focus groups, to evaluate your campus's particular needs. The AACU resources discussed above and the material in this chapter, as well as the list of resources, can guide this process. Certainly the first step in creating positive change is to identify the needs of your particular community and to evaluate existing diversity efforts. The next step is to identify areas for change. Then collectively, working for as broad a consensus as possible, groups across the whole institution can create new policies and programs to achieve those goals.

Widespread institutional change is clearly required. Allan G. Johnson demonstrates that within institutions and also on the level of personal behavior, systems of privilege and oppression work through established "paths of least resistance," which are reinforced by the dominant culture in which we all participate. "Because systems are identified with privileged groups, the path of least resistance is to focus attention on them—who they are, what they do and say, and how they do it" (Johnson 2001, 107). Looking at the realm of higher education, we can see this focusing on privileged groups clearly delineated. The curriculum focuses primarily on white men; college administrators are overwhelmingly white men too. Another path of least resistance involves limiting the analysis of a problem to the level of the individual, looking at prejudice and discrimination as an individual problem, instead of exploring racism and male privilege as institutionalized. Then, when students or faculty of color do not succeed, many blame them as individuals instead of examining the larger context. We move away from the path of least resistance when we choose to mentor students of color, teach race and gender courses, and examine inequality on our campuses, yet such a choice may entail adverse personal consequences.

Beverly Daniel Tatum points out that "there is no vehicle to cross boundaries." As we foster climates of engagement, we also have to foster ways "to cross the long-standing boundaries that separate us in American society" (Tatum 2000, 29). To create change, we must alter the paths of least resistance, which on college campuses can only occur if our efforts are comprehensive and across the institution, reinforced in the classroom, department meetings, student government meetings, committee meetings, review processes, hiring discussions, and cultural events.

Our institutions of higher education must reconsider what passes for normal, acceptable behavior. For example, if curriculum transformation workshops are offered on a regular basis, inclusive teaching should be valued in the promotion and tenure and merit review processes. An institution can make resources available to facilitate such curriculum transformation and recognize and reward those who initiate such change. In ways like these, an institution can create new "paths of least resistance," so that inclusive teaching becomes the expected norm. Establishing new paths of least resistance can produce widespread change on campuses. Institutional plans for universities and workplaces must make a commitment to diversify their top priority, so that enforcing this commitment becomes the path of least resistance.

In closing, we point to a report issued by the Educational Testing Service which reveals that minority student enrollment will rise dramatically, reaching 37 percent of undergraduate enrollment by 2015 (*Diversity Digest* 2000). Yet this level of minority enrollment will lag behind the percentage of people of color in the nation in the eighteen- to twenty-four-year-old age-group. Further, a diverse student body is insufficient to create an inclusive learning environment, and most campuses are far from achieving a diverse faculty and administration, abolishing discrimination, and creating an inclusive curriculum. With the September 11, 2001, attacks, many professors and students became deeply interested in the development of courses about terrorism, Afghanistan, Islam, the history of the Middle East, and the dilemmas of American power. The tragedy sparked a new sense of engagement and an awareness of making new connections among the disciplines and the human experience. The events alerted academics to reevaluate what they teach and how they teach it.

We are at yet another critical juncture: the student body served by our universities is becoming increasingly diverse, but we have yet to create an inclusive learning environment that meets the needs of all students. There is no way to opt out of this challenge. If we choose to do nothing, we will fail to serve our students and prepare them for life, work, and relationships in the twenty-first century. Many people, including students, faculty, administrators, and community members, have already made the commitment to create positive change. As student Shelli Romero charges us in her narrative statement at the beginning of this book, "Racism is everybody's problem." Campus community members of all racial and ethnic backgrounds can collectively advance the movement that has begun. We invite you to join these efforts and use this book as a tool to guide that process.

REFERENCES

Betts, P. 1996. Handouts from the spring 1996 University of Memphis Curriculum Integration Workshop, Diversity Seminar.

Diversity Digest. 2000. Spring–Summer. Published by the Association of American Colleges and Universities.

Higginbotham, E. 1996. "Getting All Students to Listen." *American Behavioral Scientist*, November–December, 203–11.

Johnson, Allan G. 2001. *Privilege, Power, and Difference.* Hartford, Conn.: Hartford College for Women of the University of Hartford.

Manning, K., and P. Coleman-Boatwright. 1991. "Student Affairs Initiatives toward a Multicultural University." *Journal of College Student Development* 32: 367–74.

Sergiovanni, T., and R. Starratt. 1991. *Emerging Patterns of Supervision: Human Perspectives.* New York: McGraw-Hill.

Swail, W. Scott, and Dennis Holmes. 2000. "Minority Student Persistence Model." In S. Gregory, ed., *The Academic Achievement of Minority Students.* Lanham, Md.: University Press of America.

Valverde, L. A., and Louis Castenell Jr., eds. 2000. *The Multicultural Campus: Strategies for Transforming Higher Education*, 25. Walnut Creek, Calif.: AltaMira.

Appendix: A Checklist Method of Evaluating Diversity in Your Institution

CHECKLIST 1: AREAS OF SUCCESS IN DIVERSITY PLANNING

Based on the "diversity blueprint" principles (see chapter 5 on diversity in higher education), does your institution demonstrate in the following areas that it has achieved accountability, inclusiveness, shared responsibility, evaluation, and institutionalization of stated diversity goals?

- Diversity is a stated goal of the university's mission statement, for example, a stated goal to prepare students for a diverse society; an implied or explicitly structured goal to increase enrollment of underrepresented students of color.
- The institution's media and published materials reflect and promote diversity.
- The institution values and teaches a variety of courses to educate students on contemporary and historical issues related to diversity, including courses on the following: racial/ethnic and gender inequality; ethnic communities and cultures; the social construction of race; intergroup dynamics and ideology.
- Ethnic studies and women's studies are fully supported programs that offer a major and occasionally a master's or doctorate.
- The institution participates in national/regional networks and conferences that promote diversity initiatives, and it offers resources to other institutions.

- The institution conducts its own curriculum integration workshop for faculty and presents this workshop on a regular yearly basis to new faculty.
- The institution has a strategic plan and recruitment/hiring policy to bring in new faculty of color and retain them.
- The institution has a strategic plan and recruitment/hiring policy to increase diverse representation in top management and administration to demonstrate its commitment to diversity.
- The institution has a research component to evaluate and assess diversity efforts on campus and to identify needs and effectiveness. Examples include campus climate surveys to measure race relations and levels of tolerance or the development of campus diversity plans for recruitment, retention, and presence of faculty of color, as well as for curriculum transformation.
- The institution has a strategic admissions plan for recruitment of culturally diverse students.
- The institution has a comprehensive retention plan for students of color.
- The institution has an ad hoc committee to oversee integrating race and gender into the curriculum, improving teaching effectiveness, and diversifying teaching methodology. The goal here is to serve a pluralistic student body and society as a whole.
- The institution has developed bridge programs to strengthen the educational pipeline for students coming from socially and culturally diverse school districts. Such bridge programs start as early as elementary school visitations, or they may be summer transition programs.
- The institution has regular training workshops on diversity and multiculturalism for students, faculty, administrators, and staff.
- The institution has set in place an official bias response team to investigate acts of intolerance and hate crimes and to support victims. Student conduct codes acknowledge such acts as unacceptable behaviors subject to consequences such as expulsion.
- The institution includes people of color in active roles in fund-raising efforts and setting up alumni associations.
- The institution has taken a creative and solid stance to ensure that enrollments of students from diverse backgrounds will be upheld.
- The institution has developed mentoring networks for students and faculty of color; these networks are necessary to assist with retention and/or promotion to tenure.
- Campus life departments support the formation of ethnic clubs, cultural celebrations, and multicultural programming.
- The institution has implemented and institutionalized structures to formally gather representation among students, faculty, staff, and administra-

tion to address race issues and to seek advice about fostering and increasing diversity.

- The institution rewards faculty for producing research for participating in national coalitions on race and consensus building.
- The institution has developed an institute or office focused on race, ethnicity, gender, and sexuality and the relation of these areas to curriculum development and faculty publication.

CHECKLIST 2: INDICATORS THAT NEGATIVE ATTITUDES AND INSTITUTIONAL BARRIERS PERSIST

- Presence of antidiversity sentiment. For example, the color-blind defense against diversity initiatives argues that race and ethnicity do not/should not matter; the reverse racism defense argues that all diversity initiatives are antimerit, racist, and antiassimilationist.
- Persistence of racial stereotyping. For example, the following myths circulate: minority students are underprepared and unqualified for admission; colleges are lowering standards to achieve diversity in admissions and the curriculum; or diversity initiatives cause resentment and stigmatization and promote balkanization.
- Hate groups and hate speech are present on campus or Internet sites that target young adults with racist sentiment or hate speech are promoted.
- The university does not document hate and bias crimes and discriminatory acts; a lack of publicly available documentation leads to denial of racism on campus. There may be little organized effort to provide overall safety or a cohesive crisis response plan.
- The institution has a dismal underrepresentation of people of color in faculty and administrative leadership positions; increasing diversity of teaching or professional staff is not addressed and therefore valued.
- There is poor retention of faculty of color; no priority has been given to addressing issues related to their exit.
- The institution lacks support systems for faculty of color and women; it needs to build networking opportunities and mentoring programs.
- There is a lack of promotions for administrators of color, who remain marginalized in positions dealing with EO/AA or multicultural affairs.
- The elimination of scholarships and programs once designated to students of color has not been rethought in a way that would enhance the diversity of the student body and also the experience of the students of color on campus.

- Faculty resistance to integrating race and gender into their courses has not been confronted and countered in a positive way.
- The institution does not provide incentives and rewards for faculty efforts to revise their curriculum or become involved in mentoring designed to help with retention goals.
- There is a general lack of accountability, strategic planning, and assessment for a diversity mission, which should be mandated from the highest levels of administration.
- There is a lack of resources and funding to implement necessary change to increase or enhance diversity.

Resources

BIBLIOGRAPHY FOR TEACHING
RACE AND WHITENESS

Astin, A. W. 1993. "Diversity and Multiculturalism on Campus: How Are Students Affected?" *Change* 25, no. 2: 44–49.

Brodkin Sacks, Karen. 2000. *How Jews Become White Folks*. New Brunswick, N.J.: Rutgers University Press.

Clark, Christine, and James O'Donnell, eds. 1999. *Becoming and Unbecoming White: Owning and Disowning a Racial Identity*. Westport, Conn.: Bergin & Garvey.

Dyer, Richard. 1997. *White*. New York: Routledge. Dyer examines racial representations of whiteness in the media and contextualizes these in the context of representations in Christianity and colonization.

Ferber, Abby L. 1998. *White Man Falling: Race, Gender, and White Supremacy*. Lanham, Md.: Rowman & Littlefield.

Ferrante, Joan, and Prince Brown Jr. 1998. *The Social Construction of Race and Ethnicity in the United States*. New York: Longman.

Fine, Michelle, Lois Weis, Linda Powell, and L. Mun Wong, eds. 1997. *Off White: Readings on Race, Power, and Society*. New York: Routledge. This is an anthology of articles divided into different sections such as theorizing whiteness, white performances, academic life, living whiteness, white screens, and so on.

Frankenberg, Ruth, ed. 1997. *Displacing Whiteness: Essays in Social and Cultural Criticism*. Durham, N.C.: Duke University Press.

Frankenberg, Ruth. 1993. *The Social Construction of Whiteness: White Women, Race Matters*. Minneapolis: University of Minnesota Press. A great qualitative study of how race shapes white women's lives and their daily experiences of racial structuring and privilege.

Frye, Marilyn. 1992. "Oppression." In Paula S. Rothenberg, ed., *Race, Class, and Gender in the United States: An Integrated Study*, 54–57. 2d ed. New York: St. Martin's.

Goffman, Erving. 1986. *Stigma: Notes on the Management of Spoiled Identity*. New York: Simon & Schuster.

Hacker, Andrew. 1992. *Two Nations: Black and White, Separate, Hostile, Unequal.* New York: Ballantine.

Hedley, Mark, and Linda Markowitz. 2001. "Avoiding Moral Dichotomies: Teaching Controversial Topics to Resistant Students." *Teaching Sociology* 29 (April): 195–208.

Helms, Janet E. 1992. *A Race Is a Nice Thing to Have: A Guide to Being a White Person or Understanding the White Persons in Your Life.* Topeka, Kans.: Content Communications.

Hurtado, S. 1999. "Reaffirming Educators' Judgment: Educational Value of Diversity." *Liberal Education* 85, no. 2: 24–31.

Jacobson, Matthew Frye. 1998. *Whiteness of a Different Color: European Immigrants and the Alchemy of Race.* Cambridge: Harvard University Press. Historical examination of how immigrants became white; focuses on Jews, Irish, and Greeks.

Johnson, Allan G. 2001. *Privilege, Power, and Difference.* Mountain View, Calif.: Mayfield.

Kinchloe, Joe. 1999. "The Struggle to Define and Reinvent Whiteness: A Pedagogical Analysis." *College Literature* 26, no. 3: 162–95.

Marks, Jonathan. 1994. "Black, White, Other." *Natural History,* December, 32–35.

Omi, Michael, and Howard Winant. 1994. *Racial Formation in the United States: From the 1960s to the 1990s.* New York: Routledge.

Orfield, Gary, and Edward Miller. 1998. *Chilling Admissions: The Affirmative Action Crisis and the Search for Alternatives.* Cambridge: Harvard University Press.

Orfield, Gary, with Michael Kurlaender. 2001. *Diversity Challenged: Evidence on the Impact of Affirmative Action.* Cambridge: Harvard University Press.

Roediger, David. 1999. *The Wages of Whiteness: Race and the Making of the American Working Class.* Rev. ed. New York: Verso. Examines the formative years of working-class racism in the United States. This revised version has an afterword that discusses recent studies of whiteness and the changed labor force.

Segrest, Mab. 1994. *Memoir of a Race Traitor.* Boston: South End.

Smith, Darryl G., et al. 1997. *Diversity Works: The Emerging Picture of How Students Benefit.* Washington D.C.: Association of American Colleges and Universities.

Tanno, Delores V. 1994. "Names, Narratives, and the Evolution of Ethnic Identity." In *Our Voices: Essays on Cultures, Ethnicity, and Communication.* Los Angeles: Roxbury.

Tatum, Beverly Daniel. 1992. "Talking about Race, Learning about Racism: The Application of Racial Identity Development Theory in the Classroom." *Harvard Educational Review* 62, no. 1: 1–24.

———. 1994. "Teaching White Students about Racism: The Search for White Allies and the Restoration of Hope." *Teachers College Record* 95, no. 4: 462–76.

Tatum, Beverly Daniel. 2000. "The ABC Approach to Creating Climates of Engagement on Diverse Campuses." *Liberal Education,* Fall, 22–29.

Terkel, Studs. 1992. *Race: How Blacks and Whites Think and Feel about the American Obsession.* New York: Doubleday.

Wellman, David. 1997. "Minstrel Shows, Affirmative Action Talk, and Angry White Men: Marking Racial Otherness in the 1990s." In Ruth Frankenberg, ed., *Displacing Whiteness: Essays in Social and Cultural Criticism.* Durham, N.C.: Duke University Press.

Zack, Naomi, ed. 1995. *American Mixed Race: The Culture of Microdiversity.* Lanham, Md.: Rowman & Littlefield.

USEFUL BOOKS FOR RECONCEPTUALIZING
UNIVERSITY STRUCTURES

Thomas, Richard W., Jeanne Gazel, and Ronald L. Byard, eds. 1998. *Building Community across Radicalized Lines: The Multiracial Unity Project at Michigan State University.* Unity Studies Monograph Series, no. 1. East Lansing: Multiracial Unity Project, Urban Affairs Programs, Michigan State University. 106 pages.

This book is accompanied by a video: *The Multiracial Unity Living Experience* (MULE), Michigan State University, August 1998. Running time 15:03. Documentary about MULE, the "undergraduate race relations program created to promote positive race relations through open and frank discussions and the development of genuine friendships."

The monograph and video present a program that moves beyond traditional race relations teaching and research to a program that focuses on institutionalizing a community building approach to race relations. The MULE projects take place in the residence halls and begin small, with five groups of twenty to thirty students who voluntarily join based on their interest in race issues and individual and social change. The members range from freshman to seniors, and the racial makeup is diverse. The students work on five components throughout an academic year: roundtable discussions, social activities, small group activities, community-building trip, and community service project.

The project is typically linked with an academic required course, either a history course, The Formation of a Multiracial Society: Bringing the Margins to the Center, or a social science course, Race, Class, Gender Intersectional Analysis. Leadership training components are integrated with support from schools of business and engineering. Sustainability has been achieved when its retention of freshman and sophomores are 50 percent and 25 percent, respectively. Juniors and seniors who continue become leaders with additional responsibilities.

MULE focuses on building community among students and developing community outreach components to urban–suburban/multiracial coalitions. Part of the outreach includes conducting comparative research on the historical and contemporary processes of unity among diverse peoples and making the research available to all people, organizations, and communities experiencing racial polarization.

Bowen, William G., and Derek Bok, in collaboration with James L. Shulman. 1998. *The Shape of the River: Long-Term Consequences of Considering Race in College and University Admissions.* Princeton: Princeton University Press.

An analytical study of race-sensitive college admissions and what happens afterward, giving specific data about the contributions made by students who benefited and or accessed higher education through affirmative action policies.

University of Maryland–College Park and Association of American Colleges and Universities. 1998. *Diversity Blueprint: A Planning Manual for Colleges and Universities.* Washington, D.C. Order at www.aacu-edu.org/cgi-bin/cgiwrap/www/aacu/pubs.cgi $29.00.

Excellent guidebook for college presidents, faculty, and student affairs professionals.

Tatum, Beverly Daniel. 1999. *Why Are All the Blacks Sitting Together in the Cafeteria: Conversations about Race.* New York: Basic.

Excellent work about racial barriers that provokes dialogue about race relations in schools. This psychologist, professor and dean of studies at Mt. Holyoke College, encourages readers to get past a reluctance to talk about racial issues and break the silence about racism. Why do some people self-segregate and what purposes does it serve?

Ford, Terry. 1999. *Becoming Multicultural: Personal and Social Construction through Critical Teaching.* New York: Falmer.

Part of a series on critical education practice geared for educators and teacher education programs. Presents a curriculum approach called Opening Doors to enable college students to understand other people's perspectives. Makes use of autobiographies, video viewing, text readings, dialogue journals, weekly journal sharing, scenarios, small group presentations, and guest speakers. Defines perspectives and labels; discusses two conceptual models of being-becoming multicultural; assesses implications for critical/multicultural teaching and what those teaching practices encompass for critical questioning and reflection.

Edwards, H. 1973. "The Black Athletes: 20th Century Gladiators for White America." *Psychology Today,* November, 43–52.

Reconsiders the problems of black athletes.

Lumas, Bernadette M. 1997. "Hero Today, Forgotten Tomorrow: Fulfilling the Needs of African American Student-Athletes." *McNair Journal.* Available at .

Sellers, R. 1993. "Black Student-Athletes: Reaping the Benefits or Recovering from the Exploitation." In D. Brooks and R. Althouse, eds., *Racism in College Athletics: The African-American Athlete's Experience.* Morgantown, W.V.: Fitness Information Technology, Inc.

WEB SITES

www.diversityweb.org

Foremost Web site, "a compendium of promising practices, programs, and resources" related to diversity in higher education. It is developed by the Association of American Colleges and Universities and the University of Maryland, in collaboration with Diversity Connections and DiverseCD. The site provides discussion forums, institution profiles, an online copy of *Diversity Digest,* and links. The page on inter- and intragroup relations features links to eleven current programs that work to develop community, unity, and intergroup projects, and it has an astounding set of recommended resources in seven areas:

- Research, evaluation, and impact
- Curriculum transformation
- Faculty and staff involvement
- Student involvement and development
- Campus–community connections
- Political and legal issues
- Institutional vision, leadership, and system change

www.UnitedAgainstHate.org

New virtual convention sponsored by the Hate Crimes Coalition. Informative and a way to bring people together.

www.aacu-edu.org

The Association of American Colleges and Universities represents over seven hundred accredited member institutions and works to advance and strengthen undergraduate liberal education. One of its priority areas is "establishing diversity as an educational and civic priority." The Diversity Works and Diversity Web, racial legacies and learning, described in this book, are among the initiatives developed by AACU. The monographs and books it publishes are available for purchase on this Web site. Other topics include leadership, faculty, curriculum, diversity, and global.

The AACU publishes the quarterly *Diversity Digest: Communicating Diversity in Higher Education*. Its offices are located at 1818 R Street, NW, Washington, D.C. 20009; telephone 202-387-3760. This useful sixteen-page newsletter features between eight and ten articles and news columns covering campus–community connections, diversity research, diversity news, diversity curriculum transformation, student experience, and resources. It provides in-depth coverage about college campus diversity programs, ranging from diversity conferences to affirmative action stances, college surveys on minority students, and peer advising programs to boost graduation rates. It gives an overall picture of what's happening on college campuses nationwide and stimulates new perspectives about programming and diversity initiatives. The features on diversity research offer substantive studies that professionals can use as evidence for programming or curriculum proposals.

www.naspa.org/about/index.htm

NASPA, National Association of Student Personnel Administrators, is the leading national association for college and university student affairs administrators. NASPA provides professional development through its regional and national organizations and yearly meetings. It promotes exemplary practices that enhance student learning and development and aims to be a leader in policy development. Its Web page provides links to summaries of research in a feature entitled "Diversity on Campus: Reports from the Field." Seventeen studies from colleges and universities are reported, for example, "Situational Characteristics of Positive and Negative Experiences of Same Race and Different Race Students" (University of Maryland–College Park), "The Multicultural Climate at the University of Texas at Austin," and "The Effect of Cultural Groups on Student Interaction and Intercultural Learning" (SUNY–Stony Brook).

Useful updates are provided by features on diversity in higher education and campus violence and hate crimes. Both include news and events, innovative campuses, research and publications, other resources and links, and policy and legislative updates. This publication is an excellent way to keep up with research and to network with specific colleges that share information on their diversity programming, for instance, Washington State University and its working group on hate-free universities and communities.

www.acenet.edu

ACE, the American Council on Education, has coordinated higher education since 1918 and includes community colleges and adult education. The Web site features its division of programs, including the Office on Minorities in Higher Education, which began in 1987 in response to declining minority enrollment. OMHE publishes an annual minority status report on minorities in higher education and position papers, such as legal developments related to affirmative action. The Web site also provides special link on issues—affirmative action, disabilities issues, immigration and education, minorities in higher education, women in higher education, and student aid.

YEARLY HIGHER EDUCATION
CONFERENCES ON DIVERSITY

National Conference on Race and Ethnicity in American Higher Education

NCORE holds a yearly conference during the first week of June. This is the leading and most comprehensive national forum on race and ethnicity aimed at faculty, researchers, professionals, administrators, and students. The weeklong conference features an abundance of keynote speakers and panel presentations from nationwide colleges and organizations that provide policy, planning, programmatic, curricular/pedagogic, research/assessment, training, and theoretical perspectives from around the country. The conference highlights exemplary working models and approaches. Its purpose is to assist institutions to create inclusive higher education environments, programs, and courses and to improve campus racial and ethnic relations. It sponsors many institutes on grant writing, multicultural course transformation, and effective diversity training. Its Web site is www.occe.ou.edu/NCORE.

Association of American Colleges and Universities

The AACU holds its annual national conference in January. In October of every year it hosts a three-day conference dedicated to diversity and learning: identity, community, and intellectual development. Contact the AACU at 1818 R Street NW, Washington, D.C. 20009; e-mail: info@aacu.nw.dc.us.

American Council on Education

ACE/OMHE sponsors a biennial national conference, Educating All of One Nation, to help institutions improve their comprehensive planning for minority achievement. The office provides assistance to institutions seeking to improve recruitment and retention of minority students, faculty, and administrators; phone: 202-939-9395.

National Association of Student Professional Administrators

NASPA holds its national three-day conference in March of each year. The conference includes keynote speakers, and recently the number of programs that address diversity planning has been increased. A network committee develops yearly workshops for specific issues and topics; the network for educational equity and ethnic diversity sponsored twenty-five presentations at the 2000 national conference.

TRAINING

National Coalition Building Institute (NCBI), 1120 Connecticut Avenue, NW, Suite 450, Washington, D.C. 20036. Phone: 202-785-9400; fax: 785-3385; e-mail: ncbiinc@aol.com. This organization offers a one-day workshop on prejudice reduction in various U.S. cities and its five-day Leadership Training Institute each summer. NCBI has trained and organized antiracism teams in fifty-five cities worldwide and forty campus affiliate teams at colleges and universities. Founded in 1984, NCBI works to eliminate prejudice and intergroup conflict worldwide by teaching a set of skills to enhance listening, understanding the various positions at the heart of the conflict, mapping out the concerns of each party, and reframing the issue in a way that builds bridges. At the prejudice reduction workshop, participants identify and work through stereotypes, hear personal stories about discrimination and internalized oppression, learn effective ways to intervene when confronted with prejudicial remarks and slurs, and make a commitment to be allies to underrepresented groups.

VIDEOS

The following distributors have many relevant works for consideration. Our resource guide divides the videos into two categories: those that deal directly with university or organizational issues and those that present narratives, which can be used like the narratives in this book. We suggest that you look at each distributor's Web site, from which many of our capsule annotations are drawn.

Distributors

California Newsreel, 149 Ninth Street, San Francisco, CA 94103. Fax: 415-621-6522; phone: 1-800-621-6196 or 415-621-6196; e-mail: contact@newsreel.org; Web site: www.-newsreel.org. Abbreviated below as CN.

The Cinema Guild, 1697 Broadway, Suite 506, New York, NY 10019. Phone: 212-246-5522 or 800-723-5522; fax: 212-246-5525; e-mail: thecinemag@aol.com. Abbreviated below as CG.

Filmakers Library, 124 East 40th Street, New York, NY 10016. Phone: 212-808-4980; fax: 212-808-4983; e-mail: info@filmakers.com. Abbreviated below as FL.

New Day Films, 22-D Hollywood Avenue, Ho-Ho-Kus, NJ 07423. Phone: 201-652-6590; fax: 201-652-1973; e-mail: curator@newday.com. Abbreviated below as ND.

Third World Newsreel, 545 Eighth Avenue, 10th Floor, New York, NY 10018. Phone: 212-947-9277; fax: 212-594-6417; e-mail: twn@twn.org. Abbreviated below as TW.

Women Make Movies, 462 Broadway, Suite 500, New York, NY 10013. Phone: 212-925-0606; fax: 212-925-2052; Web: www.wmm.com; e-mail: info@wmm.com (for general information); orders@wmm.com (for film and videotape orders). Abbreviated below as WMM.

Videos about Understanding Race and Ethnicity

The following videos are very effective in educating and provoking discussion about race relations and understanding racism, white privilege, racial stereotypes, and intergroup communication. Donna Wong has seen many multicultural centers or student organizations use these film showings for diversity training or student development—in one evening or in a retreat—and then facilitate discussions afterward.

Blacks and Jews, by Alan Snitow and Deborah Kaufman, 85 minutes. Free facilitator's guide. A collaborative documentary by two filmmakers, one Jewish and one black, traces a shared history of discrimination and racial conflict between these traditional civil rights allies. Donna Wong notes that on a campus like Emory, where both Jewish and African American students are well represented, this film effectively stimulates positive discussions about race and ethnic relations on campus. CN.

Blue Eyed, directed by Bertram Verhaag, 90 minutes. Diversity training with Jane Elliot. *Essential Blue Eyed* (trainer's edition and debriefing) contains on one tape a fifty-minute trainer's version and thirty-six-minute public version of *Blue Eyed*). Free facilitator's guide. This is a new video about the diversity exercise assigning adults into "blue eyed/browned eyed" identities and subjecting them to contempt and humiliation to teach about discrimination and privileges gained or lost based on personal physical features. This video includes Jane Elliot debriefing the participants and showing them and viewers how to apply its lessons to schools and work settings. CN.

The Color of Fear, by Lee Mun Wah, 90 minutes. Stir-Fry Production, 1904 Virginia St., Berkeley, CA 94709. Phone: 510-548-9695. Eight Americans (two each of Asian, European, Latino, and African descent) share experiences on the subject of race. Moderator is the filmmaker, who also serves as a guest speaker on the college tour circuit.

Sa-i-gu—Blacks and Korean Americans. CrossCurrent Media, 346 9th Street, Second Floor, San Francisco, CA 94103. Phone: 415-552-9550. This live-action documentary explores the April 1992 Los Angeles riots from the Korean American perspective. It includes news footage and bilingual interviews showing the violent aftermath of the Rodney King decision. Used recently at Stanford University in a student-sponsored meeting, it led to discussion and the establishment of a mixed-race theme house as an additional option to separate ethnic theme houses.

Oprah Show with guest author Beverly Tatum (author of *Why Are All the Black Kids Sitting Together in the Cafeteria?*). E-mail: show@interaccess.com (for Oprah online staff). This video (broadcast January 17, 2000) features lively discussion on racial identities and racial stereotyping by high school students who went through diversity awareness exercises and then confronted one another in dispelling the stereotypes and sharing their emotions and impact of being labeled. Tatum, the guest author, explains the value of self-segregated support groups and the need for intergroup communication.

VIDEOS ON RACIAL DIVERSITY
IN HIGHER EDUCATION

In Plain English: Students of Color Speak Out, by Julia Lesage, 56 minutes. Julia Lesage Video, 3480 Mill Street Eugene, OR 97405. Phone: 541-344-8129; fax: 541-346-1509; Web: www-vms.uoregon.edu/~jlesage/; e-mail: jlesage@oregon.uoregon.edu. The videotape that accompanies *Making a Difference.*

Multicultural videos: trilogy on students of color at Barnard College. Contact Candace Young, Office of the Dean of Studies, 105 Milbank, Barnard College, 3009 Broadway, New York, NY 10027. Phone: 212-854-2024; fax: 212-854-9470. (1) *About Face,* 25 minutes. Fifteen Asian and Asian American students discuss identity, family, relationships, and college experience. (2) *Indivisible.* Ten black Barnard women (alumnae and current students) tell personal experiences and challenges while at Barnard. (3) *Oyeme* (Hear Me). Latina students and mothers speak about education, religion, family, and racism while sharing their family histories.

The Multiracial Unity Living Experience. Michigan State University, August 1998.

The Rise of College Campus Racism: Causes and Solutions, 120 minutes. Production of Black Issues in Higher Education. Cox, Matthews & Associates, 10520 Warwick Avenue, Suite B-8, Fairfax, VA 22030. Phone: 703-385-2981. Julian Bond moderates this presentation, which probes the root causes of hate crimes on campus. Ten guest panelists offer analysis and solutions for colleges and universities.

Shattering the Silences: The Case for Minority Faculty, by Stanley Nelson and Gail Pellett, 86 minutes. Free facilitator's guide shipped with purchase. Special price for high schools, public libraries, and community groups. Documentary with eight faculty of color who describe the special pressures they face in majority white institutions. Helps to inform about the educational benefits of a diverse faculty and a more multicultural curriculum, including their relationship to retention of students of color. CN.

Skin Deep: Building Diverse Campus Communities by Frances Reid/Iris Films, 53 minutes. Free facilitator's guide. Frank discussion about affirmative action, self-segregation, internalized racism, and cultural identity among a multicultural group of college students. CN.

PERSONAL NARRATIVES ON VIDEO

Many of these videos are autobiographical. They give first-person accounts similar to the ones presented in this book, but at greater length and told in the form of personal histories. Like all personal narratives, they reveal a complexity of self that exceeds simple social classifications and labeling, even as the individual responds to that labeling and has been influenced by it.

Between Black and White, by Giannella Garrett, 26 minutes. This film shows four men and women who each have a black and a white parent. Each has been identified by society as either black or white, but rarely celebrated as both. All have an individual definition of who and what they are. FL.

Beyond Black and White, by Nisma Zaman, 28 minutes. This is a personal exploration of the filmmaker's bicultural heritage (Caucasian and Asian/Bengali) in which she relates her experiences to those of five other biracial women. These experiences are examined in the context of history, including miscegenation laws and governmental racial classifications. WMM.

Black Women On: The Light, Dark Thang, by Celeste Crenshaw and Paula Caffey, 52 minutes. This tape explores the politics of color within the African American community. Women representing a variety of hues speak candidly about the long-standing "caste system" that permeates black society. These women share provocative, heart-wrenching personal stories about how being too light or too dark profoundly influenced their life and relationships—from childhood through their adult years. WMM.

Brincando El Charco: Portrait of a Puerto Rican, by Frances Negrón-Muntaner, 55 minutes. Sophisticated in both form and content, the film contemplates the notion of "identity" through the experiences of a Puerto Rican lesbian photographer living in New York. Making connections to Puerto Rico and New York, the story becomes a meditation on class, race, and sexuality as shifting differences. WMM.

Coffee Colored Children by Ngozi Onwurah, 15 minutes. This lyrical, unsettling semiautobiographical testimony conveys the experience of children of mixed racial heritage. Suffering the aggression of racial harassment, a young girl and her brother attempt to wash their skin white with scouring powder. Later they share rituals to come to self-acceptance as adults. WMM.

Color Schemes, by Shu Lea Cheang, 29 minutes. Using a washing machine as a metaphor to tackle misconceptions about racial assimilation, the film presents twelve writers and performance artists from various cultural backgrounds who talk about the complexities of race in their lives. TWW.

Facing the Façade, by Jerald B. Harkness, 55 minutes. Features interviews with eight young black men and women enrolled at Indiana University in Bloomington. Although these students come from a wide variety of backgrounds, they all speak frankly—out of a sense of disappointment, sometimes bitterly, but often with a sense of humor—about their "minority" status on campus, the persistence of racist attitudes among fellow students and even some instructors, as well as other controversial issues such as racial separatism, integration, black studies programs, sexism, and prejudices within their own community based on language, behavior, and styles of hair and dress. CG.

Fuori/Outside, by Kym Ragusa, 12 minutes. The video maker, a woman of African American and Italian American descent, examines her relationship with her Italian American grandmother. A powerful bond between the two women, marginalized by color and age, survives the instability of family, class, and ethnic identity. TWW.

Great Girl, by Kim Su Theiler, 14 minutes. Drawn from personal experience, Kim Su Theiler's first film is an evocative and poetic drama about historical and cultural disorientation. A woman who came to America as a child adoptee returns to Korea looking for her birth mother and part of her history and her cultural identity. Once in Korea she finds only fragments of the picture. WMM.

High Horse, by Randy Redroad, 40 minutes. In a modern American city, from a cop to a young bike messenger, dislocated Native people search for and sometimes find their figurative and literal homes in different journeys of love, loss, and identity. TWW.

History and Memory: For Akiko and Takashige, by Rea Tajiri, 32 minutes. The filmmaker strives to find images to represent her parents' World War II internment experiences. Highly effective in the classroom. WMM.

Intro to Cultural Skit-Zo-Frenia, by Jamika Ajalon, 10 minutes. This tape explores the raw edges of identity for a lesbian/gay of color. Set to an original soundtrack, the work foregrounds the particular experiences of African American lesbians while challenging homophobia in the black community. TWW.

Introduction to the End of an Argument/Intifada: Speaking for Oneself . . . Speaking for Others, by Elia Suleiman and Jayce Salloum, 45 minutes. Using clips from feature films, cartoons, and network TV, this unique video provides a rare critique of the portrayal of Arabs in Western media, which it juxtaposes to text and location footage shot on the West Bank and used to discuss the negative influence of Arab stereotypes on U.S. views and foreign policy. TWW.

Janine, by Cheryl Dunye, 9 minutes. African American filmmaker Dunye candidly tells the story of her friendship with Janine, a white upper-middle-class girl she met in high school, and how that friendship ended. TWW.

Just Black? Multi-Racial Identity, by Francine Winddance Twine, Jonathan F. Warren, and Francisco Ferrandiz, 57 minutes. In this often humorous documentary, we meet several articulate young men and women of mixed racial heritage. Each has one black parent and one white, Asian, or Hispanic parent. FL.

Mama . . . I Have Something to Tell You, by Calogero Salvo, 31 minutes. This autobiographical video, in which the filmmaker reveals his homosexuality to his mother, explores the awkward situation of being "out" to friends but closeted to family. In this intimate dialogue his mother discusses her preconceptions, fears, and love, and he reveals childhood memories, adolescent thoughts, and fears, and affirms his present loving relationship. Other Latino lesbians and gays offer further insights into family responsibilities, death, and the importance of honesty. CG.

Memories of Tata, by Sheldon Schiffer, 52 minutes. In interviews conducted during the last months of his life, Schiffer's grandfather, Adam Morales ("Tata"), the family patriarch, discusses his notions of what it was to be a man—including the need to command respect, macho notions of sexuality, emotional outbursts coupled with the threat of physical violence, and sexist notions of child rearing. These "memories of Tata" are contrasted with the often painful recollections of his estranged wife and two daughters. CG.

Miles from the Border, by Ellen Frankenstein, 15 minutes. Twenty years after emigrating from a rural village in Mexico to an ethnically divided community in California, the Aparicio family shares its experiences of dislocation and the difficulties of crossing cultures. ND.

Mitsuye and Nellie: Asian American Poets, by Allie Light and Irving Saraf, 58 minutes. This absorbing documentary examines the lives of Asian Americans through the poetry of Mitsuye Yamada and Nellie Wong. Interviews, rare archival footage, and intimate family scenes underscore the different histories of Chinese and Japanese Americans, as well as shared experiences of biculturalism and generational difference. WMM.

None of the Above, by Erika Surat Andersen, 23 minutes. The mixed race filmmaker interviews herself and others: Leslie, a young woman of Native American, African, and European ancestry; Curtiss, whose mother is Japanese and father is African American; and Henrietta, whose family has been mixed for at least six generations and defies all categorization. FL.

Orientations, by Richard Fung and Gay Asians Toronto, 56 minutes. More than a dozen men and women of different Asian backgrounds speak frankly about their lives as members of a minority within a minority. Their commitment and outspokenness challenge the stereotype of passive Asians. TWW.

Real Indian, by Malinda Maynor, 7.5 minutes. The filmmaker describes being a Lumbee Indian who doesn't fit any of society's stereotypes for Native Americans. WMM.

Resilience, by Amy Happ, 14 minutes. This affecting memoir employs haunting imagery and personal narration to evoke the relationship between the filmmaker, her beloved stepmother, Vyola, and Vyola's battle with alcohol addiction. Recalling her experiences as an Alaskan Eskimo woman living in white middle America, Vyola describes how drinking became her refuge. Documenting Vyola's sobriety and struggle, this thoughtful, accessible film deals with racism's searing effects, the cycles of addiction, and changing definitions of family. WMM.

Seoul II Soul, by Hak J. Chung, 25 minutes. The Korean American filmmaker explores his identity by looking at the cultural ties and miscommunication in his family, consisting of his father, a black Korean war veteran who married a Korean war bride, and their three grown children. FL.

The Shot Heard Round the World, by Christine Choy and Spiro Lampros, 67 minutes. Presents the complex issues around a suburban homeowner who mortally shot Yoshi Hattori, a Japanese high school exchange student. FL.

Slowly This, by Arthur Jafa, 26 minutes. Speaking from their experiences as a Japanese American man and an African American man, writers David Mura and Alex Pate share personal and provocative stories that provide insights into complicated issues around race and masculinity. TWW.

Stories of Change, by Theresa Tollini, 57 minutes. Available in two thirty-minute parts. Portraits of four ethnically diverse women—Hispanic, Caucasian, Vietnamese, and African American—who surmount alcoholism, drug abuse, poverty, illiteracy, and cultural barriers. ND.

The Way Home, by Shakti Butler, 92 min. Conversation guide included (extra copies available at $5 each). Over the course of eight months, sixty-four women, representing a cross-section of cultures in the United States, met in councils separated by ethnicity—indigenous, Asian, European, African, Arab, Jewish, Latina, and multiracial. The women speak their hearts and minds about resistance, love, assimilation, beauty standards, power, school experiences, and more. Woven throughout are collages of historical and family photos, dance sequences, visual images, and music from over twenty cultures. ND.

Who's Going to Pay for These Donuts, Anyway? by Janice Tanaka, 58 minutes. The video maker searched for her father after a forty-year separation. The two reunited when Tanaka found him living in a halfway house for the mentally ill. Tanaka also reconnects with a more prosperous uncle who, like the father, had suffered internment. WMM.

Yellow Tale Blues: Two American Families, by Christine Choy and Renee Tajima, 30 minutes. Clips from Hollywood movie images of Asians are juxtaposed against portraits of the Choys, an immigrant, working-class family, and the Tajimas, a fourth-generation middle-class California family. FL.

About the Authors

JULIA LESAGE
ASSOCIATE PROFESSOR, ENGLISH,
UNIVERSITY OF OREGON

Alternative Media and the Making of In Plain English and Making a Difference

In the late 1970s and early 1980s, I was out of a job. After participating actively in an open admissions struggle at the University of Illinois at Chicago, I lost an academic job teaching film studies in an English department there and then two more jobs in a space of four years. I spent the next twelve years blacklisted as a radical academic. Needless to say, much of my suspicion of academic institutions and administrations comes from this experience. However, those years were fruitful ones intellectually and artistically. I had white-middle-class cultural capital as a writer and also married-middle-class-women's economic privilege. I could get intermittent employment as a visiting lecturer in colleges across the country, and my husband paid the rent and household expenses. During this time, I wrote politically oriented film studies and learned to make video—within what was then known as the guerrilla television or alternative media movement. In 1974 I, along with my husband, Chuck Kleinhans, and colleague John Hess cofounded the film journal *Jump Cut: A Review of Contemporary Media*. This journal developed articles on "third cinema," gay and lesbian criticism, and feminist film criticism, and editing the journal let me continue working with others collectively in a politicized intellectual way. All of us in the loosely connected national network of alternative media makers and critics were eager to build support for grassroots political media making both in the United States and

219

abroad. Additionally in those years, because of my interest in political media making and the potential of video as an activist medium, I learned video making through an independent producers' media workshop, the Center for New Television, in Chicago.

Since I did not have a full-time teaching position, I did this kind of cultural work by necessity outside of institutional structures. Finding structures outside the academy in which to lead a rich intellectual and creative life gave me a renewed respect for and understanding of alternative cultural institutions, the history of which dates back to nineteenth-century utopian socialism. Within a context of alternative cultural production I also learned to work in effective and frugal ways; for example, *Jump Cut* has always functioned by its three editors' "tithing" themselves to pay for expenses—each putting in about $1,000 per issue—and my own video production has been made in a similarly thrifty manner, costing several thousand dollars per tape.

Jump Cut's origins derived from the underground press movement. In the 1960s and 1970s the underground press was a vital alternative cultural force both growing from and feeding into the political movements of the time. Often impudent and anarchistic, it offered cogent political analyses not found in the mainstream press. (For example, working on such a publication in graduate school, we read the French press in the library to provide coverage of Laos and Cambodia, when there was a blackout on invasion coverage in the U.S. press.) The economic base of the press was the availability of cheap tabloid newsprint, of the sort your grocery flyer is printed on, and its editorial base was loosely formed editorial collectives in major cities and college towns throughout the United States, Canada, and Europe.

Working within the tradition of the underground press, especially with the founding of *Jump Cut*, allowed us to critique not only Hollywood as an institution and the ideological substructures of Hollywood film, but also to introduce whole new fields into film studies, an emerging academic discipline in the 1970s. Thus, in *Jump Cut*, we inaugurated gay/lesbian criticism in film studies in the United States, have had a consistent feminist critical presence in most of our articles, and pioneered special sections on African and African diaspora filmmaking, Chicano/Latino filmmaking, and Cuban and Brazilian cinema. We understand clearly that the historical role of the alternate press, especially in intellectual life, is often to move whole disciplines in certain directions, and also to provide political direction and leadership within a field for those who want to move it in a progressive direction.

My personal history during this period is significant in a number of ways, telling how members of the dominant social group—in my case, as a white, middle-class, heterosexual, married woman—often contribute to social change while still relying on unearned race and class privilege. Semiemployed, I found documentaries more economical to make than fiction, and as someone doing film studies scholarship, I consequently became interested in writing about documentary media in a theoretical way. My investment in documentary provides great personal pleasure, since I concentrate on work that I think might have a beneficial social effect—that is, I enjoy making and viewing work that has as its goal publicly asserting previously silenced realities, unacknowledged experiences, and social structures and contradictions. Furthermore, for me to pursue social issues, media making, and scholarship means that I posit knowledge as demanding action and implying it.

In the alternative media movement of this period, many progressive documentaries circulated in a rental market in schools and libraries, but this venue for distribution later shrank with the advent of cable television and cheap video distribution of fiction films. During this time, many working-class people and media makers of color also got a start in video production and turned to the documentary form. But with the advent of cable television many more independent producers now want to make fictional film. That I have not aspired to professional budgets nor to feature fiction in part derives from the position of privilege in which I am located. I have continued to make low budget documentaries that do not require the monetary investment needed for broadcast quality because I wish to do something under my aesthetic and political control, something I select as worthwhile.

My making video as an avocation has both advantages and disadvantages. On the one hand, I have always worked outside the ideological constraints of the broadcast industry. This choice lets me embrace contradictions in a tape's subject and experiments in style that would not fit into entertainment's "televisual flow." Similarly, I have developed a working style that allows me to get feedback during the preproduction stage but to take charge during production and editing, so as to actually see a politically important project through to the end in a timely and economical way. This media making avocation, as well as my politicized scholarship, bears the marks of a middle-class intellectual's individualism and independence.

During these years, as I made documentaries and wrote widely on feminist and left issues in film, I had the wonderful opportunity to teach video in and make documentaries about Sandinista Nicaragua. I had originally learned filmmaking in South America while working in Lima, Peru, from 1967 to 1970. I experienced intellectual and political renewal through living in Latin America when my husband and I had the opportunity to teach video with the Sandinista labor union, the Central Sandinista de Trabajadores, in the late 1980s and early 1990s. In Nicaragua I could also put my experience with low budget video production to good use as we two joined with working-class media makers in the shared project of building a new society. We were not only teaching media skills within that revolution but also taping video footage in Nicaragua to edit in the United States in order to make our own tapes to build solidarity with the Nicaraguan people. The shape that our solidarity video work took was largely informed by our stays with ordinary people in Managua and Estelí.

Drawing on my knowledge of Spanish and my close personal and political ties to the people I filmed, I made videos in support of the Sandinistas within what I have described as the "alternative media" tradition. In editing, I would create a work first in Spanish and then later in English. There were pros and cons to this process, and my cultural sympathies and presuppositions shaped the effect that the works had. In fact, my experience in distribution was that these works did not communicate well to a broad U.S. middle-class audience but did speak to those who came from poor rural areas in other parts of the world.

This personal experience with intercultural video making and distribution then influenced my scholarly writing on documentaries, in which I noted the differences between social action documentaries made from within a culture and those from an outsider's perspective. In fact, solidarity documentaries often distort the cultural nuances of the group being supported and ignore almost completely contradictions within that group; such a distortion regularly occurs when sympathetic media makers from a dominant culture insist on the political need "to communicate more clearly" to potential liberal supporters back home.

Translation has always fascinated me in my work in comparative literature. In making solidarity work around Nicaragua, I gained more understanding of the unequal relations in translating the needs of the disadvantaged into media works destined to circulate in mainstream distribution outlets. Sadly, the lesson I learned about translating one culture to another was a pessimistic one. Since then, all my major video work and publication management has continued within the alternative cultural tradition because nuances and contradictions not usually expressed within dominant cultural institutions more readily find an audience there.

Radical Media Making and Scholarship in the 1990s: Limits and Goals

As an associate professor in the English department at the University of Oregon, I experience a tension between my ongoing desire to contribute to social change and my desire to maintain good intellectual standing in an institution that has deeply held, conservative assumptions about professionalism. The academy is one place that women can rise via meritocracy even though they face entrenched sexism. At the same time, women academics have class privilege and unearned race privilege. Women academics work in a culturally prestigious environment with other privileged whites. With their admittance into this club, some women in my situation gain a great sense of belonging and inclusion and feel themselves full citizens of the institution. Others, including myself, understand more about the silencing, structural exclusion and invisibility of women's issues in academic institutions.

Unlike the faculty of color here, obliged to live constantly by what W.E.B. Du Bois called "double consciousness," I have a social identity as an academic that coincides with my identity as a progressive middle-class white woman. Although my life is enormously enriched when I work collectively in projects for social change, I undertake projects in terms of working toward an ideal— generally as an act of individual moral will. Unlike scholars of color, who are located intellectually as writing about ethnic experiences in the United States, I rarely acknowledge that my scholarship is about the white experience or the perspective of a white scholar. Because of my cultural capital, I understand the structure of cultural institutions. I run a small film studies journal in which I can publish my own work, and I have good contacts with other publishing venues. I successfully distribute my video work in a small-scale way. In general, I have intellectual and material access to many aspects of cultural production that mark my privilege as white. Additionally, in terms of media making, I can remain technologically downwardly mobile. Because of my teaching job and my middle-class married-woman's privilege, I do not have to aspire to professional success, to have my work shown on network or cable television, in order to gain respect from my peers and promotion at my job.

My status of privilege inflects my radical scholarship and media work with certain limitations, although these limitations may follow any cultural work that aims to speak to a larger audience, within a dominant culture that expects its cultural products to be shaped in a certain way, within certain parameters. Let me explain, with specific reference to the videotape, *In Plain English*, and this book, *Making a Difference*. Partly because of my experience in Latin America and partly deriving from my participation in the women's movement and women's studies, intellectually much of my work deals with the repressed subcultural codings of groups in struggle. These alternative perspectives, which compete with and challenge dominant versions of reality, have always fascinated me. They provide the basis on which to make media or write criticism that has an efficacy in its oppositional stance.

Because of the value I place on these subcultural codings of groups resisting domination, I am suspicious of family-of-man type works that wallow in the pathos of oppression while protesting that oppression with the claim that we are all basically human or we are all basically alike. For that reason, in *In Plain English* and *Making a Difference*, the students' voices are juxtaposed against each other, to emphasize both differences and commonalities of viewpoints. Hopefully the book's organization will lead readers to judge what might be typical or not for a student of color and to reflect on how students juggle in their own individual ways issues of color, identity, and gender all at once. At the same time, the voices in this book—the students' and the other writers'—claim the authority to represent general issues and human concerns. The whole book implicitly argues for the validity of its argument, yet it partially masks authorship by using student testimony as a phenomenological guarantee, seeming to make the witnesses the source of the argument. The students are presented as a sampling, a cross-section, the "common citizen," with a kind of democracy in the gathering and presenting of testimony and evidence. Their narratives as presented here, as in all documentary writing and media, has an artistic coherence in which connotations are reduced for the sake of argument. The editing of their voices in *In Plain English* and *Making a Difference* provides coherence and functions anthropomorphically to give a sense of intimacy.

All of these tactics reinforce one of the subtlest and most dangerous aspects of documentary: its power to keep the audience feeling transcendent, superior, and benevolent. I worry that the book's being used in the classroom might make an object of study out of the student voices, dishing them up for bourgeois intellectual consumption and keeping them in a position of perpetual subordination to the reader or teacher. I want someone to take responsibility for the pain the students of color constantly face but I know that no reader will do that. Yet I cannot fully embrace postmodernist narrative practices, which challenge all identification since these artistic practices are also reductive, often based on abstractions that border on claims to universality. Finally, rather than be paralyzed by a kind of intellectual purism, I undertake projects like the tape and this book with the trust that I and the others working on the project will do our best to enact our common goal, one that we share with the students. The students of color whose voices are recorded here act out of a great sense of service, resolved that the best way to improve the campus climate around racial issues is to once again and in the distant future educate the community at large about ethnicity and race.

ABBY L. FERBER
ASSOCIATE PROFESSOR, SOCIOLOGY,
UNIVERSITY OF COLORADO—COLORADO SPRINGS

I decided to apply to graduate school in sociology, with an emphasis on gender, after working for numerous years at homeless shelters with primarily female clients. While I had very little exposure to women's issues in undergraduate school, as a social worker I worked on a daily basis with victims of rape, domestic violence, prostitutes, elderly widowed women, and women divorced or deserted by their husbands and left penniless with few marketable job skills. This experience opened my eyes to the realities of women's lives. I grew up in a very liberal, middle-class family, with parents who always taught me that girls could do anything they wanted and modeled gender equality. Although their values enabled them to raise two strong daughters with self-confidence and high aspirations, I had no knowledge of the extent of inequality and limited opportunities which confront both women and people of color.

As a graduate student at the University of Oregon, I became involved with the Center for the Study of Women in Society (CSWS). The center is committed to exploring the intersections of gender, race, and class, and it provided me with the opportunity to take courses on black feminist thought and Asian American women, which encouraged me to begin exploring intellectually the ways in which women's experiences are structured by race. These courses challenged me to rethink traditional feminist theory and to explore the ways in which race and class shape life for everyone. While I expected to learn about many kinds of women's experiences, the ideas also challenged me to explore my own experience of race, as a white woman. These courses were pivotal to my own development as a scholar, future research agenda, and personal growth. Not a part of the regular curriculum, these multicultural courses were taught by visiting scholars. Thanks to these courses, I am doing this work today. I am a perfect example of the importance of multicultural curriculum for all students.

I first became involved in this book project as a graduate student. Debbie Storrs and I team-taught a course on women of color in U.S. society, and we became attuned to the struggles and issues facing many of our nontraditional students. We began interviewing these students and collecting their life stories to explore their experiences in higher education. When we learned that a professor on campus, Julia Lesage, was conducting videotaped interviews with students of color, we requested permission to read the transcripts and use them in our research. We were especially interested in exploring the similarities between the experiences of women and those of students of color in courses that integrated gender and race into the curriculum to understand how such courses shaped these students' experiences in the classroom. While some research had been conducted by scholars exploring resistance on the part of white students, we discovered no research exploring the experiences of minority students in these classes.

Julia graciously shared her research with us, and Debbie and I wrote an article based on that research (Ferber and Storrs 1995). Julia invited us to work with her to transcribe and organize the narratives she had collected, and I jumped at the opportunity to gain further research experience. As Julia and I worked with the narratives, we realized that the interview material contained important material that did not make it into the video. It was at this point that we decided to begin building a book around these narratives.

Surprisingly, I found that these narratives offered insight into my own struggles with race and ethnicity. As a white Jewish woman teaching and researching race, I have struggled with the issue of my own relation to multiculturalism; as a graduate student, for example, I overheard one faculty member argue that a Jewish person had no place teaching race. I believe that the student narratives in this book, while not united in their perspective, speak eloquently to this issue, and I have learned a great deal from them. I believe that it is my responsibility, as a white person, to educate myself and others about the history and present realities of race and racism, rather than expect people of color to shoulder that responsibility. At the same time, I am absolutely committed to working within my institution to increase the hiring and retention of faculty of color. The more voices and perspectives that get heard, the better. This is a conversation that everyone needs to be involved in.

Our research at the graduate level contributed to focusing on the construction of race for my dissertation. Fascinated with the newly burgeoning field of whiteness studies, I began exploring the intersections of race, which became the basis for my book, *White Man Falling: Race, Gender, and White Supremacy*. Course work, exposure to work by women of color, and these student narratives firmed my commitment to explore the intersections of race and gender. However, I decided to focus on the ways in which *whiteness* is constructed and shaped by gender relations. Much exciting work by women of color already explored the ways in which race and gender shape the lives of women of color; however, at that time, few works analyzed how whiteness operated.

Selecting such a topic was in part an attempt to explore how my own life is implicated in the politics of race. While I learned as a graduate student to reject biological and genetic explanations of race and to look instead to history, society, and culture as formative factors, researching the white supremacist movement turned analyzing the social construction of race into a personal encounter with racial politics and history.

In reading white supremacist literature, I became acutely aware of the unsettled insider/outsider status of Jews. According to white supremacist ideology, I am so dangerous I must be eliminated. Yet, in my daily life, where I am defined by most people as simply white, I am the beneficiary of unearned privilege. Like most white people, for most of my life, my race had been invisible to me. I saw race as something that shaped the lives of people of color as the victims of racism. We white people are not used to thinking about whiteness when we think about race. Consequently, we have failed to recognize the ways in which our lives are shaped by race.

It was also during my graduate school years that I experienced my Jewishness as an outsider identity for the first time. Arriving for the first day of classes, I was greeted by a fellow student with the welcome: "Oh, you're the Jewish one."

This jarring experience startled me, for it immediately othered me. Having lived in predominantly Jewish communities until that time, I had never experienced my Jewishness as a basis of otherness. Whether or not I define myself as Jewish, I am constantly defined by others as Jewish. Jewishness is not simply a religious designation one may choose, as I once naively assumed.

Whether or not I see myself as Jewish does not matter for white supremacists. Racial identity is not always a question of self-definition but involves being defined by others, as the narratives throughout this book disturbingly reveal. While reading white supremacist publications, I felt that for a few moments I could understand what it is like to be a person of color in U.S. society; but when I put down the racist, anti-Semitic newsletters and walk outside, where most people see me as white, I realize I can never really know what it is like. Cheryl Greenberg argues that two factors potentially present an obstacle to Jews fully embracing contemporary multiculturalism:

> the tension between Jewish self-perception of vulnerability and external perception of Jewish security, and the inability of most Jews to appreciate the radically different historical condition of white ethnics and non-whites in America. (Greenberg 1989, 61)

I believe, however, that the tension between vulnerability and privilege can inspire alliance with multiculturalism. It can be a source of positive tension, pushing us to explore race as a social construct as well as the history of white privilege. At certain points in time, Jews have been racialized, defined as a non-white minority. Around the turn of the last century, Jews were considered a separate, inferior race, with a distinguishable biological identity justifying discrimination and even genocide. After World War II Jews were welcomed into the category of "white" along with other European ethnic groups, beneficiaries of one of the largest affirmative action programs in history (the 1944 GI Bill of Rights). Today, Jews are considered white, and Jewishness merely a religious or an ethnic designation. This changing conceptualization of Jewish identity highlights the vulnerable, shifting borders of insider/outsider status, as well as Jews' contradictory relationship to multiculturalism. Exploring my own experiences as a Jewish/white woman, as well as the shifting territories of race and racial privilege for Jews, provides a basis for my own dedication to multiculturalism as well as my commitment to this project.

We all participate in racializing projects, and thus we all have the responsibility for examining our own positions and histories within the politics of race and racism. Privilege and oppression are a part of the same system, and there are no sidelines. Significantly, the student narratives in this book not only give voice to their own experiences of discrimination, they also decenter the experience of white college students which has so long been masked as the neutral norm. They provide us with an opportunity to grasp the extent to which all of our lives are structured and shaped by race.

DEBBIE STORRS
ASSISTANT PROFESSOR, SOCIOLOGY,
UNIVERSITY OF IDAHO

It was several years ago, as a graduate student, when I first considered participating in this manuscript. It was a difficult time in my life. I was in the midst of writing my dissertation, teaching a course, and managing my personal life. I sought advice from a senior woman of color. I recall, with some lingering bitterness, her discouraging response to the prospect of my potential collaboration on this project. Some of her concerns were well founded, focusing on the need to prioritize my research and writing activities. After all, I was in the midst of writing a dissertation on mixed racial identities and any distractions might extend the graduate process longer than necessary.

While not explicit, the discouragement I experienced was also due to the politics of representation that ravaged our campus during my stay there. Like other predominantly white institutions, my alma mater, the University of Oregon, was embroiled in numerous debates concerning race. Issues ranging from the low numbers of students and faculty of color to whether and how to best implement a required diversity course for all students served as the backdrop of my graduate experience. At the heart of these issues was the politicized notion of racial representation. In other words, what was being debated boiled down to who should be part of the university, whose history should make up the curriculum, and who should teach what to whom.

Given this milieu, it comes as no surprise that some faculty and graduate students of color were suspicious and concerned about the project and my role in it. "Who else will be participating?" they asked. Others were more pointed, asking, "Why have you been asked to collaborate on this project?" What I think they were really wondering was who had not been asked to participate and why. A good friend of mind asked the frank question, "Is this another example of the exploitation of minority students by well-intentioned but misinformed white faculty and graduate students?" Their questions challenged me to consider the purpose and role I would play in this book, but also spurred my thinking and analysis about the discourse concerning racial representation and the divisions it seemed to foster. It was only after I had completed my dissertation and secured a tenure-track position as a sociologist that I decided to fully participate in this project.

While the integrity and actions of my coeditors diminished the concerns raised by others, the stories of the students in this collection were primary in my decision to participate in the project. I was struck with the parallels in our experiences as I too have struggled and fought to position and name myself within various groups and institutions. The voices of these students, and my own personal biography, have brought to life the power of essentialist thought that, in my opinion, continues to mitigate racial coalitions and ultimately serves to reinforce racial hierarchies. People like myself, those from racially mixed backgrounds, pose a potential challenge to racial borders and racial essentialist thinking. Anzaldua's characterization of borders reveals the threat posed by those who transgress them:

> Borders are set up to define the places that are safe and unsafe, to distinguish us from them. A borderland is a vague and undetermined place created by the emotional residue of an unnatural boundary. It is in a constant state of transition. The prohibited and forbidden are its inhabitants. Los astravesados live here: the squint-eyed, the perverse, the queer, the troublesome, the mongrel, the mulatto, the half-breed, the half-dead; in short, those who cross over, pass over, or go through the confines of the normal.

What borderland inhabitants can reveal is the porous nature of category boundaries. Moving across boundaries reveals their constructed nature and "unnaturalness," explaining the threat that we pose to the hegemonic understanding of race. I often use my own racial biography as a way to begin a dialogue concerning socially and politically constructed racial boundaries and meanings when I teach about race and ethnic relations. While it feels safer to simply intellectualize our nation's racial logic, I find that using subjective experiences can help generate student interest and fundamentally reject positivistic ideas about objectivity.

The following exercise helps students understand the social construction of race as well as locate me, their instructor, as a racial subject. Because a fundamental objective of my race and ethnic relations course is to reveal the political nature of racial boundaries and meanings, I provide students with a history of U.S. racial logic, including the changing census categorizations over time (see Lee 1993). Following this brief history, I give students a synopsis of my family's racial history and then ask them how I might have been racialized in different time periods. Students discover that my race would have changed in different decades even as my family biography remains constant, revealing that race has more to do with politics than biology.

I have discovered, when I do not use this exercise, that students are curious but often afraid to ask about my race. I find their curiosity unsurprising given that race, according to Omi and Winant, is one of the first things that we notice about people. Positioning individuals within our racial schema is important because it provides us with clues to their behavior and abilities. In short, we use what Omi and Winant refer to as "racial etiquette." Once we can locate individuals within our racial categorization, we then know how to interact with them. It is often difficult for others to categorize people like myself who have ambiguous physical racial markers. Their desire to fit the world within a clearly defined racial schema has led to my being multiply positioned by others.

I find that the way I am perceived by others varies, depending on the availability of informational and racialized cues, the political context and need, and the availability of minority "others." My hometown of Anchorage, Alaska, often served as a racial marker for others to position me, incorrectly, as Native Alaskan. Those who did not have this information assumed that I was Mexican American, possibly because of the large number of Latinos who reside in Oregon. I find that in my current residence in Idaho I am often perceived as Native American due to the close proximity to the Coeur d'Alene and Nez Perce reservations.

The political context of my interactions also shapes the ways in which others racialize me. The celebration of diversity in institutions of higher education has prompted others to recognize, label, and count me as a person of color. In this politically charged environment, the presence of minorities can be misused as a stamp of approval in gauging diversity success, which often allows organizations to ignore the need to institutionalize wider structural changes. At the same time, I have found that my racialization as a person of color can be quickly cast aside when others who more firmly rooted within racial categories come on the scene.

I find the categorization of myself as a person of color used as a way to legitimize (or delegitimize) my expertise when teaching or writing about race. The elevation of personal racial experience as credentials for scholarly activities presumes homogenous experience within racial groups and reinforces the bifurcation between subjective and scholarly knowledge. These experiences, and the heightened and lived awareness of the construction of racial borders, lead me to believe that individuals like myself do have the potential to disrupt essentialist logic.

My personal response to the politics of race varies depending on context and goals. In my research on mixed race identities, I explicitly identify my biography to my subjects and audience, in recognition of how my social locations shape my research interests. Sometimes in class I discuss my mixed racial background as a way to reveal the myths of racial purity and biological essentialism. At other times, I resist the temptation to legitimize my participation in racialized situations through placing myself on the racial map of nonwhiteness and instead point to my scholarly credentials. In these situations, I try to challenge those who embrace essentialist notions to move beyond the belief that my credibility can be dismissed or accepted on the basis of my pigmentation and instead to recognize and consider whether my training, scholarly experience, personal politics, community involvement, and research experience qualify me to participate in the activity at hand.

Other situations, such as serving as a mentor for students of color, call for a more explicit discussion of my racial experiences. While there are multiple strategies we can employ, an important one is to participate in projects like this one, which illustrate, through narrative, the politicized and fluid nature of racial belonging and meaning. The students who share their stories reveal the complexities of racial representation and their attempts to position themselves as both knowledge makers and members of various communities. We share the goal of problematizing the reductive positioning we experience by others. Whether this means challenging the actual borders and making them more porous or whether this means illuminating the fluidity of meaning within borders, both actions serve to capture a more liberating representation of oneself and provides the basis for potential coalition between groups. It is with this purpose in mind that I find it meaningful and important to participate in this project.

DONNA WONG
COORDINATOR OF ACADEMIC SUPPORT SERVICES,
OFFICE OF MULTICULTURAL PROGRAMS,
EMORY UNIVERSITY

Being of Chinese descent, I wear daily a racial uniform that physically identifies me as an Asian woman—a stigma of foreignness attaches to my physical being. People ask, "Where are you from?" "What are you?" I could be Vietnamese, Korean, Japanese, Hawaiian, Nepalese, Filipino, or any other of the numerous Asian ethnic groups. When I speak, people may think I "speak English very well for a foreigner" or perceive me as American born—which I am. Born in Los Angeles Chinatown, raised in Hollywood, California, educated at UCLA and the University of Oregon, I have been a college instructor and academic counselor for the past thirteen years. I am currently an administrative professional in multicultural student affairs at Emory University in Atlanta, Georgia.

My personal experience has led me to a firm conclusion: on a predominantly and historically white campus, having staff and faculty who can relate to students of color is crucial for these students' retention and academic success. It is not that I have innate social antennae that tune in to students of color, but personal experience enables me to talk to students of color around our common perspectives. As an administrator of color, I better understand the barriers and obstacles to their having a positive college experience and graduating, I support them as they work to solve their issues, and I advocate for them when necessary.

I showed the video *In Plain English* to composition classes I taught at the University of Oregon. Migrant students from a mixture of racial/ethnic backgrounds painfully and energetically discussed the issues the tape brought up. In the essays they wrote in response to the video, they described their own experiences of being discriminated against in the public school system, in their Oregon home communities, and on campus. The discussion that the video stimulated broadened class members' understanding of prejudice, different cultures, and college life.

When Julia Lesage decided to produce a book to accompany the video, she graciously solicited my input because of my familiarity with issues concerning students of color, my direct contact with college students, and my research interests in diversity and higher education. I could also draw on my interactions with faculty and administration, having worked on various university committees that addressed race, admissions, retention, discrimination, and minority scholarships.

As this book expanded in scope to examine the nationwide bronzing of colleges, I moved to Emory University, a private institution in the South. My experience in this new setting has enabled me to get another taste of diversity in higher education and observe differences between public and private institutions. Interacting with students, faculty, administrators, and other student affairs professionals has given me many new insights about process, collaborative change, and divergences in views and strategic actions. The University of Oregon had an 11 percent enrollment of students of color, whereas Emory's decade-long diversity initiatives have reaped a critical mass of students of color—27 percent.

Given that this book is a collaborative project written between 1994 and 2001, Debbie, Abby, Julia, and I have gained a more historically grounded perspective, from which we can now address race relations and the process of change. We have asked ourselves the following questions: How are current race relations on campus different from what they were ten years earlier? What structural plans are best used to enhance racial integration and acceptance? What support systems can best counter prejudice and intergroup racism? Considering their greater numbers today, how might students of color effect changes in campus life, curriculum, and policies? What type of campus-wide and state leadership fosters racial diversity and respect? How do our job positions and race affect our work?

I answered these questions from the perspective of a student affairs administrator whose primary contact is with students of color as I work on predominantly white campuses. Collectively, *Making a Difference* contains a unique compilation of perspectives from many different stakeholders and shareholders. Hence, in reading the book *Making a Difference* or using the video *In Plain English*, faculty and administrators can gain a broader understanding of the complexities in educational equity and ethnic diversity and thus become effective allies working for diversity in the workplace. Over the years, the numbers of students of color have increased while the numbers of administrators and faculty of color have not shown parallel growth. The resultant lack of diversity among student affairs professionals, nationwide, concerns me. At the year 2000 conference of NASPA (National Association of Student Personnel Administrators), one workshop was entitled Becoming an Ally with Students of Color without Being a Person of Color. As this workshop pointed out, the lack of administrators of color creates a problem when a university is carrying out a mission to increase its racial diversity in both student enrollment and graduation rates. Thus, when it develops structural diversity initiatives to increase the enrollment of students of color, the planning must include a professional staff of color to ensure appropriate recruitment and retention strategies.

Without input from people of color and a vision to provide multicultural support systems, diversity initiatives are bound to flounder, frustrating the students. I have repeatedly witnessed compelling issues affecting students of color that are not met with the requisite attention, sensitivity, and mediation. Such issues may include the university's defending the right of free speech, an issue that often offends certain ethnic students; or an interest among students of color in having a more diverse course curriculum that includes non-Western perspectives. How these issues are handled is crucial to the campus climate, since they can polarize a college community and tear apart racial harmony.

I most effectively make a difference in campus affairs when I cull from my personal experience in order to advocate for and underscore the perspectives of students who are underrepresented or nontraditional. Drawing on my own personal experience as a minority college student, I recall seeing few faculty of color or professional staff of color in the late 1960s and early 1970s. At that time, when I was in college, it was easy to become discouraged when I was contemplating different career paths and not seeing people like me in those roles. Although I knew that I wished to be a teacher and an adviser or a counselor, I did not find a mentor while I was in college. As a result, it took me a long time to make the decision to attain advanced degrees and credentials; a nineteen-year gap exists between my bachelor's and master's degrees. There was no "educational pipeline" to move me forward because no one shed light on its trajectory and potential opportunities. But having persisted in gaining professional status, I now cherish the role I have in helping the next generation.

In retrospect, one pivotal experience transformed me into an activist. At UCLA, I witnessed and participated in the formation of an Asian American studies program in the early 1970s. Due to the enormous momentum of the ethnic pride movement and the unity of minority students, students protested and then successfully proposed new college courses to focus on underrepresented minority groups' history and experience in the United States. when we worked with other students and a few faculty, positive social change resulted. I saw the value of forcing an upheaval of traditional higher education curriculum to meet the needs of a changing society. One of the highlights for me was working on the first Asian American textbook reader of student-produced research, articles, and graphics. This book, *Roots* (1971), was used in UCLA's groundbreaking ethnic studies courses.

Today in my work in student affairs, I still find it important to go beyond traditional models of student development in order to be inclusive and success-ful in bringing diversity to higher education. Through my position as an admin-istrator, I can address complex issues that specifically apply to nonnative English speakers, immigrant/refugee students, first-generation college or low-income students, and students with disabilities. I collaborate with colleagues and execu-tive administrators to build policies that "back" diversity. We might be review-ing the institution's discrimination policies, addressing the digital gap where some students arrive with few technical skills, or recommending diversity train-ing in residence life to dispel stereotypes. Our goal is always to transform the campus to be more inclusive and interculturally sensitive.

As a person of color who values communication between diverse cultures and internalizes a multicultural frame of reference, I am able to empathize with many individuals and establish rapport with them. I can understand people's experi-ences and perceptions across cultural/racial/ethnic/class boundaries and mediate issues having to do with those boundaries that a white person may not recognize. As a Chinese American, I am more accessible to many pan-Asian American and international students. As a second-generation Chinese American, born to immigrant parents and raised bilingually and multiculturally, I can specifically empathize with college students who are from non–English speaking immigrant families. In our institutions we encounter many barriers—class, language, and race—that hinder advancement or prevent us from smoothly entering the educa-tional pipeline.

To sum up, my knowledge of myself and the issues within the community of students of color has made me a more effective student affairs professional and has enriched my personal relations. I use my position and power to reach out to students to mentor them personally so they can see the range of opportunities open to them. In this manner, I passionately serve as an agent of change and a mobilizer for diversity. I try to live promoting a vision of racial respect, accep-tance, and equal opportunity.

REFERENCES

Anzaldua, Gloria. 1987. *Borderlands/La Frontera: The New Mestiza.* San Francisco: Spinsters/ Aunt Lute.

Ferber, Abby L. 1998. *White Man Falling: Race, Gender, and White Supremacy.* Lanham, Md.: Rowman & Littlefield.

Greenberg, Cheryl. 1998. "Pluralism and Its Discontents: The Case of Blacks and Jews." In *Insider/Outsider: American Jews and Multiculturalism.* Berkeley: University of California Press.

Lee, Sharon. 1993. "Racial Classifications in the U.S. Census: 1890–1990." *Ethnic and Racial Studies* 16, no. 1, 75–94.

Omi, Michael, and Howard Winant. 1994. *Racial Formation in the United States: From the 1960s to the 1990s.* 2d ed. New York: Routledge.

Index